Barbara Kopple: Interviews

Conversations with Filmmakers Series
Gerald Peary, General Editor

Barbara Kopple
INTERVIEWS

Edited by Gregory Brown

University Press of Mississippi / Jackson

www.upress.state.ms.us

The University Press of Mississippi is a member
of the Association of American University Presses.

Copyright © 2015 by University Press of Mississippi
All rights reserved

First printing 2015
∞
Library of Congress Cataloging-in-Publication Data

Kopple, Barbara.
  Barbara Kopple: interviews / edited by Gregory Brown.
    pages cm. — (Conversations with filmmakers)
  Includes bibligoraphical references and index.
  Includes filmography.
  ISBN 978-1-62846-212-8 (cloth : alk. paper) — ISBN 978-1-62674-569-8 (ebook)
  1. Kopple, Barbara—Interviews. 2. Motion picture producers and directors—
United States—Interviews. I. Brown, Gregory, 1953- editor. II. Title.
  PN1998.3.K6655A3 2015
  791.4302'33092—dc23
                              2015015802
British Library Cataloging-in-Publication Data available

Contents

Introduction ix

Chronology xx

Filmography xxvii

Barbara Kopple Interview: Making *Harlan County, U.S.A.* 3
    Chuck Kleinhans / 1976

The Making of *Harlan County, U.S.A.*: An Interview with Barbara Kopple 11
    Gail Pellet / 1977

Filming in Harlan: Interview with Barbara Kopple and Hart Perry 21
    Gary Crowdus / 1977

Interview with Barbara Kopple (on *Harlan County, U.S.A.*) 32
    Jan Aghed / 1977

American Dream: An Interview with Barbara Kopple 41
    Gary Crowdus and Richard Porton / 1991

Barbara Kopple 49
    L. A. Winokur / 1992

Filmmaker's Knockout Punch 58
    Harlan Jacobson / 1993

Stand Up and Do Something: Barbara Kopple Speaks with Lisa Lincoln 61
    Lisa Lincoln / 1998

Woody Captured on the Spot, without a Script 67
    Michel Ciment / 1998

Woody Allen's "Wild" Concerts: Filmmaker Blows Own Horn on His European Jazz Tour 72
    Gary Arnold / 1998

Scene One: Something about Barbara 77
    Bill Kirtz / 1999

Living for the City: Barbara Kopple 80
    Steve Chagollan / 2000

Free Love, Commercialism, and Violence: Oscar-Winning Documentarian Barbara Kopple Explores Three Generations of Woodstock 82
    Jennifer M. Wood / 2001

Documentary Filmmaker Barbara Kopple Discusses Summer in the Hamptons, as Shown in Her New Miniseries for ABC 85
    Charles Gibson / 2002

Kopple on Audience Appreciation 90
    Mary Sampson / 2002

Barbara Kopple 92
    Alison Sloane Gaylin / 2004

Tales from the Front: A Conversation with Documentarian Barbara Kopple 95
    Katrina Onstad / 2005

Women Who Witness War: Female Correspondents in Iraq Are Subject of Documentary 100
    Michael Lisi / 2005

Indiewire Interview: Barbara Kopple, Co-Director of *Shut Up & Sing* 103
    Brian Brooks / 2006

Spirit in the Dark: Barbara Kopple on Filming the Group That Wouldn't *Shut Up & Sing* 109
    Damon Smith / 2007

Crossing Lines: Barbara Kopple 118
    Michael Joshua Rowin / 2008

Barbara Kopple's Shortlist 125
    Barbara Kopple / 2008

Woodstock Never Dies 131
    Jacqueline Linge / 2009

2010 IDA Career Achievement Award—The Magic of Being There: Barbara Kopple and the Subject-Filmmaker Relationship 135
    Sara Vizcarrondo / 2010

Exclusive: Barbara Kopple Talks HBO Gun Control Doc, *Gun Fight*: "Reason Is Lost" 139
    Sophia Savage / 2011

Barbara Kopple on Gun Rights, Freedom of Speech, and Virginia Tech 141
    Eleanor Barkhorn / 2011

Full Frame Day 2: Barbara Kopple and Guns 144
    David Fellerath / 2011

Shut Up & Sing: On Accidental Political Activists 147
    Rahul Chadha / 2011

Filmmaker Barbara Kopple on *Running from Crazy* and the Burden of Legacy 154
    Karen Kemmerle / 2013

Additional Resources 159

Index 163

Introduction

The documentary filmmaker's responsibilities can be daunting. Project research, fundraising, working with a crew, following "characters," identifying story lines, crafting a final product with editors, promoting the film—these are the nuts and bolts necessary to complete any project, successfully or not. Then consider a lifetime of responding to ever-changing technologies, economics, and distribution channels.

Add to the mix a producer's values, worldview, sense of fairness, and objectivity and the enterprise becomes all the more complex. In the more than fifty years since Barbara Kopple made her first unedited documentary film as an undergraduate class research project, she's learned to balance these facets of the process toward a singular goal: to give as complete and riveting a view as possible of her subject.

Throughout a lauded career that included two Academy Awards for her most ambitious labor films, Kopple has made herself readily available to interviewers from many publications and countries. Many themes repeat themselves throughout the following interviews and those excerpted in this introduction.

Barbara Kopple's early decisions about college would seem destined to lead her into a network of like-minded activists. Eager to see the world outside her privileged yet liberal upbringing in affluent Scarsdale, New York, in 1965 Kopple enrolled in Morris Harvey College (now known as the University of Charleston) in West Virginia. Here she got a taste of Appalachian mountain culture, but her focus quickly shifted to the burgeoning Vietnam War protests, as she transferred to Boston's Northeastern University. There, faced with producing a research paper for a clinical psychology class, Kopple incensed her professor by submitting a short movie about lobotomy patients she got permission to film at Medfield State Hospital. (She reports early on that she'd read you could easily operate a camera by pressing a button.[1])

It was the connections she made upon her move to New York's New School of Social Research, however, that would dramatically affect her career. Taking a cinéma-vérité film course, she met a classmate employed by Albert and David Maysles. Soon she was hired to do any and all odd jobs, working with assistant editor Barbara Jarvis, and helping with completion of the brothers' film *Salesman* and then with *Gimme Shelter*, both now acknowledged as cinéma-vérité classics. Assisting the Maysles led her to understand the value of listening to members of a production team.

The Maysles accepted input on their projects and in return staff members felt part of a community of creative teammates. For *Winter Soldier*, a film about Vietnam War vets opposed to the war, a collective produced the film, benefitting from donations collected by Jane Fonda and Donald Sutherland, who also mentored the group. From there, Kopple moved on to create her own company, Cabin Creek Films. Headlines in the newspapers inspired Kopple's decision to embark on *Harlan County, U.S.A.*: a deadly West Virginia mine disaster, corruption in the United Mine Workers, and the murder of a reformist candidate for the union's presidency.

Not surprisingly, a great deal of interest has centered on her ability to raise funding, especially considering Kopple's remarkable productivity (she's finished directing almost fifty films and television shows so far, to say nothing of commercial advertisements). She wisely notes that if you wait until you have all the money needed to make a film, you might never start.[2] Despite ever-more capable and affordable equipment, filmmaking remains an expensive proposition, though much less so than in the heyday of 16-mm film. Yet Kopple is optimistic about prospects for young filmmakers, noting the greater popularity of the reality genre today and the potential for commissions for documentary work from television networks that may help obviate the need for some of the early risks she took.

During the three years of shooting on *Harlan*, Kopple would write more than a hundred fundraising and follow-up letters. With a contribution of ten thousand dollars from the American Film Institute, Kopple continued shooting footage and cut it into short movies she could show to potential donors. Completing an astonishing amount of research on foundations and what they would and would not support, Kopple discovered that actually meeting people who might write the check is one of the most important steps in the process. When foundations turned her down, she'd ask why, show her footage, and ask for advice about who might help her.

It was an exhausting but necessary ordeal that diverted her attention from collecting the story. The grants would come in, but seldom for the amounts requested. She ignored a standard bit of advice—never invest your own money in a film; otherwise, she might never have seen the film through to completion. The decision carried consequences. At one point, she had as little as five dollars while living among the miners and was amazed at getting a Master Charge card, which replenished her stores and financed the effort for two months, though it would take her years to pay off the debt.

Such trials and tribulations might explain her reluctance to haggle over revenues from *Harlan County, U.S.A.*'s distributor. In one 1980 interview, she reported giving the distributor 70 percent of all earnings of the film for fifteen years, and allowing the company to recoup costs for film prints and advertising. She did, however, insist on provisions for benefit and reduced-cost showings.[3] Though it might seem a poor deal on the face of it considering Kopple's prolonged period of poverty, it could also be seen as a savvy move by a relatively unknown director anxious to gain the publicity for her film an experienced distributor could provide.

Kopple feels a great sense of community among fellow documentarians who view and react to each other's work and thereby help to refine it. At a recent commencement address, Kopple encouraged American University graduates to seek out such community.[4] It has been there for Kopple from the beginning, with *Harlan County* shown in rough cut at prominent documentarian D. A. Pennebaker's screening room.[5] She recounts how, later, she awaited the announcement of the Academy Award documentary winner, arms locked with other documentarians, who boosted her toward the stage. She shared the glory and opportunities of the New York premiere and of later showings with coal miners and their families, and with the singer Hazel Dickens, in particular, who generously made appearances in support of the film.

Fame counted for little when Kopple tried to finance *American Dream* in the mid-1980s. By then, she'd also directed a fictional film (*Keeping On*) aired on PBS's *American Playhouse* series, and documentary footage for the concert movie *No Nukes*. Even so, potential backers initially weren't interested in unions, meat packing, or the economically depressed Midwest during the high-water mark of the Reagan era. Being famous, she discovered, actually was a detriment to her efforts as donors preferred to give handouts to up-and-comers—not someone who already had achieved an Oscar. Pursuing the story nonetheless, Kopple soon found herself with no money again and no lab willing to give her credit to develop her film stock. The few dollars she could raise filled an office with used refrigerators to keep the film from ruin.

Fundraising's heavy-lifting seemed to lighten in the early 1990s, when production companies came calling on Kopple to undertake projects that they would underwrite. In one case, NBC engaged her for *Fallen Champ: The Untold Story of Mike Tyson*, giving her a "Movie of the Week" budget. Her parents, on hearing the news, reportedly were delighted that, finally with a salary, "Barbara got a job!"[6] As producer, director, and writer, Barbara was delighted as well that she could focus on the work of the film and not "split her brain" to also concern herself with the financial aspects of the work. She also allied herself with leftist media activist and critic Danny Schecter in the early 1990s, sharing directing credits with him on *Beyond JFK: The Question of Conspiracy* and receiving co-director credit on Schechter's *Prisoners of Hope: Robben Island Reunion* about South African President Nelson Mandela.

About the same time, Kopple was asked to document Michael Lang's upcoming Woodstock '94 concert, with both film and festival supported by PolyGram Records. As the concert date approached and costs ran over budget, PolyGram's fears of a public safety debacle a la *Gimme Shelter* led to a desperate round of cost-cutting. Lang's contract with the company was iron-clad, but, as she'd experienced before with her first work in Kentucky toward what would become *Harlan County*, Kopple's film was defunded or "orphaned." Still, she persevered and shot the event with a minimal crew. When Lang came back again to promote Woodstock '99, she shot fresh film, used the 1994 footage along with clips from Michael Wadleigh's original *Woodstock* film, and after her long financial struggle produced *My Generation* about three generations of Woodstock attendees.

In the mid-to-late 1990s, Reebok and others would hire her to make pioneering "real people" commercials and she would direct a series of specials on social issues including body image and learning differences for the Disney Channel. These assignments as well as directing gigs for the TV series *Homicide: Life on the Street* and HBO's *Oz* helped to pay bills and maintain her film company, which then geared up for future films, such as 2006's *Shut Up & Sing*.

Kopple worked on many projects during this period involving her friend Cecilia Peck, before and after 1999's *A Conversation with Gregory Peck*, a look at the actor's Q and A tour, interspersed with family life scenes. These projects include the fiction film *Havoc*, a vision of wealthy teen gang-bangers, released to DVD in 2005.

Kopple has repeatedly worked with many of the same crew members. Notably, Tom Hurwitz, the son of documentary pioneer Leo Hurwitz, has frequently filled the role of cinematographer with David Cassidy often playing the roles of producer or sound person. Kopple has also continually worked with a cadre of executive producers including Diane Sokolow, who hired Kopple to work on the Mike Tyson project Sokolow's late husband had found so intriguing. Another was Tom Fontana, also for TV, starting with a Director's Guild of America award-winning episode of *Homicide: Life on the Street* entitled "The Documentary," which features a doc within the show.

Over the years, Kopple has also collaborated with a number of talented editors, among them Nancy Baker, Lawrence Silk, and Bob Davis, as well as Bob Eisenhardt, who is also credited as a director in *Bearing Witness* and writer in *Gun Fight*. She has developed a talent for drawing in a cadre of fellow filmmakers and politically concerned supporters who bring fresh eyes where she admittedly is just too close to her characters and her footage, seeing editors as a project's "first audience."[7] She remains a part of this community today and cheers on her fellow filmmakers, including some distinguished former students she taught over a decade ago, while admitting partiality to some exceptionally powerful works throughout her interviews.

Certainly one of the most important relationships in her work and personal life was the one she maintained with Hart Perry, who matched her dedication through the three-year shooting of *Harlan County* as principal cinematographer and would return again to help film *American Dream*. The relationship with Perry grew more complicated as Perry fathered her son Nicholas, the couple broke up after seventeen years, and she and Perry then moved on to other relationships, with Kopple marrying former labor organizer Gene Carroll. Family bonds and shared political views still enabled Kopple and Perry to work together, with Perry working as cinematographer on some of her later work, as well as on his own often music- and art-related projects.

Kopple has been cautious in her criticisms of other documentary makers. What about the ethics of scripted TV reality shows or the obvious presence of the filmmaker in Michael Moore's movies? Pleased with the expanding audience for nonfiction genres, "I'm not a traditionalist," she says in her interview with Roland Legiardi-Laura. "I don't believe there's only one way to do a work. I'm more radical or open in my approach. Anything goes and you should support people who are trying to use new and innovative forms. It's the chemistry of how you relate to people or ideas."[8] Since that declaration, she herself has pursued a reality miniseries for ABC (with Sokolow) that chronicles the sites and events of a summer in the Hamptons island resort towns, a reality series for VH1 that reveals the true lives of celebrity spouses, and even a pilot for TruTV.

She cares about her causes, characters, and outcomes, but all within a framework of letting situations unfold with minimal interference from her small crew. Though the Maysles imbued Kopple with a preference for the cinéma-vérité-style filmmaking, she's never been a slave to it. She tells interviewers that she and her film crews try to be invisible so that her subjects (or characters) won't be influenced by them and that any appearance the crew does make is "garbage."[9] Yet, in the case of *Harlan County, U.S.A.*, while the filmmakers clearly employ cinéma-vérité techniques, they directly question people in the story, too. And in early interviews about *Harlan County, U.S.A.*, Kopple maintains that the presence of her camera actually lessened the likelihood of violence, one reason she often carried along her equipment even though she had no film.

When she could use it, cinéma vérité often yielded high drama, as when a union leader in *American Dream* forgot about the film crew and accidentally knocked over her microphone in his frustration at a meeting. The cinéma-vérité approach wasn't always an option, though. She couldn't shoot the Mike Tyson film that way because he was already in jail and she didn't have access to him. In any event, his manager, Don King, would have demanded editorial control in return—a deal she wouldn't make. To her great fortune, she found a treasure trove of unaired footage made when Tyson was a teenager. This project of Kopple's, uncharacteristically, also employs excerpts from many "straight" (formal) interviews collected while a short production timetable didn't allow for development of trust with sources.

She does, indeed, remain true to cinéma vérité in a film like *Wild Man Blues*, which candidly follows Woody Allen as clarinetist on a harrowing European tour with then-girlfriend Soon-Yi Previn. Likewise, the Dixie Chicks ignored the camera in the midst of their great crisis, after they criticized President Bush's war policy and experienced harsh conservative backlash. Crises are important to Kopple because not only do they divert attention from the lens, they also let her characters' natural strengths and leadership abilities emerge. Her goal, after all, as she tells Robin Finn after filming the Chicks, is "to try to tell human stories about people I think are phenomenal and whose lives are sometimes in crisis."[10] She also wants to give the audience the feeling of "being there" in the moment.

Some have criticized her portrayals of situations as lacking balance.

"It's not a matter of fair and objective," she corrects Legiardi-Laura while discussing *American Dream* in 1992. "If you're trying to give a picture of what's happening, you have to get every side of the story to be well-rounded. That's the only way people are going to understand the dynamics, the complexities and the layers within the film. Otherwise, you're making a propaganda film for the already committed and you're not going to reach out to the masses."[11] The level of access she achieved in this film and others is astounding, as she gets into places no one else does, such as being allowed to film inside the Hormel factory when others were not. She says that the time she invested in that film, living as part of the community, was key to gaining trust and access from the various factions involved in that conflict.

She also claims she is biased in her filmmaking, but that before following a subject and letting the story unfold, she first lets go of all preconceptions. Relating to her subsequent 1993 profile of Mike Tyson, she tells David Goldsmith, "It's very difficult as a filmmaker to be objective, but it's not difficult to be fair."[12]

Kopple is frequently asked about how her subjects react when they see themselves onscreen. Tyson later told her he "loved the film," Kopple told Jerry Tallmer.[13] Some other celebrity subjects were very emotional in Kopple's presence, as when the Dixie Chicks got their first look at themselves in *Shut Up & Sing* or when Mariel Hemingway first glimpsed old footage of her sister Margaux and family in 2013's *Running from Crazy*. Both of these films' intensely personal examinations allow viewers access to unknown sides of the celebrities, and invite viewer self-examination.

After the premiere of *Harlan County, U.S.A.*, the pro-union film received overwhelming acceptance from those who appeared in the film fighting the coal company on the picket lines. The feeling is that the miners have won in more ways than one. She describes them to Liz Stubbs as "running all over Eastern Kentucky screaming, 'We got an Academy Award!'"[14] Even so, some members of the United Food and Commercial Workers union such as former leader Jim Guyette, as well as union strategist Ray Rogers, may have been upset by *American Dream*'s bleak portrayal of a divided movement and thought it damaging to the cause. Yet, *American Dream* has clearly proved healing for some portrayed in the film.

No matter what side people may fall on (or whether they remain somewhere in the middle) in the increasingly complex conflicts Kopple has documented, the most important influence of the social films she often makes is in the discussions they may start. In a 1997 film she created for the Alliance for Justice on the plight of a detained immigrant, she reportedly brought enough attention to his case to move it forward. Otherwise, he'd likely have remained "voiceless." Her subsequent film on children coping with AIDS brought that issue to the Disney Channel and to families' homes, where, she has hoped, questions from children might lead to research as a family.

During her storied career, from those days she herself accepted carrying arms in Harlan County to her creation of 2011's *Gun Fight* for HBO, Kopple has learned much about the importance of guns to many people. She definitely believes that open discussion is needed about the "gun control" issue, noting that the term itself doesn't communicate one clear concept to all concerned. Another 2011 film she directed, *Fight to Live*, about access to drugs for the terminally ill, likewise raises similarly tough questions.

Gender issues are a topic frequently brought up by interviewers, and Kopple has worked on many films relating to women's issues. She was director for the fictional family segments of *A Century of Women* TV series in the mid-nineties and executive producer and director of the revealing 1998 Lifetime TV-aired *Defending Our Daughters: The Rights of Women in the World* and 2005's A&E-aired *Bearing Witness*, on the challenges facing women war reporters. Yet she does not acknowledge an extreme influence of gender on her work, and reports she has not specifically sought female filmmakers for projects.

Still, she does at times report an impact, both positive and negative, of gender on her opportunities. She has told a student publication that in the 1960s, women could "get into" the field of making nonfiction films, as opposed to making fiction films, and that once they did they found, "People would talk to you—you didn't intimidate them because you were a woman."[15] She's also noted in interviews the advantage she feels she's had in covering men's sports in docs, since she is not expected, as a man might be, to come into the situation already with a great deal of knowledge about the subject.

In the 1990s, she describes men as a "mystery" or "fascination" for her, while expressing more sureness about her understanding of women and saying she wants to continue making films (and learning) about male subjects. One such attempt, though, her 2010 *House of Steinbrenner*, focusing on the historic Yankee Stadium and family dynasty, part of ESPN's award-winning *30 for 30* anniversary series, met with mixed reviews.

New York City, where she's long inhabited a loft right in the heart of things, also has clearly had an influence on Kopple, and vice versa. Most recently, she's tackled two ambitious "New York" subject films: one on a Brooklyn soul group and another on *The Nation* magazine, headquartered in the city. Kopple has taught at New York University's Tisch School of the Arts and continues to be active in many social issue and indie film organizations in the city and state. In fact, she has frequently been a panelist for the Woodstock film festival, from which she received a Maverick Award in 2006.

Despite the fact she didn't attend the original 1969 Woodstock music concert, she made up for it with her 2009 film/TV special *Woodstock: Now and Then*. Originally aired on VH1 and the History Channel, the film in part compares the concert-goers to the similarly huge throngs who worked wholeheartedly together for the election of President Barack Obama. Seemingly overnight, the political environment in which many of her films germinated was dramatically changed.

In a recent interview for *The Hill*, Kopple not surprisingly lists mental health care accessibility as something she would appreciate the opportunity to speak about with the current president, saying she would advise him to "keep listening to people from every corner of this country . . . in the debates about healthcare, gun violence, and income inequality."[17] Decidedly, even as Kopple's career advances through changing political eras, she remains committed to her original principles.

Kopple's dream film subject, according to another recent interview with the *Glasgow Herald*, is Hillary Clinton. "I would love to know what makes her tick and makes her so strong. To see who she is really," says the filmmaker.[18] In the course of reading these collected articles, we hope you will discover some of what makes Barbara Kopple tick, what makes her so strong, and who *she* really is.

Insight and cooperation are essential to realizing a text such as this one. Without the aid of several dozen supporters, this effort would have come to nothing.

I wish to express immense appreciation to the many individuals who either directly granted permission to republish their interviews or who negotiated their terms of use, too numerous to mention all individually here. But among them are Erin Trahan, editor and publisher of Independent Media Publications in Cambridge, Massachusetts; Timothy Rhys, editor and publisher of *MovieMaker Magazine*; and Professor William Kirtz of Northeastern University's School of Journalism. Grateful acknowledgment also is owed to retired labor historian Paul Buhle, now of Madison, Wisconsin; *Jump Cut* publisher Chuck Kleinhans; Noreen Springstead, managing director of the poverty and nutrition program WhyHunger; and Andre de la Cruz, former marketing manager at *Variety*. Another debt of gratitude is due to Michael Morgera of DCA Business Media in Westport, Connecticut; David Karp and Rebecca Grunfeld at SnagFilms, Inc.; cultural critic Damon Smith; and *Bright Lights* publisher Gary Morris.

Associate Editor Michael Spain of the Albany *Times Union* arranged rights to the article printed in his newspaper, while David Fellerath provided permissions from *Indy Week* in North Carolina's Triangle area, where he worked as culture and sports editor. Brooklyn-based documentary filmmaker Rahul Chadha was a great asset in allowing publication of a Q and A session with Kopple and crew that took place at the Independent Film Channel Center in New York City. Finally, Editor Tom White of International Documentary Association *Documentary* magazine was instrumental in securing film journalist Sara Vizcarrondo's permission to use her story.

A special note of thanks goes to Lesley Allen, who as screening committee chair at the Hot Springs International Film Festival in Arkansas allowed me to view and critique more than a hundred reality-based films from around the world. That experience set into motion a chain of events that was the genesis of this work. This volume would be sorely lacking without recognition of the ever-creative film critic, filmmaker, and Suffolk University professor Gerald Peary, whose counsel and encouragement were indispensable.

As you would expect from the University Press of Mississippi, its director, Leila Salisbury, offered much-appreciated guidance and motivation. Valerie Jones, editorial associate, is to be commended for her patience, availability, and attention to detail in this process, as well.

Most importantly and fondly, this book is dedicated to my able assistant editor and wife, Holly Prall, in grateful acknowledgement of her help with all facets of this project—from gathering for our viewing most of Kopple's films, to seeking permission for article usage, to creating the polished translations of the two French publication interviews included in this volume. Indeed, her contributions to the chronology and filmography could not have been more valuable and appreciated. And I couldn't have wished for a better companion on the journey.

GB

Notes

1. Jennifer Dunning, "A Woman Film Maker in the Coal Fields," *New York Times*, October 15, 1976, 59.

2. David Goldsmith, *The Documentary Makers: Interviews with 15 of the Best in the Business* (Rotovision, 2003), 74–85.

3. Alan Rosenthal, *The Documentary Conscience: A Casebook in Film Making* (University of California Press, 1980), chapter 18, "Harlan County, USA: Barbara Kopple and Hart Perry," 303–16.

4. Liz Stubbs, *Documentary Filmmakers Speak* (Allworth Press, 2012), 63–78.

5. Barbara Kopple, "Commencement 2010: Barbara Kopple," American University School of Communication, American University, 2015. ⟨http://www.american.edu/soc/resources/ commencement-2010-kopple-speech.cfm⟩.

6. Pope Brock, "Barbara Kopple: A Firebrand Documentary Filmmaker Moves to TV to Tackle Her Latest Subject: Iron Mike Tyson," *People*, February 15, 1993.

7. Stubbs, *Documentary Filmmakers Speak*.

8. Roland Legiardi-Laura, "Barbara Kopple," *Bomb* 38 (Winter 1992).

9. Ellen Oumano, *Film Forum: Thirty-Five Top Filmmakers Discuss Their Craft* (New York: St. Martin's Press, 1985).

10. Robin Finn, "Public Lives: Behind the Lens with the Dixie Chicks and Their Fallout," *New York Times*, November 3, 2006.

11. Legiardi-Laura, "Barbara Kopple."

12. Goldsmith, *The Documentary Makers: Interviews with 15 of the Best in the Business. Rotovision.*

13. Jerry Tallmer, "Barbara Kopple: Documentaries that Sing, Shout, and Speak for Themselves," *Thrive NYC* 1, no. 23 (April 2007).

14. Stubbs, *Documentary Filmmakers Speak*.

15. John Hall, "Interview with Barbara Kopple," *Latent Image: A Student Journal of Film Criticism*, Spring 1992.

16. Kate Meyers, "Barbara Kopple's KO Punch," *Entertainment Weekly*, February 12, 1993.

17. Robin Bronk, "My 5 Minutes with the President—Filmmakers Would Talk with Obama about Issues Close to Them," *The Hill*, July 31, 2013.

18. Alison Rowat, "Kopple Plans to Go On Revealing the Facts of Life," *(Glasgow) Herald*, October 10, 2013.

Chronology

1946   Born July 30 to Alfred Kopple, a textile business executive, and Marjorie Kopple, a homemaker; raised in Scarsdale, New York.

1949   Outspoken and blacklisted Paul Robeson's scheduled concert appearances near Peekskill, New York, end in riots between local veterans' groups and fans. Kopple's grandparents, who lived in Peekskill, argued that even if people didn't believe in his politics, Robeson still had a right to sing. Kopple's grandparents and this story were an influential part in her upbringing. Once her film career begins, she will almost immediately work toward creating a fiction film based on these riots which is also to be a love story.

1961   Ernest Hemingway commits suicide in Ketchum, Idaho. His granddaughter Mariel Hemingway is born shortly after.

mid-1960s   Barbara Kopple first sees the Hamptons—Long Island, New York, ocean-side resort towns—on family vacations.

1965/66   Enrolls at West Virginia's Harvey College (now known as the University of Charleston).

1967   Involved in Vietnam War protest movement. Enrolls at Boston's Northeastern University. In clinical psychology class, rather than write a report, she makes a short film involving lobotomy patients in the Medfield State Hospital. Canadian cameraman Hugh O'Connor fatally shot while photographing a miner on rented property in Kentucky, as Kopple will later be reminded of and warned about.

1968   Disastrous explosion at Farmington Coal Mine in West Virginia kills seventy-eight men. Kopple moves to New York's School for Social Research. Meets an employee of the Maysles brothers in a cinéma vérité class and is hired to assist Albert and David Maysles during the completion of their film *Salesman* and continuing during the creation of *Gimme Shelter* (completed 1970).

1969　Kopple does not attend first Woodstock concert; Hart Perry is a young cameraman for Michael Wadleigh's iconic film. Joseph Yablonski challenges long-time incumbent Tony Boyle for the presidency of the United Mine Workers; Joseph Yablonski, his wife, and his daughter, are then murdered by the order of the corrupt union official.

1970　Miners for Democracy develops with the aim to reform the union. Its leaders, from rank and file miners, include Arnold Miller, Mike Trbovich, and Harry Patrick. Kopple will read about these events, decide to make a film, and seek funding.

1971　Kopple continues to learn as an assistant. With donations gathered in part by Jane Fonda, Donald Sutherland, and filmmaker Barbara Jarvis's mother, Lucy, a film executive, nineteen filmmakers including Barbara Kopple work cooperatively, Kopple on sound, to film the testimony of veterans invited to Detroit to testify about atrocities in the Vietnam War and then to edit the footage into the film *Winter Soldier*.

1972　Around this time, Kopple does some sound for Peter Davis's *Hearts and Minds* project. *Winter Soldier* is shown and wins an award at the Cannes Film Festival but receives little television air time. In the first national election where all eighteen-year-olds have the right to vote, Kopple helps shoot footage at the Miami Republican convention, at which Allen Ginsberg and others opposing the Vietnam War are in attendance, about the Young Republicans for Nixon—part of which will be restored and screened at the Berkeley Film and Video Festival in 2011. She also is on the all-female crew for the film *Year of the Woman* at the Democratic convention, where Shirley Chisholm seeks the Democratic nomination.

Arnold Miller is elected president of the United Mine Workers, and work growing enrollment in the union begins. Kopple, who will name her company Cabin Creek Films, to remember the poverty of Cabin Creek in West Virginia, starts filming miners' music, black lung problems, and union history with a large crew. However, backer

	who'd pledged continued support changes his mind; she's filmed much footage of Arnold Miller related to Miners for Democracy but its executive board concludes it will not back her film without their control of it. She applies to many foundations to try to secure funding.
1973	Miners in Harlan County, Kentucky, vote to become part of the United Mine Workers but the mine owner, Duke Power, declines to sign a contract, prompting a strike in June. Kopple moves there with assistant director Anne Lewis and cameraman Hart Perry; they will live with the workers during the thirteen months of the strike, returning to New York for fundraising efforts periodically, as well as to Harlan after the initial strike to follow up.
1976	*Harlan County, U.S.A.* premieres at the New York Film Festival with miners and their relatives in attendance. Kopple helps found the Film Fund, to help filmmakers with backing of, fundraising efforts for, and usage of film and video media projects related to social issues. Hart Perry's *Valley of Tears* will be a film that receives some assistance from this fund.
1977	*Harlan County* wins the Academy Award for Best Documentary Feature (of 1976) and many other awards as well as being theatrically successful.
1979	Kopple begins to develop feature drama tentatively titled "Peekskill." Along with Haskell Wexler, directs documentary footage for social issue concert film, *No Nukes*. Cabin Creek Center for Work and Environmental Studies has tax-exempt status.
1981	Son (Hart) Nicholas Kopple-Perry is born to her and Hart Perry. Kopple completes first fiction film, *Keeping On*, dealing with unionization of textile mill workers in the South. She had long considered producing and directing a film about efforts to organize workers in a J. P. Stevens textile mill; Ray Rogers, who will later be shown in her film about a meatpackers' strike, was involved in that ultimately successful textile workers' campaign in North Carolina.
1983	*Keeping On* is broadcast on PBS's *American Playhouse*. Kopple's later soundperson, Alan Barker, works on Margaux Hemingway's project filming her family.
1985	United Food and Commercial Workers' Local Union P-9 in

Austin, Minnesota, headquarters of Hormel, goes on strike in August and Kopple begins documenting the subject of *American Dream*. Kopple is a juror for the Sundance Film Festival which grows out of the U.S. Film Festival.

1988 Barbara Kopple and Hart Perry split up after seventeen years, according to Perry. Kopple will marry Gene Carroll, former labor organizer and writer who teaches at Cornell University in labor studies.

1990 *Out of Darkness: The Mine Workers' Story* completed: directed by Kopple and Bill Davis, produced by Gene Carroll, and featuring the Pittston Coal Company strike. *Harlan County, U.S.A.* is chosen for inclusion in the National Film Registry of the Library of Congress. *American Dream* debuts at the 1990 New York Film Festival.

1991 *American Dream* wins the Academy Award for best feature-length documentary (Barbara Kopple and Arthur Cohn, as its producers, both receiving the award) and many film festivals' and other prestigious awards, continuing into 1992.

1992 *American Dream* is released after a delay due to one backer demanding immediate repayment; the project as a whole during filming had been nearly out of funding and was rescued when Bruce Springsteen answered pleas and gave $25,000 to help the endeavor be completed.

1992–93 For NBC TV, Kopple produces and directs *Fallen Champ: The Untold Story of Mike Tyson* (with son Nicholas credited as "fly hand"), which wins many awards including the Directors Guild of America (DGA) Award for Outstanding Directorial Achievement.

1994 *A Century of Women* series about women's history and issues, for which Kopple directs modern fictional family segments, is released. Kopple begins to film preparations for the 1994 Woodstock concert, but then funding is removed by PolyGram. Kopple continues work on a film about the concert despite lack of funding and other difficulties with completing and releasing her film.

1995 As a location co-director for a film directed by Danny Schechter, five years after Nelson Mandela's final release, Kopple goes to Robben Island, South Africa, to film Mandela's return to the prison he'd been held at for eighteen years.

1996 — Kopple films Woody Allen and his jazz band on a twenty-three-day tour throughout Europe. Margaux Hemingway fatally overdoses on phenobarbital.

mid-to-late 1990s — Kopple teaches at New York University's Tisch School of the Arts graduate film school. Her students include Lucy Walker, Nannette Burstein, and Brett Morgen.

1997 — Kopple and Cecilia Peck meet working on documentary about fiftieth anniversary of the Cannes Film Festival. They will soon begin working together, including collaborating on *A Conversation with Gregory Peck*, which includes parts of Cecilia's father, Gregory Peck's, Q and A tour. First commercials Kopple directs are aired: "documentary-style" commercials featuring Saudi Roundtree for Reeboks—much "real people" advertisement work will follow. Directs "The Documentary" episode of *Homicide: Life on the Street*, for which she wins a DGA Award. Two other episodes of *Homicide* and one of *Oz* will follow in later years.

1998 — Directs "Friends for Life: Living with AIDS," the first of a series of four Disney Channel specials, three on social issues, and the last about Texas students' production of the play *High School Musical*. Completes *Defending Our Daughters: The Rights of Women in the World*. Receives Irene Diamond Lifetime Achievement Award from Human Rights Watch Film Festival, presented by Alan J. Pakula, as well as several awards for *Wild Man Blues*, her film based on Woody Allen's jazz tour. Screenplay entitled *Joe Glory*, about Peekskill Riots at Paul Robeson concerts, is completed for her by Jeffrey Stanley in this year, the centennial of Paul Robeson's birth.

1999 — Shoots Woodstock '99 concert which will become part of the film *My Generation*.

2001 — *My Generation* debuts on Starz Encore. Kopple films summer in New York's Hamptons to create reality miniseries for ABC TV.

2002 — *The Hamptons* is shown on ABC.

2003 — Kopple becomes involved in Discovery Docs program. Invasion of Iraq occurs and Natalie Maines of the Dixie Chicks makes anti-war, anti-Bush comments during their Top of the World Tour, prompting conservative backlash back home. MTV refuses to accept an "advocacy" commercial

	which Barbara Kopple and her staff volunteered their time to complete in which appear young people and marches opposing the war. Idea for movie about female war reporters develops.
2004	Is an executive producer for Danny Schechter's *Weapons of Mass Deception* analysis of media coverage. *Harlan County* has been restored and preserved and is screened when Kopple is honored with the Charles Guggenheim Symposium at the Silverdocs/AFI (American Film Institute) Festival.
2005	Kopple wins Clio Awards and an international ANDY Award for Sprint PCS ads she directed. Kopple and co-director for *Shut Up & Sing*, Cecilia Peck, begin to follow and film the Dixie Chicks. Kopple's *Bearing Witness*, about female war correspondents, screens as part of the opening night "Why War?" section of the Full Frame Film Festival. Kopple completes direction of full-length fiction feature, *Havoc*, starring Anne Hathaway and Bijou Phillips as affluent L.A. teens involved with gang culture. Evan Perry, Barbara's son Nicholas Perry's half-brother, commits suicide at fifteen years old. His parents Hart and Dana Perry will later make the film *Boy, Interrupted*, about him.
2006	*Shut Up & Sing* premieres at the Toronto Film Festival and Kopple and Peck win multiple prestigious awards. Ironically, the commercials for this free-speech themed film are initially refused airing by NBC since they deal with a "public controversy." The Criterion Collection releases DVD of *Harlan County*.
2007	Kopple continues being honored with awards, particularly those for outstanding women. Becomes part of Documentary Channel's new volunteer advisory board. When campus massacre at Virginia Tech leaves thirty-three dead, Kopple records the aftermath to include in film she is directing about guns in America.
2008	Kopple helps judge the AFL-CIO "Turn Around America" video competition. She is hired to film Bon Jovi's "Lost Highway Tour" and help document the band's work. She also follows Dr. Jack Kevorkian lecturing at the University of Florida for a film project on him then in development. Pilot show created by Kopple, *The D.C. Sniper's Wife*, airs on TruTV.

2009	Kopple films reminiscences for *Woodstock: Now and Then* cable TV project and also Yankee spring training for *House of Steinbrenner* to air on ESPN in 2010.
2010	*Woodstock: Now and Then* is nominated for an Outstanding Arts & Culture Programming Emmy Award. Kopple receives Honorary Doctorate of Humane Letters from American University School of Communication.
2011	*Gun Fight* is released on HBO and shows at the International Documentary Film Festival Amsterdam (IDFA). Kopple films philanthropist Ellen Ratner at work, including in Sudan, and the result, *A Force of Nature*, premieres at the Woodstock Film Festival. The Kopple-directed film *Fight to Live*, about FDA regulation of drugs for use by those with terminal illnesses, is completed; later it will be released for purchase through the Internet.
2012	Begins filming for a documentary about *The Nation* magazine.
2013	Another Kopple-directed film, *Running from Crazy*, addressing suicides and healing in the Hemingway family, premieres at the Sundance Film Festival; the featured Mariel Hemingway and her daughter Langley are in attendance. The film is released theatrically first with plans to later show it on the Oprah Winfrey Network cable channel. Also, a film for which Kopple was executive producer and for which money was raised through corporate sponsorship and on the Internet, *Running Wild: The Life of Dayton O. Hyde*, is released. Kopple tweets for people who experienced the 1939 World's Fair and completes five-minute film focusing on it for *Vanity Fair*, *The 1930s*, featuring Lucy Jarvis. Son Nicholas Kopple-Perry, D.O. is doing his residency in child and adolescent psychology.
2015	*Hot Type: 150 Years of The Nation* premieres, honoring the magazine's anniversary. Kopple is reportedly editing a film about Sharon Jones & the Dap-Kings, a Brooklyn-based soul group, and another film about homeless veterans.

Filmography

As Director—Films

WINTER SOLDIER (1972)
Debuted at the 1972 Cannes Film Festival; released in Beta SP and Digi-Beta, on DVD April 2006 by Milliarium Zero
Director: Winterfilm Collective, i.e., Fred Aranow, Nancy Baker, Joe Bangert, Rhetta Barron, Robert Fiore, David Gillis, David Grubin, Jeff Holstein, Barbara Jarvis, Al Kaupas, **Barbara Kopple**, Mark Lenix, Michael Lesser, Lee Osborne, Lucy Massie Phenix, Roger Phenix, Benay Rubenstein, Nancy Miller Saunders, Michael Weil
Cast: John Kerry, Scott Camil, Rusty Sachs, Ken Campbell, Vietnam Veterans Against the War
16 mm, b&w and color, 95 minutes

HARLAN COUNTY, U.S.A. (documentary) (1976)
Premiered New York Film Festival Oct. 15, 1976, Almi Cinema 5 Distributing; aired on PBS 1978; rereleased Criterion Collection DVD 2006
Producer: **Barbara Kopple**
Director: **Barbara Kopple**
Associate Director: Anne Lewis
Cinematography: Hart Perry (principal cinematographer), Kevin Keating
Sound Recordist: **Barbara Kopple**
Editing: Nancy Baker (director of editing), Mary Lampson, Josh Waletsky (sound editor)
Music: Hazel Dickens (score), Merle Travis (score), Nimrod Workman, Sarah Gunnings, Florence Reese
16 mm, 103 minutes

NO NUKES: THE MUSE CONCERTS (1980)
Distributed by Warner Bros.; MGM/CBS Home Video 1981
Executive Producer: Sam Lovejoy

Producer: Julian Schlossberg, Danny Goldberg
Director: Danny Goldberg, Julian Schlossberg, Anthony Potenza
Documentary Footage Director: **Barbara Kopple**, Haskell Wexler
Cast: Jackson Browne, David Crosby, The Doobie Brothers, John Hall, Graham Nash, Bonnie Raitt, Gil Scott-Heron, Carly Simon, Bruce Springsteen, Stephen Stills, James Taylor, Jesse Colin Young
103 minutes

OUT OF DARKNESS: THE MINE WORKERS' STORY (documentary) (1990)
Released on VHS 1990; available on DVD
Executive Producer: John Duray, Greg Hawthorne
Producer: Gene Carroll
Associate Producer: Dena Mermelstein, Shelly Silver, James Green
Field Producer: Gene Carroll, **Barbara Kopple**, Gary Fritz, John Duray
Director: **Barbara Kopple**, Bill Davis
Associate Director: Darryl Orr
Writer: Gene Carroll, John Duray, James Green
Cinematography: Gary Fritz, Kevin Keating, Mathieu Roberts, Mark Hay, Phil Parmet, Richard Chisolm, Jim Morrisette
Sound Recording: Gary Fritz, Mark Hay, Brian Hoffert, Richard Pooler, William Porter, Thomas Szabolcs, Brian Tooke, Dennis Towns
Main Title Design: Joanne Flaherty, Cathe Ishino; Computer Graphics: Shaun Pritchard
Editing: Bill Davis, Shelly Silver, Stefan Bruck
Music: Tom Juravich (performer), Michael Aharon (score)
Best Breaker Boys: Nicolas Kopple-Perry, Russell B. Ginsberg-Davis, David Massimo-Duray
Color with b&w sequences, 100 minutes

AMERICAN DREAM (documentary) (1990)
Released March 18, 1992, distributed by Prestige: A Division of Miramax Films
Producer: **Barbara Kopple**, Arthur Cohn
Associate Producer: Ernest Hood, Jonathan House, Molly Ornati, Gail Rosenschein, William Susman
Director: **Barbara Kopple**
Cinematography: Peter Gilbert, Kevin Keating, Hart Perry, Mark T. Petersson, Mathieu Roberts,

Sound Recordist: **Barbara Kopple**
Title Design: Cathe Ishino
Editing and Co-Director: Cathy Caplan, Lawrence Silk, Tom Haneke
Music: Michael Small (score), Sylvia Reed (coordinator)
Best Boy: Nicolas Kopple-Perry
Cast: Lewie Anderson, Ray Rogers, Jesse Jackson (among others)
16 mm, 98 minutes

BEYOND JFK: THE QUESTION OF CONSPIRACY (documentary) (1992)
Distributed by Warner Bros. Home Entertainment Group
Executive Producer: Danny Schechter, Rory O'Connor
Senior Producer: Stuart Sender; Supervising Producer: Gwynne Thomas
Director: Danny Schechter with **Barbara Kopple**
Writer: Danny Schechter
Cinematography: Kevin McCafferty, John Hanlon, Henry Zinman, Dasal Banks, Gary Griffin, Leigh Wilson, Bill Starling, J. Rolan Barry
Audio: Gary McCafferty, Gene Huelsman, David Jamal Banks, Edna Snow, John Collins, Karl Suchman, Tom Richards, J. Rolan Barry
Design: Cathe Ishino
Editing: Bruce Follmer (supervising editor)
Music: Christopher Burke (original music)
Cast/Interviewees: Kevin Costner, Jim Garrison, Oliver Stone, Gary Oldman
Narrator: Ike Pappas
90 minutes

PRISONERS OF HOPE: ROBBEN ISLAND REUNION (documentary) (1995)
Released by Videovision Entertainment
Producer: Anant Singh
Director: Danny Schechter
Co-Director: **Barbara Kopple** (for Robben Island), Ken Kaplan (for Johannesburg)
Cinematography: Craig Matthews, Peter Baker, Shafiek Cassim
Sound: Simon Rice, Pierre Rommelaere, Chevan Rayson
Art Direction: Wynand Posthumus (titles), Rosalind Lurie (title design)
Editing: Henion Han
Cast: Gcina Mhlophe (narrator)
60 minutes

PRESIDENTS' SUMMIT FOR AMERICA'S FUTURE: PRESIDENT'S SERVICE AWARD (documentary) (1997)
Segment Producer and Director: **Barbara Kopple**

WILD MAN BLUES (documentary) (1997)
Released April 17, 1998, distributed by Fine Line Features
Producer: **Barbara Kopple**, Jean Doumanian
Associate Producer: Kathleen Bambrick Meier
Executive Producer: J. E. Beaucaire
Director: **Barbara Kopple**
Cinematography: Tom Hurwitz
Sound: **Barbara Kopple,** Peter Miller
Editing: Lawrence Silk
Music: Eddy Davis, Woody Allen, Dan Barrett, Simon Wettenhall, John Gill, Cynthia Sayer, Greg Cohen; also music by Nino Rota performed by the Czech Symphony Orchestra
Cast: Woody Allen (Himself), Soon-Yi Previn, Letty Aronson (Herself—Woody Allen's Sister), other family, tour, and band members, etc.
16 mm, 103 minutes

WITH LIBERTY AND JUSTICE FOR ALL (1997)
An Alliance for Justice presentation of a Cabin Creek Films production
Executive Producer: Nan Aron
Producer: Esther Cassidy, Kristi Jacobson, **Barbara Kopple**, Linda Saffire
Associate Producer: Jennifer Norton, Cecilia Peck
Director: **Barbara Kopple**
Cinematography: Tom Hurwitz, Don Lenzer
Sound: Peter Miller, Mark Roy
Editing: Aaron Kuhn
Original Music: Art Labriola; Bruce Springsteen and Indigo Girls (use of songs)
Cast: Jesus Collado-Muñoz, Stephen Converse (attorney), Paul Ahua, Michele Meyer-Shipp (attorney), Lucas Guttentag, The Honorable Denny Chin
~32 minutes

THE ROAD HOME: STORIES OF CHILDREN OF WAR (documentary film—part of multimedia presentation and performance) (1999)
Project Conceived and Directed by Lawrence Sacharow
Film Director: **Barbara Kopple**

MY GENERATION: WOODSTOCK 1969, 1994, 1999 (documentary) (2000)
Dolmen Home Video (Germany, Italy, USA); debuted on Starz Encore channel 2001
Producer: **Barbara Kopple**; Mikado Film (Roberto Cicutto and Luigi Musini), Polygram Diversified Ventures (Rick Finkelstein), Schulberg Productions (Sandra Schulberg), Solaris (Gregory O'Connor, Gavin O'Connor, Josh Fagin)
Director: **Barbara Kopple**, Tom Haneke
Screenwriter: **Barbara Kopple**
Cinematography: Tom Hurwitz
Editing: Tom Haneke
Music: The Who, Cocker, Joplin, Metallica, Chili Peppers
Cast: Henry Rollins (Himself), Michael Lang (Woodstock Producer)
Color and b&w, 16 mm and digital video, 103 minutes

DANCE CUBA: DREAMS OF FLIGHT (documentary) (2004)
Premiered at 2004 Miami Film Festival
Producer: Cynthia Newport
Director: Cynthia Newport, **Barbara Kopple**, Boris Ivan Crespo
Cinematography: Don Lenzer, Roberto Chile, Tom Hurwitz
Sound: Ira Spiegel
Editing: Deborah Dickson, Richard Hankin
Music: Chucho Valdés (score)
Cast: Alicia Alonso, Fernando Alonso, Donald Saddler, Silvia Rodriguez, Carlos Acosta, Septime Webre, Laura Urgelles, Lorna Feijóo, Pedro Acosta, Trey McIntyre, Angela Grau, Miguel Cabrera, Cortney Palomo, Victor Gil, Jonah Gonzalez
Color, 24p high definition video, 105 minutes

HAVOC (drama) (2005)
Distributed by New Line Cinema, Media 8 Entertainment—appeared at film festivals, released on DVD in the U.S., and shown in theatres in Europe
Executive Producer: Sammy Lee, Jonas McCord, Andreas Grosch, Andreas Schmid
Producer: Jack F. Murphy, John Morrissey, Stewart Hall
Co-Producer: Lars Bjorck, Stefan Jonas
Director: **Barbara Kopple**
Story: Stephen Gaghan, Jessica Kaplan
Screenplay: Stephen Gaghan

Cinematography: Kramer Morgenthau
Art Direction: Loren Basulto
Production Design: Jerry Fleming
Editing: Nancy Baker, Jerry Greenberg
Music: Cliff Martinez (score), Swan K. Clement, Michael McQuarn (supervisor)
Sound: Trip Brock
Cast: Anne Hathaway (Allison), Bijou Phillips (Emily), Shiri Appleby (Amanda), Michael Biehn (Stuart Lang), Joseph Gordon-Levitt (Sam), Matt O'Leary (Eric), Freddy Rodriguez (Hector), Laura San Giacomo (Joanna Lang), Mike Vogel (Toby), Raymond Cruz (Chino), Alexis Dziena (Sasha), Channing Tatum (Nick), Johnny Vasquez (Manuel), Luis Robledo (Ace), Sam Hennings (Mr. Rubin), Cecilia Peck (Mrs. Rubin), Josh Peck (Josh Rubin), John Morrissey (Richard), Robert Shapiro (Himself), J. D. Pardo (Todd Rosenberg), Terri Hanauer (Lt. Kovaleski), Sam Bottoms (Lt. Maris)
85 minutes

SHUT UP & SING (documentary) (2006)
Released October 27, 2006, distributed by The Weinstein Company, DVD released 2007
Producer: **Barbara Kopple,** Cecelia Peck, David Cassidy
Co-Producer: Claude Davies
Director: **Barbara Kopple**, Cecelia Peck
Cinematography: Christine Burrill, Luis Lopez, Seth Gordon, Gary Griffin, Joan Churchill
Title Design: Number 17, NY; Bonnie Siegler & Emily Oberman
Editing: Bob Eisenhardt, Jean Tsien, Aaron Kuhn, Emma Morris
Music: Dixie Chicks, Charlie Robison
Sound: Giovanni Di Simone, Alan Barker, Jason Blackburn, Peter Miller; Additional Sound: **Barbara Kopple** and others
Cast: Martie Maguire, Natalie Maines, Emily Robison, Simon Renshaw
Shot on videotape, 91 minutes

EDGE OF MADNESS (drama) (2007/08)
Green Dog Films
Producer: Jason Gurvitz, Yan Fisher Romanovsky, Phyllis Carlyle
Director: **Barbara Kopple** (unclear if Kopple's involvement continued throughout filming)
Screenplay: Geno Havens

A FORCE OF NATURE (documentary) (2011)
Premiered at the 2011 Woodstock Film Festival
Executive Producer: Bruce Ratner, Michael Ratner
Producer: Suzanne Mitchell, **Barbara Kopple**
Associate Producer: Madeleine Akers, Kelly Brennan, David Cassidy
Director: **Barbara Kopple**
Cinematography: Gary Griffin, David Sosnow
Editing: William Davis
Cast: Ellen Ratner
46 minutes

FIGHT TO LIVE (documentary) (2011)
Premiered at Woodstock Film Festival 2012; VOD released by Gravitas Ventures 2014
Producer: Hilary Birmingham, **Barbara Kopple,** Carla Woods
Director: **Barbara Kopple**
Director of Photography: John Hazard
Editing: William Davis
Sound: Carlos Albores, John Garrett, Malcolm Hirst
81 minutes

DECADES SERIES: THE 1930s (2013)
Released September 30, 2013, on *Vanity Fair* website
Producer: **Barbara Kopple**
Director: **Barbara Kopple**
Cinematography: Alec Bohem, Isaac Brown, Gary Griffin, Mark Petersson, Chris Villafuerte
Editing: Bill Davis
Sound: David Cassidy, Giovanni Di Simone
5 minutes

THE 1930s, BY BARBARA KOPPLE, BEHIND THE SCENES (2013)
Director: **Barbara Kopple**

YOUR TAX DOLLARS AT WORK (2014)
For Vulcan Productions and Cinelan's *We the Economy: 20 Short Films You Can't Afford to Miss*, released through various media
Series Supervising Producer: Damon Smith
Producer: David Cassidy, Ray Nowosielski
Director: **Barbara Kopple**
6 minutes

HOT TYPE: 150 YEARS OF THE NATION (2015)
Premiered at Museum of Modern Art's Documentary Fortnight series, February 27, 2015
Producer: **Barbara Kopple**, Suzanne Mitchell
Director: **Barbara Kopple**
Director of Photography: Gary Griffin
Editing: Richard Hankin
Music: Max Avery Lichtenstein, composer
93 minutes

As Director—Television

KEEPING ON (drama) (1981)
Broadcast on American Playhouse, PBS, February 8, 1983
Executive Producer: Lindsay Law, **Barbara Kopple**
Producer: Coral Hawthorne
Director: **Barbara Kopple**
Screenplay: Horton Foote
Cinematography: Larry Pizer
Art Direction: John Lawless
Editing: Lora Hays
Music: Charlie Morrow
Cast: James Broderick, Rosalind Cash, Danny Glover, Carol Kane, Marcia Rodd, Dick Anthony Williams, Carl Lee
~75 minutes

CIVIL RIGHTS: THE STRUGGLE CONTINUES (documentary) (1989)
Producer: **Barbara Kopple**
Co-Producer: Esther Cassidy
Director: **Barbara Kopple**

LOCKED OUT IN AMERICA: VOICES FROM RAVENSWOOD (~1992)
Show 511, aired on PBS stations in 1994–1995 season
We Do the Work Series Producers: Ed Herzog, Rhian Miller, Patrice O'Neill
Producer: **Barbara Kopple**, Bill Davis
Director: **Barbara Kopple**, Bill Davis
Cinematography: Kevin Keating, Gary Griffin, J. Philip Dickson, Tim Flaherty
Sound: Peter Tooke, David Peterson
Graphic Design: Jody Bortner

Editing: Bill Davis, Jeremiah Birnbaum (assistant)
Original Music: Chris Burke, Second Language
Best Boys: Nicolas Kopple-Perry, Russell Ginsberg Davis
30 minutes

FALLEN CHAMP: THE UNTOLD STORY OF MIKE TYSON (documentary) (1993)
Broadcast January 1, 1993, NBC; Sony Pictures Home Entertainment, domestic video distributor
Executive Producer: Diane Sokolow, Sam Sokolow
Producer: **Barbara Kopple,** Richard Stratton
Associate Producer: Jeremiah Birnbaum, Lynn Vogelstein, Sam Sokolow
Director: **Barbara Kopple**
Writer: **Barbara Kopple**
Cinematography: Eric Gasteiger, Tom Hurwitz, Kevin Keating (director of photography), Michael Marton, Dave Meador, Phil Parmet, Mathieu Roberts, Alicia Weber, David Yosha
Still Photographer: Christopher Farina
Art: Carole Kabrin
Editing: Bill Davis, Leon Gast, Lawrence Silk (senior editor)
Visual Effects: Adam Zucker
Animation: Rob Issen
Music: Michael Bacon, Richard G. Mitchell
Sound: Paul Cote, Tommy Lockett, Brenda Ray, Peter Tooke
Shot on film and edited on video, 93 minutes

A CENTURY OF WOMEN (series): WORK AND FAMILY, SEXUALITY AND SOCIAL JUSTICE, IMAGE AND POPULAR CULTURE (documentary with fiction component) (1994)
Released 1994, TBS Productions
Executive Producer: Jacoba Atlas, Pat Mitchell
Producer: Kyra Thompson, Lynne Tuite
Director: Sylvia Morales (documentary segments), **Barbara Kopple** (fictional family segments)
Screenwriter: Jacoba Atlas, Heidi Shulman, Lynn Roth
Director of Photography: Ellen Kuras
Production Design: Conrad E. Angone
Editing: Judy Reidel, Michael Mayhew
Music: Laura Karpman (score)

Cast: Justine Bateman, Olympia Dukakis, Jasmine Guy, Talia Shire, Madge Sinclair, Brooke Smith, Teresa Wright
Narrator: Jane Fonda
95 minutes

HOMICIDE: LIFE ON THE STREET: "The Documentary" (drama) (1997)
NBC
Created by Paul Attanasio based upon the book by David Simon
Executive Producer: Barry Levinson, Tom Fontana
Supervising Producer: James Yoshimura; Co-Executive Producer: Jim Finnerty
Director: **Barbara Kopple**
Story: Tom Fontana, James Yoshimura, Eric Overmeyer
Teleplay: Eric Overmyer
Cinematography: Jean de Segonzac
Production Design: Vince Peranio
Editing: Jay Pires
Music: Douglas J. Cuomo; Music Supervisor: Chris Tergesen
Cast: Richard Belzer (Det. John Munch), Andre Braugher (Det. Frank Pembleton), Reed Diamond (Det. Mike Kellerman), Michelle Forbes (Dr. Julianna Cox), Clark Johnson (Det. Meldrick Lewis), Yaphet Kotto (Lt. Al Giardello), Melissa Leo (Sgt. Kay Howard), Max Perlich (J. H. Brodie), Kyle Secor (Det. Tim Bayliss), Barry Levinson (Himself)
60 minutes

DEFENDING OUR DAUGHTERS: THE RIGHTS OF WOMEN IN THE WORLD (documentary) (1998)
Aired on Lifetime Television for Women
Executive Producer: **Barbara Kopple**
Supervising Producer: Linda Saffire; Senior Producer: Kristi Jacobson, Judith Moses, Susan Ryan
Associate Producer: Cecelia Peck, Jesse Moss
Director: **Barbara Kopple**
Director of Photography: Christine Burill, Joan Churchill, Stephen Lighthill
Sound: Peter Miller, Janet Urban, Aerlyn Weissman
Studio Director: Mark Gentile; Set Designer: Mitchell Greenberg
Editing: Lawrence Silk (senior editor), Nanette Burstein, Aaron Kuhn
Music: Art LaBriola, Peter Gabriel (additional music)
Cast: Meryl Streep, Host
50 minutes

HOMICIDE: LIFE ON THE STREET: "Pit Bull Sessions" (drama) (1998)
NBC
Created by Paul Attanasio based upon the book by David Simon
Executive Producer: Barry Levinson, Tom Fontana
Supervising Producer: Julie Martin, James Yoshimura; Co-Executive Producer: Jim Finnerty
Producer: Anya Epstein, David Simon
Director: **Barbara Kopple**
Story: James Yoshimura, Julie Martin
Teleplay: Sean Whitesell
Cinematography: Alex Zakrzewski
Production Design: Vince Peranio
Editing: Ken Eluto
Music: Douglas J. Cuomo; Music Supervisor: Chris Tergesen
Cast: Richard Belzer (Det. John Munch), Andre Braugher (Det. Frank Pembleton), Reed Diamond (Det. Mike Kellerman), Peter Gerety (Det. Stuart Gharty), Clark Johnson (Det. Meldrick Lewis), Yaphet Kotto (Lt. Al Giardello), Kyle Secor (Det. Tim Bayliss), Jon Seda (Det. Paul Falsone), Callie Thorne (Det. Laura Ballard), Paul Giamatti (Henry Tjarks), Toni Lewis (Det. Terri Stivers), Laurie Kennedy (Felicity Weaver), Tony Fitzpatrick (Tony), Granville Adams (Off. Jeff Westby), Kevin Grantz (Stanley Bradshaw), Ralph Tabakin (Dr. Scheiner)
60 minutes

FRIENDS FOR LIFE: LIVING WITH AIDS (documentary) (1998)
Debuted on World AIDS Day—A Disney Channel Original Special; distributed by Disney Educational Productions
Executive Producer: Laurie Meadoff
Senior Producer: Susan Ryan; Supervising Producer: Linda Saffire
Producer: **Barbara Kopple**, Kate Hillis, Amy Shatsky-Gambrill
Associate Producer: Cecelia Peck
Director: **Barbara Kopple**
Photography: Kyle Kibbe, Dyanna Taylor, Peter Pearce, Tom Hurwitz, Bob Richman, Don Lenzer
Sound: John McCormick, Eric Williams, Michael Lonsdale, Peter Miller
Graphic Art: Amanda Junquera
Editing: Doug O'Connor
Music: Carlos Alomar
27 minutes

HOMICIDE: LIFE ON THE STREET: "Self Defense" (1999)
NBC
Created by Paul Attanasio based upon the book by David Simon
Executive Producer: Barry Levinson, Tom Fontana, Jim Finnerty
Supervising Producer: Eric Overmyer; Co-Executive Producer: Julie Martin, James Yoshimura
Co-producer: Sara B. Charno
Director: **Barbara Kopple**
Story: Eric Overmyer, David Simon
Teleplay: Yaphet Kotto
Cinematography: Alex Zakrzewski
Production Design: Vince Peranio
Editing: Ken Eluto
Music: Douglas J. Cuomo; Music Supervisor: Chris Tergesen
Cast: Richard Belzer (Det. John Munch),Giancarlo Esposito (Agent Michael Giardello), Peter Gerety (Det. Stuart Gharty), Clark Johnson (Det. Meldrick Lewis), Yaphet Kotto (Lt. Al Giardello), Toni Lewis (Det. Terri Stivers), Michael Michele (Det. Rene Sheppard), Kyle Secor (Det. Tim Bayliss), Jon Seda (Det. Paul Falsone), Callie Thorne (Det. Laura Ballard), Austin Pendleton (Dr. Griscom), Haviland Morris (Eleanor Burke), Paul Butler (Clifford Ramsey), Clayton LeBouef (Col. Barnfather), Ellen McElduff (Billie Lou), Jay Spadaro (Salerno), Zeljko Ivanek (ASA Ed Danvers)
60 minutes

OZ: "Out o' Time" (1999)
Aired September 1, 1999, HBO
Created by Tom Fontana
Executive Producer: Barry Levinson, Tom Fontana, Jim Finnerty
Supervising Producer: Bridget Potter
Director: **Barbara Kopple**
Writer: Tom Fontana
Director of Photography: Craig DiBona
Production Design: Gary Weist
Editing: Jay Pires
Music: David Darlington, Stephen Rosen; Music Supervisor: Chris Tergesen
Cast: Rick Acevedo, Adewale Akinnouye-Agbaje, Ernie Hudson, Terry Kinney, Rita Moreno, Harold Perrineau, J. K. Simmons, Lee Tergesen, Eamonn Walker, Dean Winters
58 minutes

A CONVERSATION WITH GREGORY PECK (documentary) (1999)
Aired on Turner Classic Movies and on PBS as part of *American Masters* in 2000; included in Universal's Legacy Series 2005 *To Kill a Mockingbird* DVD set
Producer: **Barbara Kopple**, Cecilia Peck, Linda Saffire
Assistant to the Producers: Nicolas Kopple-Perry; Best Boys: Harper Peck, Zack Peck
Director: **Barbara Kopple**
Cinematography: Don Lenzer, Tom Hurwitz, Sandi Sissel
Sound: Peter Miller, John McCormick, Michael Lonsdale
Opening Titles: Tony Lover, Liberty Studio; Closing Titles: Tony Lover, David Bruce, Lis Cherry
Editing: Bob Eisenhardt
Music: Art LaBriola
Cast: Gregory Peck and family
97 minutes

LEARNING FOR LIFE: KIDS AND LEARNING DIFFERENCES (documentary) (2000)
Released December 2000, The Disney Channel and Disney Educational Productions
Executive Producer: Laurie Meadoff
Producer and Director: **Barbara Kopple**
Supervising Producer: Linda Saffire; Senior Producer: Susan Ryan
Producer: Kate Hillis, Amy Shatsky-Gambrill
Cinematography: Don Lenzer, Hart Perry
Sound: Michael Lonsdale, John McCormick, Peter Miller, Brenda Ray, Ron Yoshida
Editing: Doug O'Connor
Music: Carlos Alomar
24 minutes

CONFIDENT FOR LIFE: KIDS AND BODY IMAGE (documentary) (2002)
Distributed by Disney Educational Productions
Executive Producer: Laurie Meadoff
Producer: **Barbara Kopple**, Linda Saffire, Kate Hillis
Associate Producer: David Becker, Tania McKeown, Mary Woods
Director: **Barbara Kopple**
Co-Director: Linda Saffire
Cinematography: Don Lenzer, Kyle Kibbe, Tom Hurwitz
Sound: Peter Miller, John Murphy, Matt Quast, Brenda Ray, Matt Sutton

Editing: Doug O'Connor
Music: Carlos Alomar
27 minutes

(ONCE UPON A TIME IN) THE HAMPTONS (documentary/reality miniseries) (2002)
Limited theatrical release in May 2002 under the title *The Hamptons Project*; on ABC, shown in two, two-hour installments on June 2 and 3, 2002
Executive Producer: Diane Sokolow
Producer and Director: **Barbara Kopple**
Producer: Linda Saffire, Jerry Kupfer
Field Producer: Suzanne Mitchell, Amy Shatsky-Gambrill
Additional Field Producer: Cecilia Peck, Daniel Voll
Associate Producer/Field Producer: Rachael P. Goldstein, Claude Kaplan, Tania McKeown, Margery Mailman, Michael Sutton, Marijana Wotton, Kristi Jacobson
Director of Photography: Don Lenzer, Nancy Schreiber, Kirsten Johnson
Sound: Peter Miller, Gabriel Miller, Roger Phenix, David Foerder, Brenda Ray, Matt Sutton, Paul Wilson
Editing: Lawrence Silk, Jean Tsien, Jennifer Robinson, Doug O'Connor
Music: Michael Bacon (score)
Cast: Christie Brinkley, Billy Joel, others
shot on videotape, 240 minutes

I MARRIED . . . (nonfiction TV series) (2003–2005 (aired))
Aired on VH1
Executive Producer: Kate Hillis, Laurie Meadoff, **Barbara Kopple** (from resume)
Producer: David Cassidy, Claude Davies
Director: **Barbara Kopple**
Cast (featured in different episodes): MC Hammer and wife Stephanie, Darius Rucker and wife Beth, Omarosa Manigault-Stallworth and husband Aaron, Carnie Wilson and husband Rob, Sebastian Bach and wife Maria, Uncle Kracker and wife Melanie, Sammy Hagar and wife Kari
30 minute shows

BEARING WITNESS (documentary) (2005)
Premiered at the Full Frame Film Festival 2005 on opening night, made for A&E Indie Films, aired on TV in 2005

Executive Producer: **Barbara Kopple**, Nancy Dubuc (A&E)
Producer: **Barbara Kopple**, Marijana Wotton
Associate Producer: David Cassidy
Director: Bob Eisenhardt, **Barbara Kopple**, Marijana Wotton
Idea: Maryam d'Abo
Cinematography: Richard Connors, Joan Churchill, Richard Parry; Additional Cinematography: David Becker, Dominic Cunningham-Reed, Bruno Girodon, Luke Geissbuhler, Lucjan Gorczynski, Tamara Goldsworthy, Kristi Jacobson, Tom Kaufman, John Murphy, David Niblock, John Ryan, Pascal Sentenac, Marijana Wotton
Sound: John Murphy, Marijana Wotton; Additional Sound: Ahmed, John Wesley Blackman, Mahmoud Batout, David Cassidy, Yuri Reitsen, Chris Renty, Hussein Soliman
Graphic Design: The Nuncle Group
Editing: Bob Eisenhardt
Music: Joel Goodman (score)
Cast: May Ying Welsh, Mary Welch Rogers, Molly Bingham, Marie Calvin, Janine DiGiovanni
90 minutes

ADDICTION: "Steamfitters Local Union 638" (short segment for longer documentary and website resource) (2007)
Premiered on HBO March 2007, freely available on HBO *Addiction* multimedia website Executive Producer: Sheila Nevins
Producer: John Hoffman, Susan Froemke; Co-Producer: Micah Cormier
Segment Director and Producer: **Barbara Kopple** (directors of other segments: Jon Alpert, Joe Berlinger, Kate Davis, Susan Froemke, Liz Garbus, Chris Hegedus, David Heilbroner, Eugene Jarecki, Ellen Goosenberg Kent, Albert Maysles, D. A. Pennebaker, Alan Raymond, Susan Raymond, Bruce Sinofsky, Jessica Yu)
Editing: Paula Heredia
10 minutes (segment)

HIGH SCHOOL MUSICAL: THE MUSIC IN YOU (docu-musical) (2007–2008)
Shown on Disney Channel and DisneyChannel.com (short clips in late 2007 followed by a half-hour show in January 2008)
Producer: **Barbara Kopple**
Field Producer: Craig Hymson
Associate Producer: Kelly Brennan
Director: **Barbara Kopple**

Director of Photography: Gary Griffin
Sound: James Baker, Daniel Brooks, Michael Jones, Michael Gonzalez
Graphic Design: Vincent MacTiernan, Bill Glenn Davis
Editing: William Davis, Douglas O'Connor
Music: Disney Channel
30 minutes

THE D.C. SNIPER'S WIFE (documentary pilot) (2008)
Aired on TruTV
Executive Producer: Bonnie Dry
Producer: **Barbara Kopple**, Williams Cole, David Cassidy
Associate Producer: Kelly Brennan, Craig Hymson
Creator: **Barbara Kopple**
Director of Photography: Foster Wiley
Cinematography: Ian Cook, Tom Kaufman, Mark Stoddard
Sound: Bob Silverthorne, Paul Rusnak
Graphic Design: Theo Stewart-Stand
Editing: Jason Szabo, William Davis
Music: Art LaBriola, Skooby Laposky
Cast: Mildred Muhammad
60 minutes

WOODSTOCK: NOW AND THEN (documentary) (2009)
In August 2009 premiered on VH1 (episode 124 of VH1 Rockdocs) and shown on the History channel
Executive Producer: Michael Lang; for History: Julian P. Hobbs; for VH1: Shelly Tatro, Jeff Olde, Brad Abramson, Stephen Mintz
Producer: **Barbara Kopple,** Suzanne Mitchell
Co-Producer: Ashraf Rijal
Associate Producer: Lee Blumer, Kelly Brennan, Julia M. Finn; Associate Producers for Woodstock Ventures: Joel Rosenman, Jennifer Roberts
Director: **Barbara Kopple**
Writer: Martin Torgoff
Director of Photography: Hart Perry
Cinematography: Gary Griffin, Mauro Brattoli, Christine Burrill, Tamara Goldsworthy, David Becker, Jon Else, Lee Daniel, Bill Mills, Mike Harrison, Mario Signore, Alec Boehm, David Sosnow, Ashraf Rijal
Sound: William Tzouris, Ryan Carroll, Giovanni Di Simone, Jonathan Chiles, Susumu Tokunow, John Hollis, David Pruger, Phillip Harris, David Layton, Michael Jones, Scott Charles, Zach Horton, Zachary Stauffer, Dina Moore, Brian Murrell, David Cassidy

Graphics: Lucjan Gorczynski, VH1 Graphics: Amanda Havey
Cartoonist: Rogerio Nogueira
Editing: Bob Eisenhardt (supervising), Emir Lewis, Michael Culyba (music)
Music Clearance: Rick Eisenstein, Diamond Time Ltd.; Maureen Daugherty, Cabin Creek Films; VH1 Music and Media Licensing: Ty Kistler, Shari Rothseid, Paul Short
89 minutes

HOUSE OF STEINBRENNER (documentary) (2010)
ESPN Film part of *30 for 30* series, premiered on ESPN, September 21, 2010
For ESPN Films: Executive Producer: Keith Clinkscales, John Dahl, Joan Lynch, Connor Schell, John Skipper, Bill Simmons, John Walsh; Producer: Mark Durand; Consulting Producer: Mike Tollin, Associate Producer: Libby Geist
Producer: **Barbara Kopple**, David Cassidy, Nicole Renna
Associate Producer: Kelly Brennan, Ashraf Rijal
Director: **Barbara Kopple**
Cinematography: Mario Signore, John Hazard, David Cassidy, Gary Griffin, Ashraf Rijal
Sound: Jonathan Chiles, David Cassidy, Ryan Carroll, Michael Barnett
Graphics: Lucjan Gorczynski
Editing: Tom Haneke, Bob Eisenhardt
Music: Pump Audio53 minutes

GUN FIGHT (documentary) (2011)
Premiered on HBO in April 2011
Executive Producer for HBO: Sheila Nevins; Senior Producer for HBO: Lisa Heller
Producer: **Barbara Kopple**, Marc N. Weiss, Williams Cole
Director: **Barbara Kopple**
Writer: Bob Eisenhardt
Cinematography: Gary Griffin, Christine Burrill
Sound: Daniel Brooks, Giovanni DiSimone, Robert Silverthorne
Graphic Design and Visual Effects: Lucjan Gorczynski
Editing: Bob Eisenhardt
Music: Music Box LLC
89 minutes

RUNNING FROM CRAZY (documentary) (2013)
Premiered at Sundance Film Festival 2013; aired on OWN April 27, 2014
Executive Producer: Erica Forstadt, Mariel Hemingway, **Barbara Kopple,** Lisa Erspamer, Oprah Winfrey
Producer: David Cassidy
Director: **Barbara Kopple**
Cinematography: Andrew Young, Michael Call, Boone Speed, Phil Parmet
Editing: Michael Culyba, Mona Davis
Sound: Alan Barker
100 minutes

Featured In

Reporters and Reporting: "Part 4: The Power of Investigation" (1989), directed by Jean Brard and Pierre Zucca
We Do the Work (show 513): "Recording the American Experience" (1994–95), The Working Group
Cinéma Vérité: Defining the Moment (1999), directed by Peter Wintonick
Conversations in World Cinema: Barbara Kopple (2001), The Sundance Channel
Independent View: "Barbara Kopple and Susan Seidelman" (2001), directed by Danny L. McGuire
Indie Truth: An Inquiry into the Documentary (2002), directed by Carl Bessai
These Amazing Shadows (2010), directed by Paul Mariano and Kurt Norton
Bring Your Own Doc "Sundance 2013 Special Ep. 3: *When I Walk, Running from Crazy, After Tiller*" (2013), directed by David Minick

Other Credits

Executive Producer:
   Gail Sheehy's New Passages (1996), New World Television Productions
   Weapons of Mass Deception (2004), directed by Danny Schechter
Producer:
   American Standoff (2002), directed by Kristi Jacobson
   Small Steps: Creating the High School for Contemporary Arts (2007), directed by David Becker
   Running Wild: The Life of Dayton O. Hyde (2013), directed by Suzanne Mitchell

Producer, Sound Recordist, and Editor:
  Richard III (1970), starring Rip Torn
Segment Producer:
  "Nails" on *Real Sports with Bryant Gumbel* (1995), HBO executive producer Ross Greenburg (Kopple apparently also acted as director)
  "U.S. Wrestling Team" in *Sports Illustrated Olympic Special: A Prelude to the Games* (1996), Executive Producer Paulette Douglas
Field Producer and Sound:
  In Our Hands (1983), produced by Robert Richter and Stanley Warnow
Location Producer:
  Hurricane Irene (1987), directed by Hart Perry
Consulting Producer (and appears in):
  The Making of "Harlan County USA" (2006), produced by Johanna Schiller
Advising Producer:
  Selfie (2014), directed by Cynthia Wade
Production Assistant:
  El Salvador: La decision de vences (los primos frutos) (1981), directed by Cero a la Izquierda Film Collective
Sound:
  Through the Wire (1989), directed by Nina Rosenblum
Sound Tech/Recordist:
  The Year of the Woman (1973), directed by Sandra Hochman
Additional Sound:
  El Salvador: Another Vietnam (1981), directed by Glenn Silber and Tete Vasconcellos
  Hells Angels Forever (1983), directed by Richard Chase, Leon Gast, and Kevin Keating
  Valley of Tears (2003), directed by Hart Perry
Assistant Editor:
  Friday the 13th: The Orphan (1979), directed by John Ballard
Cinematography:
  Bagels, Borscht, and Brotherhood—Allen Ginsberg (2011), directed by Marc Weiss
Additional Camera:
  Boy Interrupted (2009), directed by Dana Heinz Perry

Barbara Kopple: Interviews

Barbara Kopple Interview: Making *Harlan County, U.S.A.*

Chuck Kleinhans / 1976

From *Jump Cut: A Review of Contemporary Media*, no. 14, 1977, 4–6. Reprinted by permission of Chuck Kleinhans.

I first saw *Harlan County, U.S.A.* in October at the Toronto film festival, a few days after it premiered at the New York festival. The next day I met the filmmaker for an interview. Barbara Kopple impressed me as a vibrant, frank, hardworking, and tough-minded person, and I immediately liked her as much as I liked the film.

We began by talking about her background. She began filmmaking by making a film instead of writing a term paper for a clinical psychology course in college. The experience hooked her on filmmaking, and later she went to New York and worked with the Maysles brothers on *Salesman* and many of their other films. Her political commitment had begun in college with participation in the antiwar movement, and finally she wanted to make her own films to express her own convictions.

In 1972 she began filming the Miners for Democracy movement led by Arnold Miller. When the Boyle machine was ousted from the union leadership, the union began to move on organizing the unorganized, and miners in Harlan County responded. The strike for union recognition began, and Kopple moved to Harlan to cover it for the next year.

Chuck Kleinhans: When you were filming it, what use did you see for the film?
Barbara Kopple: I was very lucky. Because I had a camera in my hand, I could talk to the union leadership, the coal operators, the gun thugs, the UMW organizers and the rank and file. It was an incredible influx of information. And then I could communicate and relate that to the people in different courses of the struggle. I wanted to let the struggle emerge

and try very hard not to manipulate it. Of course, when you make films they get manipulated, because it comes from a certain point of view. But I also saw the film and see the film now as a great organizing tool. I think that films in themselves never change people, but films are really good bases to have discussions around and to take things to a higher level. There's a lot of uses for the film, particularly in the coal fields and in other trade unions. It's a film that the general public should be able to look at too.

Kleinhans: It must have been a temptation with the immediacy of the issues just to stop and say, "Well, I'll make a short film," or "I'll stop because I have this great footage and the issues are there." Yet you went on and showed the whole length of the strike and its aftermath.
Kopple: It wasn't only thinking what kind of things should be in it. It was also feeling that I was engaged in a struggle, and that even if I didn't have any film in the camera, it was important for me to be there because having a camera there kept down violence. Also, the people there really needed to know that there were other people that cared about them and supported them. It was a part of my life. I was there, and I lived there for a long time, and I lived with them, and I wanted to stay.

Kleinhans: Where were you coming from politically when you started to make the film? Did the process of making the film change you? What did you learn?
Kopple: I guess it changed me tremendously. When I went in there a lot of the people were really backward. I was able to watch change happen: people starting their own newspapers, people starting to study and read politically. We'd all read together and have little study sessions, things like that. It made me learn that you can't do anything by yourself. In order to achieve something or in order to win some kind of victory, you all have to be united under the same ideas or the same cause. It taught me a lot about criticism and self-criticism—that it wasn't on a personal level, that it was on a political level that depended on the survival of everybody. It also taught me what it meant to be in a life or death situation where nobody was going to help me. The only power you had came from that community, and if that community went against you, you were dead. And those are some very powerful lessons.

Kleinhans: Did you choose people to film who you felt were politically strong to begin with?

Kopple: The main thing that I had to deal with was being there at the right time because lots of different things were going on and really letting the people emerge. Different people came out at different times and became very strong, like the woman with the long black hair, for instance. When the women were having a low morale fight, she sort of cinched it all up by saying, "I'm not fighting for men, I'm fighting for a contract." And the very old woman who said "I've been through all this in the thirties; they may shoot me. But they're not going to shoot the union out of me." Different people emerged, particularly the women, because the men were served court injunctions. There's no way that you're gonna win a strike having three people in the picket line. It's just not gonna happen. So the women had to come out. All of these women had a long tradition of unionism. That's all they heard from the time that they were kids. It was also the first time that these women were able to actively do anything in their lives and feel their own power and really come alive. There was no way of stopping them. And they were much stronger than the men. I filmed everything that you could possibly film to try to bring more of the men's role, but the men in Appalachia are very low key. The women are very tough and very strong, particularly during the strike.

Kleinhans: I was surprised, but also I was very intrigued, by the scene where one woman is accused of being a troublemaker, of being lazy, and then she responds by saying that another woman is a marriage breaker. Why did you decide to leave that in?

Kopple: I feel that a lot of films that show struggle just show people moving straight forward. But strikes have their ups and strikes have their downs. To be really together and to show a film that's really gonna work with other people and their struggles, you have to show the low periods as well as the high periods. But you also have to show them getting back together again. And I think that that's what that scene ended with. It's very important because in any kind of political work that we do, you bicker with each other, you have periods of deep depression and you take it out on each other. The thing is to go through that—it's a criticism; it's a criticism of the working class, which is very healthy I think. And I like that scene a lot.

Kleinhans: Another thing I like about the film is the portrayal of Miller, and particularly that moment when someone starts to argue with him and he says, "Let's step outside." It's a perfect portrayal of his role. But how do you analyze him? Do you think it's the man or the institution?

Kopple: Doing that last section of the film was difficult because during the editing of that there was a split between the union's vice-president and the president. There was a lot worse that could have been said about Miller and his collusion with the coal operators. I was real nervous about doing it because I felt that I had a political responsibility, and that if this film ever reinforced the right, the vice-president, that I would be very upset by it. So it took a lot of thinking, a lot of figuring, a lot of discussions to try to figure out how to handle that section of the film. It was handled very lightly with the footage that I had.

I had very definite personal feelings about Miller, but it was just a real struggle in dealing with that section of the film, and dealing with it in a way that people—miners and other people—would understand more who their enemies were, and where the power really had to come from. I had to do it without coming out and showing it in such a way that might endorse something that's worse. That was really one of the main political decisions of the film—not to do that.

Kleinhans: I thought that one of the side benefits of the film—obviously not the main intention—was how powerfully it spoke to radicals about the power of working-class people. The film did not romanticize the workers. Yet it showed the incredible strength that they had, and the fact that their strength in many ways comes out of the fact that they don't have a choice about fighting. They really have to fight for everything that they want. A lot of times I get the sense that people with a middle-class background find it all too easy to either romanticize or to criticize without understanding the contradictions involved or the source of working people's strength. There's a young man who says that the miners have to keep struggling, and that when they had the big march, people should have gone out to the mine itself.

Kopple: And expropriated the machine gun and the mine itself. He was also saying there's two types of ways to run strikes, and that you've got to move right on to the next struggle.

Kleinhans: Is that your own feeling? I mean, is that the message that you're trying to underline in the film? That's the sense that I get. I didn't know if that was your sense.

Kopple: I agree with him. I think that he made a really good analysis of what was happening. It was really terrific that thousands of miners came in, but they didn't deal with the real issues. When they were gone, the people there were still left alone having to struggle. I agree with that. I think if you don't keep on fighting, and you—you might lose everything that you've gained. So you've got to pull it forward. You've got to take it forward. I agree with him.

Kleinhans: I was impressed by one thing. The whole business with Boyle was stated in a very clear and unexaggerated way. You could easily have spent an awful lot of time on Boyle and really made the whole thing melodramatic between the good guys and the bad guys, and you chose not to. It showed an awful lot of restraint. I think the issue's so dramatic especially since in the media it was so clear that Boyle was such a rat. He looks like a rat.
Kopple: I think hissing the villain sometimes gets you away from the points that you really want to deal with. And if you give somebody long enough, they hang themselves eventually.

Kleinhans: Another thing that was understated was the situation of the mother and the wife of the man who was shot. You had the footage of the funeral and you had the interview with them. It's very difficult. Either it becomes terribly maudlin and sentimental—and I didn't get that sense at all—or else it becomes almost careless or just tossed aside. It seemed just right. Did you have to work a lot to get that in the editing? There was a real sense that the camera wasn't intrusive, as it is so much with television documentary.
Kopple: They really wanted us to be there. They were kept at the hospital for three days, and he was kept alive by machines. He was dead; you lose part of your brain, and you're not there anymore. It was a tremendous period of suffering for them. And they were very strong people, the mother in particular. She broke down at the funeral, but in the hospital while she was waiting to hear the news she just said, "That's what my son was shot over . . . he was shot for the union, and I don't want my kids ever to be a yellow-backed scab. I want them to be a union man."

And then she told stories about her own life growing up. They were just very strong people. That miner's death also was the only reason that the union and the government and the coal operators got together. Because otherwise there would have been civil war. Those people were arming themselves and getting ready to go out that night and just kill anybody that they saw that was not for the union.

Kleinhans: How did you feel about the issue of violence?
Kopple: I feel that . . . yeah, you have to change your tactics. If someone's

shooting at you, you've gotta shoot back. And I was glad when that happened. That was a tactical change that came from the workers themselves. I'm sure glad there were guns there. That might sound strong to people in other areas, but in this area . . .

Kleinhans: I don't think anyone who sees the film could think that.
Kopple: Even now I've been hearing this whole liberal thing of "ban the gun." I don't think they should ban the gun. It's very important to have ourselves armed.

Kleinhans: When the thugs came down and attacked the camera . . . what happened?
Kopple: Oh, it was just an incredible scene. We'd all gotten together by a supermarket at about 4:30 in the morning. Suddenly we see a scab caravan go by. So like idiots, all of us—the rest of the people hadn't come—get in our cars and go up to the picket line. The scab caravan stopped at the gas station, where they always stopped. It was pitch black out, and suddenly we hear this gunfire—semi-automatic carbines. We don't know where it's coming from; it's sort of like lighting up the sky. Then as the gun thugs started to come up, it stops, so it had to be from across where the company was. Then the scabs went through, came back, got me first, got the camera, and then beat the shit out of people. Basil, the head gun thug, put a gun into one of the black miners', Bill Worthington's, belly, pushed him into the bushes. People were getting beaten with pipes and things. But it was very dark, so in the film, you can't see much but Basil walking around with his gun. They sufficiently scared and intimidated people and then went right back across the bridge. It was a very scary scene. I wasn't scared when it was happening because I was so angry. They pushed me up against the rocks, and I just started swinging to keep them off of me. They took each one of us individually and did that to us. The cameraman, Hart Perry, was yelling, "The camera's broken, the camera's broken," and that's all they really wanted to do was to make sure that we weren't functioning.

Kleinhans: How did you finance the film?
Kopple: I used to write letters for money from miners' homes; I'd be sitting there with maybe five dollars in my pocket. I used to race back to New York City, show little pieces of it to different groups. I'd try to find places that would let me Xerox hundreds of grant proposals and I'd spend days collating them and writing them out and writing zillions of

fundraising letters. I learned so much about fundraising from foundations that I could write a book about it. It was a tremendously painful experience to have to keep dealing with it because I couldn't relate to it. I'd be in Harlan and I'd have to come home and try to figure out how to do a fundraising pitch and how to talk to these people, and it was very hard. People supported it, but I sometimes had to bleed to get anything. I just had to give so much and go so far out just to get anything to keep going.

Kleinhans: Did you have any choice in that? You had no other way of financing it?
Kopple: No other way. I went to a few producers who'd say, "Why is a little girl like you doing a film like this?" Foundations were the only way. It was just weird because it's the excess of capitalism that's supporting this film, and they're supposed to be doing humanitarian, kind of educational things. So I had to do research on all the different foundations to see what they'd funded in the past, show them stuff that would just really try to knock them out, and then try to talk about it. I didn't enjoy it. I met a lot of really good people out of it, and a lot of good people came forward to support it. But it's so difficult for independent filmmakers or people who are making films about social issues to get funded. It's a really negative system because they get you to compete against all your peers. Maybe there's ten people that are gonna get grants and a hundred people have proposals. Right? I mean, it's a lousy deal.

Plus they never give you what you ask for. You ask for a thousand dollars and they give you one dollar. So they make you do it 999 times more. They think it's healthy for you.

Kleinhans: Well, now you face the other end of it—distribution.
Kopple: I don't even know what questions to ask. It's something that I'm not going to rush into. The things that I have to have in a contract are: that the film will not be recut; that the film will be able to be used by workers for free or the cost of the mailing or whatever they can afford; that it can be used for political benefits—things like that. And also I want to pay off my debts, and I want to have enough money to begin another film. I don't think that's asking for a lot. The film cost over $200,000 to make and it took four years. But from the way people talk, you're lucky if you get a couple of thousand dollars just to keep going. And I'm torn because I want it to be distributed on a really wide level so that a lot of people can see it. But I also have to deal with the realities of what I'm capable of doing and what I'm not capable of doing. And I'm not capable

of having all of these debts over me. There's no way in the world I can ever pay those off. And I just don't know if foundations are going to continue to fund the films that I want to do. So I've got to have something just to be able to begin, to get a little footage so that I can start the same routine over again of, you know, raising money to do another film.

Kleinhans: What do you want to do? What's your next film?
Kopple: I want to do a film on the Black Belt in the South and the struggle for unionization, particularly, at a J. P. Stevens textile mill that's been struggling to be part of the union now for fifteen years. It will show the movement of industry north to south, and be an investigation into what the civil rights movement was all about too. It's another big one; it might take another three years, but I really want to do it. I've got a lot of research to do and a lot of thinking to do. . . .

Kleinhans: It will be worth waiting for.

The Making of *Harlan County, U.S.A.*: An Interview with Barbara Kopple

Gail Pellet / 1977

From *Radical America* 11, no. 2 (March–April 1977): 33–42. Reprinted by permission.

In 1973, miners at the Brookside mine in Harlan County, Kentucky, went on strike after the mine owners refused to sign a contract with the newly formed local of the United Mine Workers (UMWA). Barbara Kopple, a filmmaker who had been documenting the Miners for Democracy movement, moved to Harlan to live with and film the miners and their families during the struggle. Their story is shown in her recently released film, *Harlan County, U.S.A.* The film is in color and runs 103 minutes. It is distributed by Cinema 5 Distribution Inc., 595 Madison Ave, New York, NY.

Gail Pellet interviewed Barbara Kopple in February 1977 for *Radical America*.

Gail Pellet: How did you get involved in filming in Harlan County?
Barbara Kopple: I was originally hired by the Miners for Democracy, a rank-and-file movement in the United Mine Workers (UMWA). But then I got so involved with people in the coal fields—the miners and their families—that I wanted to do a lot more than make a film about the Miners for Democracy movement.

To explain this movement, it's really necessary to go over some history of the UMWA. From the early thirties John L. Lewis ran the union as a dictatorship. That dictatorship continued under Tony Boyle, who was appointed president by Lewis in 1963. From the thirties to 1968 there had never been an election.

Boyle's regime did little organizing. They negotiated sweetheart contracts. He controlled the locals by appointing officials who shared his politics. You know, coal mining is one of the most dangerous industries in this country. Yet Boyle made health and safety demands on the companies only when absolutely forced to. For example, in 1969 the Farmington mine blew up and seventy-eight men were killed. The mine had been inspected sixteen times before and had been shown to be dangerous, but the coal operators just asked for more extensions.

Joseph "Jock" Yablonski was the first guy brave enough to run against Boyle. That was in 1969. Then Yablonski and his wife and daughter were murdered, and miners really got angry. They wanted leadership that could respond to the needs of the coal miners. So a rank-and-file movement developed—the Miners for Democracy—and three rank-and-file miners emerged as leaders: Arnold Miller, Mike Trbovich, and Harry Patrick. Miller had spent twenty-six years in the mines, and fought for the black-lung movement. Trbovich fought for autonomy at the local level. And Patrick fought for compensation for widows and disabled miners.

Part of their platform was to organize the unorganized. And so in 1973, at the Brookside mine in Harlan, Kentucky, miners voted to become part of the UMWA. This was a test case for the new reform movement. That's how Harlan began this time. But there's a history in Harlan. Harlan County came to be known as "Bloody Harlan." In the thirties the UMWA under John L. Lewis came in. During the strike people were thrown out of their homes by the companies. There were no strike benefits, so people literally starved. The company brought in gun thugs and scabs. One morning the miners went into the hills and opened up on them. Miners and strike breakers were killed. They called it the battle of Evarts. John L. Lewis got very scared and pulled out, leaving the miners to their own destiny. A number of miners spent fourteen to nineteen years in prison. Later in the 1950s, during the period of mechanization, thousands of miners were unemployed. That's when the UMWA really lost its hold in the coal fields. In 1964 they tried again to organize in Harlan County, but Tony Boyle signed sweetheart contracts and it was just as bad as before.

The miners were getting twenty-six dollars to work eight-, ten-, or twelve-hour days in the mines. It takes an hour to get from the beginning of the mine to the face where the actual work is being done, and you wouldn't get paid for that hour. The safety conditions were terrible. Suppose you and I were working under a roof and I heard a crack. I could come out, but they might say to you: "OK, you have six kids. You need the work and the money. You keep working under that roof." Workers were being divided like that. And safety inspectors were people who had come out of the company, so the company would take them to places they wanted them to see. Little or nothing was done about violations. There was no job security. If you wanted to strike about something or if you felt that something wasn't right, you'd be fired automatically. The miners had absolutely no rights.

GP: But in the film we see Miller, after winning the UMWA presidency on a reform platform, compromise the right to strike.
BK: Right. People had felt him to represent a strong, honest reform leadership that was really going to respond to their needs. But you see Miller change during the course of the film. The last section of the film includes the vote for a national coal contract. It was the first time in union history that the miners were able to ratify their own contract. You see on a rank-and-file level what a contract can mean. Is it enough to have five-day vacations? Is that really enough time to get the coal dust out of your lungs? But then Miller compromised the miners' right to strike. The last part of the film says who your enemies are; you've got to fight against the coal operators and the government. In 1975 120,000 miners went on wildcat strike; and in the following year they struck again when coal operators violated grievance procedures. Sometimes people think that once you get a good leader, you don't have to fight anymore. Everything's going to be taken care of. Of course we know that's not so, and the miners know that's not so. So the fight is still continuing. And as the young miner says in the film. "It's got to be a fight that comes from below." That's what the film is about.

GP: What in your own personal background led you to producing this kind of film?
BK: I grew up on a flower and vegetable farm in Shrub Oak, New York. I grew up with my grandparents, my parents, and my brother. They were all left-liberals. I went to school in Boston and got involved in the anti-war movement. Then I got into filmmaking, doing sound and editing. I worked primarily on social-change films such as *Winter Soldier*, a lot of things for *Bill Moyers Journal* on television. But I knew that I really wanted to do films that had content, that moved people forward. For five years I had been working until three or four in the morning seven days a week for other people, and I really wanted to do something that I cared about.

As I started to do *Harlan County, U.S.A.*, I realized that nothing in the world was going to stop me from telling that story. I don't think of myself as a producer/director, just somebody who knows how to make films, which is a way I can contribute to communicating the political things I believe in. To experience and learn but also to bring that experience back and share it with other people. We wanted a film that workers everywhere would be able to look at. What we were trying to do with the film was make it honest, from the rank-and-file people. Trying not to manipulate it. Letting them speak. That's why there's no narration in the film. We didn't want narration with rhetoric or some heavy imposed thing that didn't naturally come out of where the people were.

I filmed in the coal fields for three years. Making the film was a day-to-day process. The only thing I was concerned with was being able to continue for another day. It was a life-and-death struggle down there, and we just wanted to continue working. If you stick with people long enough, you can see clearly in which directions they are moving. That's why I think staying in a place over a long period of time is really necessary when you're trying to do some kind of in-depth study of what's happening. Three years isn't long enough, but we were able to get a glimpse of the changes taking place.

This kind of film can only happen with a small group of tightly knit people who know how to work and move quickly in different situations. The crew had to be politically motivated so we could have discussions after every few days of filming and taping, analyze what we were getting, and figure out where we were going from there. Like what it meant to watch grown men crawling in twenty-three to twenty-nine inches of space in the mines, or that if a man works fifteen years in a mine you can presume he has black lung.

GP: What kind of relationships did the film crew have with miners, their families, the sheriff, and company representatives?
BK: Well, when we first arrived at Brookside it was about four in the morning. It was foggy and misty. And there they were. State troopers with clubs; women with sticks. We figured we couldn't just get out of the car and say "Hello, we're New York filmmakers and here we are," so we got an organizer we knew to introduce us to the picketers. At first they didn't trust us, they didn't tell us their real names. The women said they were Martha Washington, Florence Nightingale, and Betsy Ross.

A week later we got in a very bad car accident. They have incredible mountains there with no lights and no guidelines, and we were pushed off of Pine Mountain by some strike breakers. We rolled right over the mountain. The car landed on the hood, so we all crawled out of the windows, took our equipment, and walked all battered and bruised to the picket line because we promised the people that we would be there. After that they realized we really cared about them, that we were dedicated. So we lived with the miners in their homes for thirteen months.

During the last couple of weeks of the strike they used to shoot up the miners' homes at night. We took mattresses to put them around the small homes, and we'd be sleeping on the floor with a kid here and a dog there. The men had porch duty at night taking turns sitting with shotguns. There wasn't any indoor plumbing, so at night we had a buddy system. One night my friend and I were going to the bathroom. He had an M-1 and I had a .357 Magnum. We could hear the gunfire down below. And suddenly there was a rustling in the bushes and we both pulled out our guns and a dog ran out of the bushes. That was the kind of terror we were living with. There was no one there to help us except the coal miners and their families. We owe our lives to them: they protected us and supported us.

I guess we kept down a lot of the violence by being on the picket line. Even if we didn't have any film we would go out there and pretend to be filming. The gun thugs at that point really didn't know who we were or where we were from. We'd also stop the scab caravan every now and then and try to ask them questions. Anytime Hart Perry, the cameraman, would ask a question, they would walk away. Whenever I asked a question they would talk to me in a very patronizing way. I didn't mind; I was just glad that they were saying something. They also told us that if they ever caught us alone at night they would kill us. The state troopers would warn us continuously that we better get out because three years ago another film crew was shot up down there. The cameraman was killed. Nobody was prosecuted for it. One morning, about four or five a.m., the gun thugs opened up on us with semi-automatic carbines. I was the first beaten up, and then Hart Perry. All of us realized at that time, even if we had been naive before, that we could be killed at any moment.

GP: How did you manage to get into jails and courthouses to film?
BK: When the miners and women were put into jail we just followed them in. We stayed in there until we were kicked out.

In the courtroom scene we were really lucky. I used to use a wireless mike, and whenever I thought I wasn't going to be able to film, I would mike somebody ahead of time who was going to participate. In the courtroom scene a lot of miners and women were confronting the judge—who was a coal operator—for putting them in jail for being on the picket line. The woman I had put the wireless mike on happened to be the one to speak. She's the one who said "The laws aren't made for working people." For filming in that situation, we opened the doors of the courtroom in the back, "pushed" the film two f-stops, and shot.

GP: In the film you follow the very important role that women played during the strike, but you don't really get a sense of their lives. Can you explain that?
BK: All their lives women had heard about unionism. From their grandfathers, their fathers, their husbands, their sons. They watched their men die of black lung or become maimed or killed in the coal mines. For the women in this film this was the first time that they really came out and did anything in a mass. The courts said that there could only be six miners on a picket line. Once they came out there was no way to stop them. It was something deep down that they had been hearing about all their lives.

They also had their own club, called the Brookside Women's Club. They did other things. For Thanksgiving they cooked turkeys in a big hall where everybody had Thanksgiving dinner together. Questions were raised, study groups were formed, we started a newspaper, people learned how to use an AB Dick machine. Everybody wrote and everybody was supposed to write, whether it was about food stamps or day care or the school system or just everyday kinds of oppression.

GP: There seemed to be some tension in the film between men and women. Was there more you chose not to show?
BK: I think that the conflict you're talking about was a result of low morale. Attacks on the miners by the strike breakers were stepped up. They were shooting into people's homes. It was a long time on the picket line, and they were getting very scared. So the striking families started fighting among themselves.

As far as men endorsing the fact that women were going on the picket line, there were problems in some of the homes, but the women did it in a mass. The men knew of no other way that they could win the strike if it wasn't for the women. But when things got really violent the men didn't want the women there.

GP: But then, at one of the meetings, Lois, who appears to be the most militant person in the film, pulls a gun out of her dress.
BK: And one of the men says "What's taken you so long?" So you start to

see not only a change of tactics by the miners and the women, but also a change in understanding. The miners need the women out there.

GP: Do you think the fact that your film crew and production crew were largely women had any significance in the final product?
BK: As far as women working on the film, that wasn't anything intentional. It just so happened that the women who worked on the film were people who were involved and committed to the subject. There were a lot of men that were committed political people too, and there wasn't in my mind any distinction between men and women. It was people who really cared and wanted to move things forward on that level.

GP: Mountain music, coal miner's music, permeates the film. Who wrote and performed the music?
BK: Well, at one of the rallies in the film you see Florence Reece, who wrote "Which Side Are You On?" during the labor struggles of the thirties in Harlan, singing it again in the seventies. Then at a couple of points in the film you see Nimrod Workman. He'd tell us old stories about the things he went through in the thirties and forties, and then he'd just burst into songs that he wrote himself. His daughter, Phyllis Boyens, sings with him in one segment. Hazel Dickens is really the main singer throughout the film, even though you don't see her. She's a coal miner's daughter, and she wrote songs like "Matmington," "Black Lung," "Cold-Blooded Murder," and the last song of the film, "They'll Never Keep Us Down." She wrote the last one especially for the film in a week. All the music in the film, except Merle Travis's "Dark as a Dungeon," was written by coal miners, miners' wives, and their daughters.

GP: There are only a couple of moments in the film where we see black miners, and one is a particularly racist incident with the strike breakers. Are there many blacks living in Harlan County, and is racism an issue?
BK: In Harlan County there's a very small black population. There is some racism, but there's a united feeling among the progressive miners. During the thirties the coal operators would go to the South and bring trainloads of black miners to use as strike breakers. When the black miners found out what was happening, they became the most militant on the picket lines. Recently racist issues have been stepped up by Klan activities.

GP: What happened when you screened *Harlan County* down there? What was people's response to the film?

BK: We were to screen *Harlan County* at the multi-purpose center where everything happened in Harlan—the meetings, the funeral of Lawrence Jones, who was the miner killed during the strike, and the contract signing took place there. A goat was hung by the center, so armed miners stood at the door before the screenings.

For me it was the most important screening that I could have ever witnessed. The people lived through the strike again. They screamed at the strike breakers, they cried through the funeral of Lawrence Jones. A man who was dying of black lung was wheeled in on a big silver hospital bed. It was incredibly dramatic. I was extremely nervous wondering what they would think about some of the scenes. I sat in the back with my hands over my face, but they really liked it. I left them a print, a projector, plus rewinds and materials they would need to clean and repair the film. It's being shown all over the coal fields. Miners and their wives are going around as speakers with the film. They're using it for study groups to raise consciousness—and funds. It's bringing the people in the coal fields closer together.

GP: How was the film funded?

BK: It was extremely difficult. We were given $9,000 to begin working on something to show other potential donors. Money was raised from foundations, church groups, individual donors, and loans. I did massive amounts of proposal writing, sometimes applying to the same foundation three times. I wrote desperate letters from the coal fields to wealthy liberal people . . . 117 letters with proposals. When they didn't write back, I did follow-up letters. It's a tremendous amount of work. Astonishingly enough, I got a Master Charge card and for two straight months we lived on Master Charge. We got film and everything that we needed. My bill is astounding; I'm still paying it off.

I think one of the most important things in raising money is that you have to meet the people who might fund you, and you have to be able to show them past work so they sense you know what you're doing. You have to learn how to write proposals and answer all the different kinds of questions that foundations might ask you about distribution or your production plan. You've got to really learn how to do a budget and how to be able to put things together concretely in terms that they understand. It's a very hard and long process to get funding, and it came in little tiny bits. I'd get anywhere from $5 to $27,000 as grants. Some of this will be made easier, I hope, by a new group in Cambridge, the Film Fund, a foundation for social-change films.

GP: *Harlan County* was the last film shown at the New York Film Festival last year; and it got the first standing ovation of the festival, plus rave reviews. Did that surprise you?
BK: Yes. We'd been working very hard. Editing had taken nine months. And trying to figure out how to structure it and get all the things we wanted in it was very draining. Our morale was low. We had a "rough cut," but it wasn't all fitting together; yet we decided that we would show it in rough cut to the New York Film Festival, and thought maybe that would be the final impetus we needed to finish after four years of working on it. When the selection committee screened it, they loved it. The film was finished the day before the festival, and we had a press screening that for us was the greatest thing. The miners' wives and some of the miners came up, and Hazel Dickens, who wrote a lot of the music, came up with her group and sang. Psychologically it was wonderful. It was a very scary time for me, because it was something I'd hidden in the closet for four years and had no idea what the reaction of other people would be. Plus talking in front of a lot of people, being responsible for what we were doing in bringing the coal miners and their wives there. I didn't know how they would feel about it. I mean they might have hated the film, right? But it was a wonderful couple of days.

GP: How is the film being distributed?
BK: The film was $60,000 in debt, and I had the choice of self-distribution or going with a commercial distributor. Self-distribution would mean trying to borrow a tremendous amount of money, and maybe at the end of a year being over $200,000 in debt. And I guess I needed to let go a little bit and go onto something else, so I chose a commercial distributor.

The film has been running for several weeks in New York, and is scheduled to open in Washington, Lexington, Charleston, and Cincinnati in the next month. And, of course, it is being screened for rank-and-file groups and community groups wherever people want it. That was one agreement I fought for with the distributor.

Time will tell. It needs a lot of grass-roots and community support and rank-and-file support if it's going to do well. If it does well it will say that people in this country want some kind of alternative, that they want to see films that make them think and feel something. It will bring people in this country a lot closer together over issues and organizing.

There are a number of new films being distributed independently right now: *Hollywood On Trial*, about the McCarthy period; *Union Maids*, about three working women in the thirties and how they lived through those struggles; and *On the Line*, about unemployment and the march for jobs and the rent strike at Coop City in New York. They are more professionally produced, well thought out, and not your usual kind of documentary where the camera is shaky and the sound is bad. They're produced by people who have really paid their dues working in the film industry, learning their craft so they can make the best kind of political films they can.

The films of the thirties, like *Scottsborough Boys* and the *Little Republic Steel Strike*, were important to me. It was during a very rough time in this country. People's lives were on the line—people like those who started the Film and Photo League in New York, or like Leo Hurwitz, who did *China Strikes Back* and *Native Land*. They were under gunfire and blacklisting, yet they were filming something valuable to our history.

GP: What are your future plans?
BK: I have two ideas. One is a film on a J. P. Stevens textile mill in North Carolina, where people have been trying to join a union for thirteen years. J. P. Stevens owns 189 mills, and every time there's a disturbance at one of them they shut it down. That's usually the only industry in the area, so people are afraid to go on strike. The second idea would be a dramatic re-enactment of the Triangle Fire.

GP: Do you think you've been changed by the experience of making the film on Harlan County?
BK: The main thing I learned is that if you stick together you can win. The film would not have happened without a lot of committed filmmakers and friends playing a lot of different roles. In Harlan the strike wouldn't have happened nor have been won, and probably more people would have died, if there weren't a lot of committed people working together united with the same ideas. That's really important, particularly now in a country where people are sometimes afraid to change things. In Harlan, people who were totally oppressed in every kind of way were courageous enough to take their lives and their destinies in their own hands and fight to change things.

Filming in Harlan: Interview with Barbara Kopple and Hart Perry

Gary Crowdus / 1977

From *Cineaste Magazine*, Summer 1977, 23–25. Reprinted by permission.

Barbara Kopple, director of *Harlan County, U.S.A.*, and Hart Perry, principal cinematographer on the film, were interviewed by *Cineaste* editor Gary Crowdus.

Question: How did the project get started and how was it financed?

Barbara Kopple: The film got started in August, 1972—just a few years after Yablonski, his wife and daughter had been murdered—when a rank and file movement within the United Mine Workers called Miners for Democracy began an attempt to bring democracy to their union. They were trying to get rid of a dictatorship that had been in the UMW for many years, to bring in a leadership that was responsive to the rank and file. They wanted the right of autonomy at a local level, the right to ratify a contract, things like that.

Three rank and file coal miners emerged—Arnold Miller, who had worked in the mines for twenty-six years, had fought for black lung benefits, and who also had black lung himself; Mike Trbovich, who had been Yablonski's campaign manager and who fought for autonomy at a local level; and Harry Patrick, the secretary-treasurer, who fought for compensation for disabled miners and widows. At that time I was able to raise enough money—nine thousand dollars—from a man who was going to produce the entire film, and so we started filming during the Miners for Democracy period.

Q: Who were the other people working with you?

BK: On the first shoot we had a crew of about seven people, including Marc Weiss, the production manager, Michael Abramson, who was going to be the co-producer and co-director, Kevin Keating, who was the cameraman, Shane Zarintash, who was the assistant cameraman, and Dick Donovan, who did the lighting, so it was a really big crew at first. At that time we thought we were going to be totally financed and everybody was paid to work on the film.

We got back and showed the footage we had on the Miners for Democracy movement, but things didn't work out as we had hoped. So there we were with all this film, wanting to go on, having gone through the coal fields, having met people who'd talked about the thirites, having gotten into the music, the history of unionism, and so on. When the new reform leadership got in, the miners at Brookside in Eastern Kentucky voted to become part of the UMW, but Duke Power, who owned the mine, said no, so this became test case for the new reform leadership, and that's how the filming in Harlan started. We did a lot of fund-raising work to be able to go down to Harlan, and the first grant that came through was from the American Film Institute for ten thousand dollars.

Hart Perry: It was about this point that I started filming in Harlan, going down for several months at a time. For instance, we'd be cutting some footage to show for fund-raising—because at that point the production budget was only covering film stock and transportation—and the miners would call up and say, "Listen, you got to come down, something's happening," and we'd go down. The filming wouldn't have been possible without the support of the community—in a *real* way, because we were living with them.

I met the foreman of the mine—he's the guy who sets off the dynamite in the first scene of the film—at a grocery store when I was shopping for baloney. We started talking, and he said he was working at this nonunion mine, and so we arranged to film there. Also, since we were living in Harlan, we made ourselves available. We could wait for months on end, shooting very little, just waiting for the story to evolve, patiently recording it.

But the key to the filming in Harlan, as far as I was able to tell coming into it, was the way Barbara had been able to establish a rapport with the people. She was able to develop a good rapport with the union organizers. And the women, Lois and Bessie, are indeed good friends. It's part of Barbara's ability to relate to people. It's more than just making a movie because in a documentary like this there's a fine line between relating to people and manipulating them.

BK: The thing that happened was that we were there for so long that people didn't recognize us a lot of times without our gear on. For instance, in strategy meetings, to figure out who was going to be on the picket line, Lois would say, "OK, Hart, are you going to be there?" and "Barbara, are you going to be there?" And we'd have to say, "Shhh, Lois, you're not supposed to say that." And she'd say, "Yes, I know, but are you gonna *be* there? I have to put your name down." So they'd lose consciousness of us as filmmakers. Anne and I were members of the Brookside Women's Club. We all started a paper together called *The Harlan Labor News*, on which people learned how to use a mimeograph machine, and everybody wrote for it. Incredible things happened just living there and being part of that community.

Q: I know you gathered a lot of stock footage on various aspects of the story—the history of the UMW, scenes from "bloody Harlan" in the thirties, footage on strip-mining, and so on. How much of this material were you able to use?

BK: Well, everything made the film except strip-mining. The really important thing, as far as the vision that I had, was that people be able to understand what the miners were fighting for—you know, what is this union, what's its history, what's it based in, what's the union doing today, and where is the union going?

Actually, we were editing the film all along. Whenever we got back, Anne Lewis and I would cut the film, not for clarity or anything, just cut it into little vignettes to do fund-raising with. We started narrowing it down chronologically, beginning with the earliest history and moving up until we got about halfway through Harlan, when Anne left the project and moved to Virginia. Originally both of us were going to edit the film, but it was much too close for me to do it once she left—in fact it was probably too close for both of us since we had too many emotions tied to it, we didn't know what was clear to other people and just because we liked something didn't mean that other people were going to be responsive. So Nancy Baker started working on it and she became the chief editor who went all the way through the entire nine months of editing.

There were also a lot of assistant editors, some of them who had never worked on a film before, but who were really politically committed. To me it was just incredible that these people would come every single day and really struggle to put the film into shape—and it was a very hard film to put into shape, sometimes you'd think your brains were coming out of your head because things just didn't connect or didn't work. Everybody would work on a different section—like the old history, or the Miners for Democracy, and someone would have the Harlan section, and someone else would have the national coal contract section—and all these were sort of broken down. We used to have mass meetings around the table—because everybody used to eat lunch together—and we'd discuss stuff politically. We'd screen all the material and then have structure meetings to deal with questions like whether the film should be a chronological film—for instance, I never thought that the nucleus of the film would really work around Harlan, because how would you get into Harlan, and cut out of Harlan and then get back into Harlan?

During these structure meetings, we'd all view the footage and discuss where things worked and where they didn't work—and you were politically responsible for what you said, you couldn't just say, "Well, it doesn't work, it doesn't have flow, it doesn't have characters, or whatever." If you criticized it, you had to come up with something else that might work. It was an incredible experience because there were a lot of different people coming from a lot of different places, with fresh ideas, including some people, for example, who before then hadn't known anything about the miners' movement.

It was an incredibly wonderful process, although it was also a very painful and very difficult process. I don't think it could have been done without all those energies and all those ideas and all those committed people struggling with it. The way the editing was done was the most inspiring thing for me, because the rest of it was an incredible struggle just to keep going from day to day, worrying about where money was going to come from, going to the union headquarters and being treated terribly by the union bureaucrats, wondering if you were going to lose your life the next day, and coming home and wondering why you were doing it and then going to the coal fields and realizing why you were doing it.

HP: Barbara's vision for this movie was, for me, one of the most remarkable things about the whole project. Not only the vision, but how—in the face of indifference and criticism and lack of support and money—how despite these odds she kept this vision alive. There were many, many low points we went through but she kept the idea of the film alive for four years, actually almost five years.

BK: They would say [pinches her cheek], "Why is a pretty little thing like you making a film?"

Q: The impression one gets from the film, though, is that the sexism you encountered actually helped you to make the film.

BK: It's true. People weren't intimidated by me at all. Basil and I would have lots of discussions—a lot of things that aren't in the film. For instance, he'd say, "Where are you from?" And I'd say, "From New York." So he'd say, "You're nothing but a New York Yankee?" And I'd say, "That's right" And then he'd say, "What are you doing in Kentucky? Do you like Kentucky?" I'd say, "Yes," and he'd say, "You don't sound like you do." And we'd just have these discussions back and forth, but if Hart or any other male on the crew would open his mouth, Basil would just walk away.

HP: Basil flirted with Barbara. He's a real character in the movie because we felt it was important to try to show the other side. I think Basil identified very closely with John Wayne, and the role he plays in the movie is a traditional John Wayne role, and he thought of it as that. He was acting within the prerequisites of the unique culture of that area—if someone tries to force something on you, you take out your gun and stand up for what you think is right.

Q: During the shooting, the presence of the camera on the picket line seemed to assume a real political importance.

BK: I think that it kept down the violence a lot. . . .

HP: [Laughs] . . . Apart from getting pistol-whipped ourselves!

Q: Were you the one operating the camera during the scene when the strikebreaker rushes the cameraman and knocks him over?

HP: Yes, and there's a story behind that. We got there at 4:30 in the morning and were there on the picket line getting ready to shoot, when all of a sudden this submachine gun started shooting. Barbara recorded this, so in the film those are the sounds you hear and you see the lights of the cars. At that point the picket line scattered, everybody started running. I lost contact with Barbara and I set up with Anne who had the sun-guns.

It really pissed me off—I wasn't scared, I was just pissed—because I knew they were shooting over our heads. There were two strikebreakers nearby, one in the back seat of a car with a Thompson submachine gun partially hidden under his raincoat, and another guy standing by the car, so I took up a position right near them. At the same time, the scabs were coming down the road, driving with one hand and shooting their pistols out the window up into the air with the other—it was like a Wild West show, a noisy affair but not particularly lethal.

The highway narrowed to one lane right at the entrance to the bridge, so Anne and I set up shining the sun-guns in the faces of the drivers of the scab cars as they were turning to go across the bridge. That's the reason why Basil—because he's actually blinded by the sun-guns—rolls down his window and points his gun at me. At that point, I figured, "Oh, oh, I've taken this too far." But then they went across the bridge and stopped firing.

We had just hooked up with Barbara again, and had set up and turned on the sun-guns to film, when all of a sudden these two guys came running at us. I got separated from Barbara and Anne—I was about thirty feet away, partially knocked down a ravine. They had tried to smash the camera, and this guy hit me in the face with his pistol and chipped my front teeth. I got up and the camera was still working, so I kept on shooting although I didn't put it up to my eye because I knew I'd just get hit again. I was filming this scene—which is the greatest scene in the movie but you can't see it because it was too dark at 4:30 in the morning—where Basil Collins comes up to Bill Worthington, who's black, and sticks his gun in Bill's stomach. Bill took his gun and stuck it into Basil's stomach, and then a strikebreaker came up with a loaded .357 magnum and cocked it and put it up to Bill's head. I was around five feet away, with the camera at 9.5, and the lens sort of sagging, recording this, thinking to myself, "Jesus, should I be filming this in case they murder him, or should I turn around and film this guy getting beaten up by strikebreakers?" Luckily, nothing happened. None of this was filmed through the eyepiece, though, because after we got beaten up, everything was filmed from the hip at a wide angle.

BK: We were all beaten up. When they started to come across I realized they were coming for us, and I figured, "Well, they're not going to hurt a woman as much as a man," so I got in front of Hart and sort of went up towards them, but then, Boom!, they got me out of the way, they got Hart, and they got Anne. Different guys took each of us individually and beat us up. I was carrying the tape recorder and I had a long "fishpole" mike, so I just started whipping that around just to keep them off me. After it was over, after they let us up, I found Anne and she was OK, but we couldn't find Hart.

HP: They had trashed the camera pretty good—there was about six hundred to eight hundred dollars worth of damage and I had to gaffer-tape the lens together. But I knew I had footage of Basil pointing his gun at me and that's a felony, flourishing a deadly weapon, so we went to a judge and got a warrant for Basil's arrest. The next day there was the stand-off picket line, where they put the car across the road and we filmed them pointing their guns at the strikebreakers. Then the sheriff came up and tried to get them to take the car off the road. While I was filming this I got the idea—because we had the warrant right there—and I told Anne to go get the warrant and that's why the camera is running when she comes into the frame with the warrant for Basil's arrest. So that whole scene happened spontaneously even though it was manipulated a little bit.

Q: The death of Lawrence Jones carries a lot of emotional weight in the film and seems to have been a crucial element in the settlement of the strike. Is that an accurate portrayal of the events?

BK: It was, it was. If Lawrence Jones hadn't been killed and galvanized things, the situation there would have become bloody Harlan to the nth degree, it would have been civil war.

Q: There's also a hint of pressure from Washington.

BK: Yes, after that the government came in, the union came in. . . .

HP: I mean, all hell was going to break loose.

BK: People just came out of the woodwork after that. We saw people we'd never seen before and these guys were loaded to the gills with guns and everybody was in favor of all-out guerrilla warfare, of killing them the next day, I mean, it was unbelievable, if something hadn't been done, I think everybody would have killed everybody else.

Q: Was the role of women in the strike as important as the film implies?

BK: Yes, these were women who had heard about this sort of thing all their lives and when this happened there was no way of stopping them. They formed the Brookside Women's Club which raised money for medical benefits for the strikers and their families, and once they were needed on the picket line their strength was incredible. Among Appalachian people, by the way, the men are usually a lot more low-key than the women....

HP: The women were much more articulate.

Q: The situation seems very similar to that portrayed in *Salt of the Earth*.

BK: Well, it wasn't exactly like *Salt of the Earth* because in Harlan the men didn't try to keep the women off the picket line. There were some little family squabbles, but they also realized that if it wasn't for the women, nothing could happen.

Q: I think the film is very honest in the way it deals with the Miners for Democracy, especially later in the film when it becomes clear that there are serious problems regarding Miller's leadership. That must have been a difficult situation for you to deal with.

BK: Well, there were lots of arguments about the ending, and the first idea for the ending that I came up with was to do something about nationalization of energy, but that would have looked as if it had been just dropped in there and wasn't really natural. Most of the people felt that the film should end after Harlan, and there were bitter fights about that, but it was my feeling that the film had to go on, you just can't leave it at a sensational ending and think that things are going to be OK. It's very important to let people know who their enemies are, and what happens when you depend on leadership. We wanted to show that there has to be some real tight control from below because without that you're just a victim of whatever the leadership turns out to be.

A lot of people criticized that—that's the politics of the film, I guess. The last ten minutes of the film is done in a much different style, it's a more newsy kind of thing, dealing with the national coal contract, the wildcat strikes and things like that. We wanted to show that even though they got a contract, it wasn't exactly what they wanted, it was a pretty bad contract, and they had to continue struggling to push their demands, so the film goes all the way up till 1976.

Q: Has the union leadership seen the film and, if so, what do they think of it?

BK: Well, this is only hearsay, but reportedly Arnold Miller recently saw the film and said he was going to buy out the opening night at the theatre in Washington. That's very surprising, and the only thing I can think is that it's a political thing he has to do to get him back into office.

Actually, during the Miners for Democracy movement we travelled all around with Miller and got some really intimate footage that's not in the film—hunting with his son, interviews with him talking about what he felt about workers taking over control of production, and so on, but it just didn't make sense within the structure of the film to use them. I spent a lot of time with him because it was a perfect entree into a lot of different places.

HP: The support from the union was up and down.

BK: Trbovich thought the film was going to be an agit-prop film for Miller, and since he wanted to be the president and there had been a feud between him and Miller from the very beginning, he wanted to kill the film. The executive board had originally voted to give us $20,000 with no strings attached, but Trbovich brought it up before them again, saying that they should have right of approval of the film, which he knew we would turn down. He also did a whole red-baiting number on me because I brought *Salt of the Earth* down to Harlan. Finally the executive board and Miller saw it as a bad political risk and pulled away and that was the last I had to do with Miller.

HP: It depended a lot on the individuals involved—the organizers down in Harlan really supported us, but it was completely different down in District No. 6. We filmed some scenes in Harlan of these two guys from District No. 6 who came to this big rally and they went after some left-wing people who were hanging out, selling papers, and beat them up and burned their papers. During the voting on the contract in District No. 6, these same two guys were doing the same thing—when anyone came in from the outside with papers, and of course they were all left-wing, they'd beat 'em up and burn the papers.

Q: You seem suspicious.

HP: I was frankly suspicious. They didn't really seem to me to be like the regular coal miners we'd come to know, many of whom were friends. They were a different sort of people.

BK: They *were* coal miners . . . they were part of a vigilante group infiltrated by the Klan. The most backward kind of stuff is in that area. I mean, there are sections where black people live and they can't go out after a certain time and they can't go where white people live, yet when they work in the coal mines they work as a team and there's a lot of camaraderie.

Q: Is the film going to be shown theatrically in the South?

BK: Yes, it's going to be shown in Lexington, Cincinnati, Charleston, Atlanta, and in North Carolina—right in Duke Power territory—it's going to be opening all over the South. It's also going to show in Detroit, Chicago, Boston, Los Angeles, San Francisco, Washington. . . .

Q: A few weeks ago you were concerned that the film might not open outside of New York City. When did all this happen?

HP: Right after *Harlan* made the fifty top-grossing films list in *Variety*. In one small theatre in New York, against competition like *King Kong* and *Marathon Man*, it was forty-fourth out of fifty.

BK: The film is doing everything that I hoped in my wildest fantasies it would be able to do—it's going to open in showcase theatres all around New York, it's going to have a national break and be shown theatrically on a mass level which is something that I just never expected could happen.

HP: It's a curious vindication of independent filmmaking because with all the other independent films I've done, after the film is made it's shown to a limited audience. The fact that a film made in this fashion—one that involved a real struggle to make it and which was sustained a lot through political commitment and emotional feelings toward the subject, not for the regular film production reasons which is that you're getting paid for what you're doing—films sustained by those reasons usually find a small audience. So this has been a really extraordinary experience.

BK: I think the important thing that's really come out of it is for the miners and the women down there, because now it's much easier to get a national campaign going. For instance, after the strike when the Klan moved in and Bessie was in jail for allegedly kidnapping the wife of a Klansman, it was real hard to get support for that, it was hard to get people to send telegrams, to write letters—we were still editing the film at that point. It's much easier now, people can't wait to talk to her now or to other people in the film. It's a lot easier, the contacts have been made, the story is out, and people can really start to relate to it. That's really vital.

Interview with Barbara Kopple (on *Harlan County, U.S.A.*)

Jan Aghed / 1977

From *Positif*, October 1977, 26–31. Translated from French by Kader Souma and Holly Prall. Reprinted by permission.

Q: The music seems to have a large part in the thematic structure of your film. It also seems to have such a place in people's lives that their struggle would be harder without it.
A: Miners are geographically isolated from each other. They are in Kentucky, in West Virginia, in Pennsylvania, in Ohio, Alabama. . . . The cultural history of Appalachia is characterized by the fact that songs were written to try to communicate. In this way all the tragedies are like the happy events. And they are written with the blood and guts of the miners, by the miners themselves, by their daughters or their wives. This is a very important part of the culture, to make the struggle a little easier and to communicate in order to be less isolated from one another.

Q: You lived in West Virginia?
A: Yes, for two years.

Q: So, you heard a lot of country music.
A: Especially bluegrass.

Q: The country music of your movie is certainly very different from that of Nashville.
A: Sure! It is entirely written by the people themselves. It's their music. It is a music of struggle, the struggle of people who do not want to be victims and who want to fight for what they believe.

Q: Were you familiar with this kind of music before you made the movie?

A: Yes, but not as familiar as after having done it!

Q: Sara Ogan Gunning, for example, how did you find her?
A: These are the traditional singers of this music for many years. Many of them were blacklisted, for example Florence Reece who sang "Which Side Are You On?" in the thirties in Harlan County, and who reappeared in the seventies. Labeled as communist, she had been forced to leave: they were tortured and their houses searched—it is the kind of story that has not stopped happening since the beginning of trying to establish trade unionism in the United Mine Workers.

Q: In the thirties, in Harlan, there was also a communist union, the National Miners' Union, and it is through this ideology that Sarah Ogan Gunning wrote the song "Come All You Coal Miners" that ends with a vision of the capitalist system, sinking into "the darkest pits of hell." This ending is not found in your movie and one doesn't find this communist connotation in the version of the song heard there.
A: That's right. It is rather used for the struggle of women and to show that they are beginning to talk about the fights of Harlan. During the thirties, in Harlan, there were real battles. John L. Lewis was the president of United Mine Workers; the miners were armed and ambushed the strike breakers; a lot of miners were killed, a lot strike breakers as well; and Lewis withdrew; miners were sentenced to fourteen years and even nineteen years in prison. That was when the National Miners' Union appeared. They were very strong. They really did a lot of work organizing; their leaders were tortured, blinded, expelled.

Q: At that time, a committee made up of leftist writers, led by Theodore Dreiser along with John Dos Passos and Samuel Ornitz, came to Harlan to investigate the charges of miners and violence. The work of this commission produced "Harlan Miners Speak—Report on Terrorism in the Kentucky Coal Fields." Did you know that report when you were preparing your movie?
A: Yes. And in fact, in Harlan in the seventies, the United Mine Workers tried to conduct the same kind of investigation. It brought trade unionists, humanists, philosophers, and all kinds of people for a new public investigation, like in the thirties where the miners testified. But this time, it was more a question of publicity and therefore different from the events of the thirties.

Q: It is a very pleasant surprise the appearance in the movie of Florence Reece. How did you get her in the movie, when she is very old and lives far from Harlan?
A: She was in Tennessee at that time. Her husband is dying of silicosis. In fact, he just had an attack and I don't know how he is doing right now. But the events of Harlan were very important for her. She often came, we met at the picket line and she provided considerable support to the morale of people. She sang in front of the court when women were thrown in jail, she sang at the picket line and during the marches.

I think it is very funny that you, a Swede, have heard about Harlan County. I mean, if an average American is asked about Harlan, he responds: "You mean Harlem?" Americans, you see, have no idea about the origin or the fight of the trade unions of their own country. It is a part of national history that is neglected or forgotten despite its enormous importance.

Q: Have you shown the movie to Harlan residents and, if so, what was their reaction?
A: What followed the strike, was the intervention of Ku Klux Klan. And any person with progressive ideas, of whatever sort, was a victim of intimidation. The woman who in the film stands up in court to say "the laws aren't made for the working people in this country," was thrown in jail on the charges of kidnapping the wife of a member of the Klan and crossing the state border with her. At that time, there were paramilitary demonstrations; there were bomb attacks, against the homes of the people who had interracial relations; the headmaster of the high school had students make dresses and hoods for the Klan; the atmosphere was rather brutal. When I arrived with the movie, the Ku Klux Klan hung a goat with KKK on his stomach near the place where we were going to project it, where in the movie the funeral and strategic meeting happen, and also the signing of the contract, etc. . . . So it had to be an armed screening. The miners protected the outside. Altogether it was very passionate. By watching the movie in this tense atmosphere, people relived the whole strike. They cried out against the strike breakers, they were crying during the funeral of Lawrence Jones; the man who was dying of silicosis was brought on his big hospital bed to see the movie. It was incredibly dramatic.

Q: Were there reactions from the company?
A: Not for the moment. I participated in a TV show called *Good Morning*

America after the release of a small clip of the film where the miners and ourselves had machine guns and semi-automatic rifles; I was questioned on that topic and I answered that Eastover Mining Company had hired thugs. Whereupon the director of the company wrote to request a transcript of the interview; he was so outraged that he intended to prosecute—but that was it. During the strike—the union investigated it—there were proven murderers that emerged at Eastover's as security guards. So I would have liked he start his prosecution!

Q: About the thug, Basil Collins, the man waving a gun at night in the truck, he is an intriguing character in the movie. After the strike and the eruption of violence, did he stay and live in Harlan?
A: Of course. He is still a mine foreman.

Q: How could he survive in the community after such a thing?
A: It was necessary that the scabs go back to work alongside those who made the picket line and even during the strike the unionists were living near the scabs. We were asking the miners: "How can you do this?" It is a tradition: if your father was union in the thirties, you fight for the union today and if your father was a scab during the thirties, you yourself are a scab today. Sometimes they are even neighbors. This situation obviously raises a lot of resentment among certain members of the community. A lot of Harlan's scabs have joined the Ku Klux Klan and Basil was a member of the John Birch Society.

Q: How many people were actually at the camera for the making of this movie?
A: Hart Perry was the photographer, I am on sound, and Anne Lewis was an assistant.

Q: Despite your small number you managed to be in the right place at the right time.
A: We were living there, in the miners' homes; they were feeding and taking good care of us and without them we wouldn't have survived.

Q: Is this why you have reached this amazing intimacy and synchronization between a camera on one hand and the miners and dramatic violent events on the other?
A: Because we were living with the miners and became good friends with them, it did not seem natural to be without equipment or not filming.

Everyone was thus comfortable. And they were violently excited about events. As for us, what we especially wanted to film, was the behavior. During the shooting we thought about using techniques of fiction, that is to say to evolve the characters, film the interaction between people, and not interviews or people talking directly to the camera. We wanted the camera to be descriptive.

Q: The miners sensed in you a great loyalty to their cause, otherwise they would not have allowed this intimacy to be established.
A: Certainly. They clearly understood that we sympathize with their cause, their fight, and their actions.

Q: And how could the miners be persuaded about that feeling? For example, how much loyalty did they credit you with at the time of your first contact with the miners and their families?
A: This happened over a period of time. I started shooting during the Miners for Democracy movement. In 1969, the assassination of Yablonski, his wife, and his daughter sparked a whole movement in the mines known as Miners for Democracy: the miners had more than enough of living and working under the dictatorship laid down by the union president Tony Boyle and they wanted a leadership that matched their needs. In these circumstances, from the masses of the miners emerged Arnold Miller and a few others, who had spent from twenty to twenty-six years in the mines, leading the fight for a local plan. Part of their platform then was to organize the unorganized. Thus in 1973 the miners of the Brookside mine voted to join the United Mine Workers and this became a new element to change the direction of the union. So, as I filmed the whole Miners for Democracy movement, it followed naturally that I was going to Harlan County. A lot of people who worked on Miller's campaign were organizers in Harlan County. When we arrived there, the strike had already been going on for fifteen days.

Arriving in Knoxville in Tennessee, we drove for two and a half hours on bad roads and I asked one of the officials: "Where should we go?" He replied: "Continue to go straight. When you reach the bridge, cross it and you will see the people." That's what we did and it was very . . . like rainy, foggy; we got there around five o'clock in the morning; women were sitting there with sticks. The state troopers were also there with their clubs. We realized that we could hardly leave the car and say: "Hi! I am a filmmaker from New York and I came to film you." We were afraid that everyone would start hitting us. So we turned around, crossed back over the bridge and asked the officials to come introduce us. Regarding the women, they began by being incredibly suspicious. They said they were called Florence Nightingale, Martha Washington, etc., not wanting to give us their real names. I believe it took a good week for them to tell us what picket line we should go to and things like that, for them to trust us and talk to us. They were very suspicious.

But then they really broke the ice. These are great personalities. They were also great in the movie, if I can talk that way. But, contrary to what is often said, this is not a movie about women. It is a movie about people.

Q: All right, but without having the label "movie about women," it celebrates much the
activism, the energy, the outspokenness, and the courage of women, do you agree?
A: Certainly. This is what happened: the judge, who was a worker for the mine, had decreed that there would only be six strike picketers authorized. Everyone knows that a strike cannot be won with only six people on the picket line. So it was up to women to take over. They were women who have heard all their life their grandfathers and fathers talking about the unions, but for most of them it was the first time they were taking a position. When they got started, there was no way to stop them. They were more and more militant and became the main force that ensured the success of the strike.

Q: Despite all the warm scenes in the community, all the scenes of solidarity, of activist joy and optimistic fight, the movie is steeped in an atmosphere of violence, of threating danger, and there were also moments more terrifying, because they were more authentic, than any Hollywood movie. I think for example of the scene where the scabs, revolver in pocket, get through the crowd of picketers: a "nonviolent" scene very violent, very frightening!
A: We were told they were going to kill us (the thugs of the company). This atmosphere of violence is part of daily life in Harlan. Everyone has a revolver. It is not illegal. No one hides it. We were told that if we were caught at night we would be killed. During the last weeks of strike, the scabs really took it far. For example at night they shot on the miners' houses. Among other things we had a buddy system to go to the outhouse. One evening, my cameraman and myself went out, him with an M1 rifle and me with a Magnum .357—it was just to go to the toilet! We heard gunshots and noises in the bushes. We were so scared that we both

drew our guns and a dog ran out. It was really terrifying. At night men guarded the entrance. They sat under the porch all night and we slept in the houses on mattresses laid on the floor. We were scared. And everyone knew that the only force and protection came from the people. And this was what made us feel at the same time incredibly strong.

Q: What kind of audience is there in the United States for a movie like this?
A: What happens with this film is very surprising. When I was shooting the movie I was thinking that no one would ever see it. I was imagining that the unionists, the miners, and maybe some of my friends would be the only audience. Then the film, shown at the New York Film Festival, received three standing ovations from the public. We have today a commercial distributor and the movie is in fifty cities. We heard yesterday that the movie came out in Boston where it is generating more revenue than *Rocky*, *Marathon Man*, and *Black Sunday* and is the second most successful in the city. It works incredibly well. It really fits as a commercial movie. For me, this means that the people of this country maybe want something else other than remakes of *King Kong*; that maybe people want movies that make them think and affect them, that they are able to understand not only the problems of their countries but also those of others and maybe other movies like mine can follow and find a mass market.

Q: You worked on *Hearts and Minds* by Peter Davis?
A: Yes, I did part of the sound.

Q: It was an important movie from several points of view, but one which, at the same time, did not follow its own logic, in the sense that it never questioned the American system. He managed to leave out the capitalist system and therefore ended up not making an American movie that took a more liberal position!
A: You are right. But I think it was important for what he said and that showing it in all the places where Peter has is a political coup in America. But to me also it poses problems: I thought that it showed the Vietnamese people as victims not as the big revolutionary force they were. But it was shown in many places and many people were influenced by what they learned from this film. I don't think that the movie industry in

general can change or recruit people: it is only a collective experience shared by people and a starting point for advancing issues and ideas.

Q: In any case it seems to me that, from a critical point of view, your movie advances the issues and ideas of American society far more than *Hearts and Minds*.
A: The end of the movie really gave us a hard time, as it needed to complete the film but also give it a political meaning. It was a difficult decision to make because we were thinking to finish by asking for the nationalization of energy. But it would seem completely out of place because it was not part of the rest of the film. Furthermore we did not want to finish the movie on a kind of sensational moment, like the funeral and the signing of the contract, without advancing a little further. It was only natural to show the new leadership at work, so people can see what role the government and the companies play then.

Q: The movie delivers a very strong political message in the sense that it takes a very clear position, for the mass of the union workers, against the established leadership, when it shows the dangers of corruption attached to the leadership and declares that initiative should come back to the base in the local unions. This is a fairly clear political position.
A: The power comes from below! Obviously this position that the film takes is heavily criticized, especially by the union bureaucrats. What the miners were feeling and what they were trying to say, is that, we cannot trust any kind of leadership, everything needs to be controlled by ourselves. With the arrival of Arnold Miller, the whole movement Miners for Democracy started, so that there was no longer any opposition from the base, at least visibly. In the United States it is very easy for union management to be corrupted, you earn four times more than workers and the whole perspective changes. Power corrupts and absolute power corrupts absolutely. Any kind of corruption, even the most mild, must be considered in this context: coal mining constitutes the most dangerous industry there is and if there is any kind of corruption the victims will be the miners. They cannot accept the slightest trace of dishonesty or collusion.

Q: How much footage did you shoot?
A: We recorded fifty hours of film—enough material to make separate

films on silicosis, the safety of miners, the history of unions and Harlan, corrupt unions, strip-mining and underground mining, the national coal contract—on many different topics in Harlan County. After all, the filming lasted more than three years. Editing took nine months—it was a very difficult film to put together. One of the bright sides is that it was a collective work. Many people worked on it; they came every day to my house in New York; there were some who had never worked on a film before but who felt politically engaged to work on this one; others participated in the entire editing process. We projected a rough cut of ten hours: people were watching and could not just say: "It's not working because the characters do not evolve, or because of the rhythms or something else." It was necessary to propose a solution. If you were commenting, you had to suggest another choice. It was a very cerebral and difficult way of editing, that demanded a lot of energy but it was very beneficial for me who was so close to the material because it allowed me to see what others thought according to their own perspective.

Q: Do you plan to continue making documentaries?
A: Yes, but I think the next movie I want to make is a movie about the Triangle Shirtwaist fire. In 1911 in New York, while unions were just beginning to organize, 153 women in the factory lost their lives. There was no improving the working conditions; it was forced labor; the emergency exits were closed. I would like to make a movie on this subject. It would be a fiction movie, after real people and real events. If I cannot find the money for the movie, I might make another documentary right away.

Interview at Cannes in May 1977 and originally translated from English by Jeannine Ciment.

American Dream: An Interview with Barbara Kopple

Gary Crowdus and Richard Porton / 1991

From *Cineaste Magazine* 18, no. 4 (December 1991). Reprinted by permission.

Barbara Kopple is a two-time Academy Award winner, having won the Oscar for Best Feature Documentary for *Harlan County, U.S.A.* (1976) and for *American Dream* (1990). She began her film career in 1968 working on the Maysles brothers' documentary, *Salesman*. She subsequently worked as an editor, camerawoman, and soundwoman on numerous documentaries before beginning production on *Harlan County, U.S.A.* in 1972. She also worked as co-director on the documentaries *Winter Soldier* (1972) and *No Nukes* (1980), directed a narrative feature entitled *Keeping On* (1981) which aired on PBS's *American Playhouse,* and more recently produced and directed the documentary *Civil Rights: The Struggle Continues* and co-directed (with Bill Davis) *Out of Darkness: The Mine Workers' Story*, a feature-length documentary on the one-hundred-year history of the United Mine Workers of America. Last year, *Harlan County, U.S.A.* was one of twenty-five selected by the National Film Registry as a "National American Treasure," guaranteeing its protection and preservation under the Film Preservation Act of 1988.

Kopple's latest feature documentary, *American Dream*, premiered at the 1990 New York Film Festival and is now set for a nationwide theatrical release in early 1992 by Miramax-Prestige Films.

Cineaste: Did winning an Academy Award for *Harlan County, U.S.A.* make it any easier for you to produce *American Dream*?
Barbara Kopple: No, it was harder to make this film because the times were more difficult. Funding for the arts was being slashed, some artists were under attack, and the tax write-off for film production investments had disappeared.

The subject matter of the film also made it difficult to get funding, because it was the Reagan era and nobody seemed interested in workers and unions any more. People said, "Unions are dead. Why are you wasting your time on this? Give us something on South Africa or anything else, but we don't want to hear about unions." To me unions are not dead. This film is also about economic crisis—it deals with what people read about in the newspapers every day.

It was also a difficult subject to make a film about because it was so complex, with so many different layers, and with so many different stories that needed to be followed. *Harlan County* was much easier in a sense because it was more black and white, it was "Which side are you on?" This one was different because I wanted to show what was happening from different people's perspectives.

On one hand, I was filming the local union leadership and a community in flux. These were people who felt they'd been betrayed because they were working for a profitable company, one where their grandfathers and fathers had worked, and they had been told they would never make less than they were making. When their wages were suddenly cut from $10.69 to $8.25 an hour, they felt a sense of shock and outrage. The corporate headquarters was in Austin, and it was a very paternalistic system, so of course they were going to fight back. On the other hand, there was the international union's point of view, and Lewie Anderson, who headed the meatpacking division wasn't a bad guy, he just had a different vision. He represented nearly two hundred thousand meatpackers nationwide and he was seeing wages being cut in some places to $6.50 an hour. He had a different strategy because he knew that the Austin workers were on the top end of the scale and he felt that you had to fight to bring the bottom people up. It was a very complex situation.

Cineaste: One of the strengths of the film is that it enables us to see the varying perspectives of the international union, the local union, and the local union's dissident faction. How were you able to film inside each of these groups?
Kopple: I think they let us in because they trusted us to give everyone a fair shake. I screened *Harlan County* for both the international and the local people. I also knew Ray Rogers from the J. P. Stevens campaign, so, when I showed up in Austin, I wasn't a stranger. Ray's policy was to get as much media as possible to tell P-9's story. Harlan County was closed, there was no media, you were on your own. People carried handguns and if somebody said, "I'm going to kill you," you could bet they would

try. Austin was a middle-class community and very different. The media was exciting to them, media was going to tell their story, and that was a big part of the Corporate Campaign.

I had trouble sometimes with the international because they'd say, "Union meetings are sacred. You can't be in there." But I'm very persistent, so I'd give long speeches in front of all these packing house guys as to why they should let me film their meetings. Some of them never got comfortable with it, and others sort of enjoyed it, or whatever. But we didn't get in people's faces, we kept a low profile. There were only two of us doing the filming, the cameraman and myself, and I do the sound on all my films. We tried to move around quietly because it's their show, not ours.

Cineaste: Were there times when you nevertheless felt that your presence added another dynamic to the events?
Kopple: I guess it always does but I think that for some of these meetings we were really insignificant and that they just forgot about us.

Cineaste: There's one scene where Lewie Anderson blows up and knocks over a chair....
Kopple: Yeah, and my microphone. He didn't know we were there. They were dealing with survival, with a real life crisis, so most of the time they really did forget that we were there.

Cineaste: You didn't seem to have the same kind of access to the management point of view or the labor/management relations.
Kopple: We have an interview with Chuck Nyberg, Hormel's executive vice president, and Richard Knowlton, the CEO. We also shot management press conferences and management interviews, but they always said the same thing.

Cineaste: We thought perhaps they refused to grant an interview because they knew who you were.
Kopple: No, they knew who I was, but I wasn't blocked. In fact, I was one of the few people who got in the plant to film. I couldn't believe it. But there weren't a lot of labor/management negotiations because the company wouldn't talk to them. They wouldn't even be in the same room with them, so they had arbitrators going back and forth. We actually filmed a scene where the arbitrators explain the company position

but it became too time-consuming, in film time, to explain that these were the arbitrators, so we used a bit of narration as a shortcut.

Cineaste: The film portrays a very complex situation, but, in the end, the audience is pretty much left to make their own interpretation of events, to decide whose strategy was right. Was it a conscious decision not to be more forthcoming with your own interpretation?

Kopple: I don't feel that way. I don't think that one strategy was right and one strategy was wrong. I felt these people were stuck in a situation where everybody had different feelings about what was happening and were being forced to make real life choices. It wasn't about who was right and who was wrong. These were all people who cared about workers. I wanted to show the audience the horrible dilemma that confronts people caught in an economic crisis, when everything, including long-held beliefs, starts to unravel.

Cineaste: In a sense, the dilemma was that almost any strategy would have been problematic.

Kopple: Absolutely. I mean, economists are still trying to figure it out. For me it wasn't a matter of right or wrong strategies, it was a matter of saying, "We can't let this kind of thing continue. This has to be stopped."

I wanted the film to be a reflection of what people have to go through when they're faced with this kind of crisis, to show the tough decisions they have to make, like whether or not to cross a picket line. This plant had been union for fifty-two years, these guys were all good union men, their grandfathers and fathers who worked at Hormel had been union. One of the main tenets of unionism is that you do not cross a picket line and yet these guys had to decide whether or not to cross a picket line to get their jobs back. You can see how painful it is to be forced to make that decision. As one guy says, how do you reconcile your feelings as a breadwinner with your belief in union solidarity? Do I cross the picket line so l can feed my family or do I stay out for the things I believe in?

Cineaste: The film's closing rendition of "Solidarity Forever," in light of the tragic events we've just seen, as well as some of the information conveyed in the final title cards, seems almost ironic. What was your intention?

Kopple: Well, it wasn't supposed to be ironic. What it meant to me was a sort of regrouping of things that people believed in, that a sense of hope and a willingness to stand up and fight for your beliefs was still alive in these people. Maybe you don't win every battle but each one changes you and makes you smarter, so that scene was meant to be moving, to be reflective, about past generations and struggles, and to convey hope for the future.

Cineaste: In *Harlan County*, you very effectively interwove historical and contemporary sequences, but there's little sense in this film of a historical memory of the strikers or the people in Austin. There was a sit-down strike in 1933 and the I. W. W. was involved in the formation of the meatpackers' union in Minnesota. It's almost as if the 1985 strike was a reawakening of that radical tradition. Did you have a historical sequence in *American Dream* that had to be eliminated at some point?
Kopple: No, there wasn't any archival stuff that we could get our hands on, except for the Hormel corporate promotional film from the 1950s. *Harlan County* lent itself to more of a historical treatment because it dealt with the history of coal mining and the long struggle for unionism. *American Dream* is more of a contemporary film about the Reagan era, about wage concessions and economic crisis. I don't think it's a film that calls for that much sense of history—discussing a strike fifty-two years before wouldn't have fit here.

Cineaste: Did you use the same collective method of editing on this film that you did for *Harlan County*?
Kopple: The editing was very difficult because there were two groups of editors. With the first group, just as we had screened everything and taken notes and figured out where we were going, they all had to leave for personal reasons, including serious illnesses in their families, and I had to start all over again. The new editors were Larry Silk, Tom Haneke, and Cathy Caplan, each of whom came in at different times. They were phenomenal. For example, Cathy came here as an assistant, just to sync stuff up, but she was here throughout the shooting, so she knew every bit of footage we had. When we got back, Larry came in, and after Larry was here for several months, Tom came in, and by that time Cathy had also become an editor. Everybody would take sequences to cut, and then swap sequences, and we'd talk collectively about them, so it was similar to what I did with *Harlan County*.

Cineaste: Were there major sequences of the film that you had assembled but couldn't include in the final cut for one reason or another?
Kopple: Yes, for example, there was a whole section of the film that

stayed in until the last three months. When I started the film, I had read about plant closings, and the first place I went to was Worthington, Minnesota, where it was rumored an Armour plant was going to close. The first scene I filmed there was a husband and wife sitting on their front steps and talking about how the plant was going to close but, since they had a clause in their contract that enabled them to move to another plant, they'd be OK. Suddenly, the phone rang and, as he went in to answer it, we continued filming his wife who was talking about how bad things were. A minute or two later he came out, looking very strange, and said, "Cut." But we kept rolling as he sat down and told his wife that he'd just been told they were selling all the Armour plants and that "We won't be going anywhere." Both he and his wife burst into tears. He looked at her and said, "What am I going to do. Meatpacking is all I know."

I shot incredible stuff in Worthington. I filmed people with their families and they'd say things like, "I don't understand why this is happening. I never did anything wrong. I never missed a day of work. I've always been a good worker." We filmed another guy packing up his family, like a scene out of *The Grapes of Wrath*, with mattresses piled on top of the truck, driving to Texas to try to find work. The material we had was incredibly moving, it really conveyed a sense of people who felt powerless, and it worked so well dramatically because then Austin was so vivid and full of life.

Cineaste: So the Worthington material was intended as the film's opening sequence?
Kopple: It was. First it was twenty minutes, then fifteen minutes, and we really tried to save it. It set a tone of what was going to happen, but it just didn't work, because we were afraid the audience would say, "Why did you get us involved with those people, and now you're taking us somewhere else and we have to learn about these people. Where are you going to land?" So it just didn't work, but it was the most heartrending footage.

Cineaste: You've used a somewhat more traditional music score in *American Dream*.
Kopple: Well, there really weren't any meatpacking songs. We thought of using songs by Mellencamp or Springsteen or James Taylor, but none of that music grew naturally out of the film's subject as it did in *Harlan County*, where we had a wealth of coal mining songs about mine disasters

and so on. In *American Dream* we basically used music for underpinning. For example, remember the scene where people are being arrested for civil disobedience? By that point in the film, the audience knows that the strikers probably aren't going to win the strike, so we didn't want to use real sound there to involve the audience in the action. We made the natural sound almost subliminal and used music to distance the audience from the action. You sense that they're still struggling, but you're not so caught up in the action as you were in earlier scenes.

Cineaste: What did Jim Guyette, Ray Rogers, and Lewie Anderson think of the film?
Kopple: All three of them were up on stage with me when the film was shown for the first time at the New York Film Festival, and that was pretty scary for me. They all said really nice things to me at the screening but none of them really sat down afterwards with me and talked about it. I think Ray and Jim feel there was too much of Lewie Anderson in it. Lewie Anderson felt that it was fair, that it showed all points of view, and that it was a good union film.

Cineaste: Have you shown the film to the people in Austin?
Kopple: Yes, we showed it earlier this summer at the local high school where over two thousand people showed up. They were really very emotional because it was the first time since the end of the strike that all of these people were together in one room, and you could just feel the electricity. I was petrified, absolutely petrified, because they had gotten different reports about the film from Jim Guyette and Ray Rogers, and so they were all just waiting to see for themselves. Well, the lights went out, and there was not a sound throughout the entire showing—a few boos when a company spokesman or Sheriff Goodnature appeared, but otherwise dead silence, not even coughs. I didn't know what was happening. Then, at the end of the film, all two thousand people were on their feet, clapping, with tears in their eyes. They loved it, and people came up to me and said things like, "I don't know why you were afraid to show this, it's wonderful," "It's going to help the healing process here in Austin," and "We would do it all over again." The response was really great and I was just so happy.

Cineaste: I guess you don't get many moments like that.
Kopple: Not enough, because that's a screening and an audience that you really care about. It's their story.

Cineaste: Will *American Dream* get a nationwide theatrical release like *Harlan County, U.S.A*?

Kopple: Yes, we expect to sign a distribution deal very soon and it should be in theatres by the winter. Documentaries are movies and need to be shown in theatres. There should be alternatives to *Terminator II*. People should also be able to see films that reflect their own lives, their own sense of history. Documentaries have drama and passion and narrative stories.

Cineaste: So you believe that documentaries could reach theatrical audiences if distributors and exhibitors were more imaginative in promoting and marketing them?

Kopple: Sure. *Harlan County* did really well. It showed in theatres all over the country and was number nineteen on *Variety*'s list of fifty top grossing films. More recently, films like *Roger & Me* and *Paris Is Burning* have done extremely well. When they're marketed properly, documentaries can be very successful, and there should be more of them in theatres.

Barbara Kopple

L. A. Winokur / 1992

From the *Progressive* 56, issue 11 (November 1992). Reprinted by permission.

To hear Barbara Kopple tell it, it's not easy being a maker of documentary films. Despite the two Academy Awards she has under her belt, funding for new projects is still hard to come by. And she admits that being on the road, often for months—sometimes years—at a time, "can certainly take its toll on your emotional and personal life."

But with her indefatigable spirit, Kopple takes it all in stride. "I figure nothing is really easy," she explained during an interview last spring at her downtown Manhattan loft. "And filmmaking enriches me as a person and gives me more of a quality to my life, a chance to give back to people what they're giving to me." And Kopple has been doing just that. Having been described as an "activist filmmaker," she is best known for her films about labor conflict, but her latest triumph is a piece on former boxing champ and current prison inmate Mike Tyson. It's scheduled to air this season on NBC television as *Movie of the Week*, the first documentary to run in this prime-time slot.

"It's a portrait of a man with many layers, a story of rags to riches and back to rags," she says. "I try to deal with human issues in my films. That's most important to me, to look at human beings and how they change over periods of time and what forces impact their lives."

Earlier, this New York–area native brought to light the struggles of eastern Kentucky coal miners in her acclaimed 1976 film *Harlan County, U.S.A.*, for which she received her first Oscar. Then, in 1991, a repeat performance: this time, Kopple walked away with the prize for *American Dream*, a poignant portrayal of the 1985–86 strike at the Geo. A. Hormel & Company meatpacking plant in Austin, Minnesota. The film cost nearly $1 million and was about five years in the making, she says.

Kopple got her start by apprenticing with documentary filmmakers David and Albert Maysles, of *Gimme Shelter* and *Salesman* fame. Among her credits, Kopple has directed or co-directed *Winter Soldier*, a film about Vietnam veterans; *No Nukes*; *Keeping On*, a dramatic feature about union organizing among textile workers in the South that aired on PBS's *American Playhouse*; *Civil Rights: The Struggle Continues*; and *Out of Darkness: The Mine Workers' Story*. Kopple also was asked by film director Oliver Stone to co-direct a documentary on the assassination of President John F. Kennedy that would serve as a companion piece to his feature-length motion picture *JFK*. The film, *Beyond JFK: The Question of Conspiracy*, has been shown in Europe but not yet widely viewed in this country.

What's next? "A film about love and relationships," she teases. "One that comes from the soul."

Question: In both *Harlan County, U.S.A.* and *American Dream*, you've chosen to focus on labor. Why?
Barbara Kopple: It's not so much labor as it is workers whose lives are in crisis. People who are willing to stand up and risk the things that are important to them in times when it's not that easy to do.

Harlan County, as you might remember, is a film about coal miners in eastern Kentucky fighting for the right to have a union. In getting that union, they were machine-gunned with semi-automatic carbines; a miner was killed by a company foreman; women took over the picket lines—all to have a union, a union of their choice. Doing that film taught me what life and death are all about, what it means to stand up and fight for the things you believe in and to risk everything that you have.

With *American Dream*, I had been reading about plant closings and wage concessions, and wondering where labor was and how the industrial landscape had changed since I made *Harlan County*. So it was a natural flow for me to make *American Dream*.

Q: Let's talk about *American Dream*. You started filming in Worthington, Minnesota, where, at the time, an Armour meatpacking plant was rumored to be closing. But then you switched gears, having been captivated by the struggle of Local P-9 of the United Food and Commercial Workers in Austin, which was about a hundred miles away. What was it about P-9 that caused you to leave Worthington behind?
Kopple: Starting with the Worthington struggle was a very important catalyst for me, because, in a sense, it really set a tone for the time. And the tone for the time was that people felt powerless; people felt it was their fault that this plant was closing and that kind of economic crisis was happening to them.

But I became depressed, wondering where the spirit was that I knew in Harlan County. Then I heard Jim Guyette, the president of Local P-9, talking on the television news about how P-9 wasn't going to take it and was going to fight back against Hormel. I realized then that the energy was there. So I went to Austin.

Q: Was it his spirit?
Kopple: Well, it was the spirit of the whole community. They were going to fight back and do something to change their situation at a time in our country of some of the worst plant closings and wage concessions.

Q: The legacy of Reaganomics?
Kopple: Absolutely.

Q: In *Harlan County, U.S.A.*, there are the good guys and the bad guys. The issues that are presented are much more black and white. But *American Dream* is far more complex. And tragic, perhaps.
Kopple: A lot of people say *American Dream* is tragic. And to me, the fact that these kinds of things can happen in America is tragic.

American Dream is a gray film for me. What you have is a town, Austin, Minnesota, which is headquarters to Hormel and where everybody knows everybody else. You have a local union made up of people whose grandfathers and fathers worked at the Hormel plant. You also have a company where the chief executive, whose father had been the plant manager, grew up working in the plant.

People were promised that they would never make any less than what they were making. But Hormel saw everybody else cutting wages and wanted to remain competitive. So when the company cut wages, even though it was profitable, from $10.69 to $8.25 an hour, people felt betrayed. Within one family alone, maybe there would have been more than two hundred years of being part of this company.

That's how they looked at it. Father, grandfathers, brothers, uncles—if you add up all those years, like twenty or thirty years apiece, it could total about two hundred years to have invested your life in a company.

Add to this the parent union, the United Food and Commercial Workers, whose strategies were in conflict with those of the local union. The national had its meatpacking division headed up by Lewie Anderson, whose strategy was: You don't take a profitable company which is paying a good wage and fight it; what you do is you go after the others who are traditionally anti-union paying the workers $6.50 an hour and unionize them and bring them up to a higher level.

So you had all these things tied up in Austin. That's why it's gray. For me, it would have been very easy to have taken one particular position or another, but I felt that what people in this country need is some sense of truthfulness. Some sense of really being able to look at a situation and see what kind of decision you would make if you were in the position of P-9, or the parent union, or even the company.

Q: There's been a lot of criticism over the years that parent unions are out of touch with their rank and file. Clearly, we saw some of this in the UFCW/P-9 struggle. Yet you chose to give a lot of play to Lewie Anderson, chief negotiator for the meatpacking division of the UFCW parent. Why?

Kopple: Lewie Anderson was one of the many layers that I had to deal with, but I don't think I made him instrumental. I just filmed what was happening. One of the great things about documentaries is that there are no actors and there are no scripts; you simply follow real-life people and events.

Q: What can you say about the role played by Ray Rogers, head of Corporate Campaign, Inc., who was hired as a labor consultant by Local P-9 to assist with its fight against Hormel?

Kopple: Ray has devoted his whole life to helping the underdog and working with rank-and-file people. To me, he had an impossible task. I mean, this kind of economic crisis was happening all over the country and he was hired to do a job. He has a great heart. He's really courageous. He was hired to fight the company and embarrass it in any way that he possibly could to get the workers what they wanted. He did everything within his capabilities.

Q: *Harlan County, U.S.A.* conveys a bitter contempt for scab workers. From the point of view of the camera, we as viewers are one with the striking coal miners, never overstepping these bounds. But in *American Dream*, we come close to crossing the line.

Kopple: In *Harlan County*, it never would have dawned on me to interview a scab as I did in Austin. The scab workers in Harlan County, I found out later, were released from the local prison and paid a small fee, or were let out on work furlough, to mine the coal. It was a definite union-busting technique by the company that turned into violence later on. And these people didn't live in the community. Nobody knew where they were from. I wouldn't have filmed them. No way.

But in *American Dream*, it was different. I don't think anybody had ever filmed what it is that goes on in people's minds that leads them to make what is probably one of the toughest decisions of their lives—to cross a picket line. I wanted to know what was happening with them. And I wanted to be responsible, because these guys are good guys. Their grandfathers were union and their fathers were union, and the mandate of unionism is you do not cross a picket line no matter what. You're confronted with these guys who were in opposition to a lot of the local union tactics but who stuck it out for most of the strike. But then they reached a point where they just didn't know what to do. And their dilemma was: Do I cross a picket line to get my job back, or do I stay out on strike for the things I believe in?

They faced a crisis that for me was so complex because American workers shouldn't have to face that kind of crisis. All these people wanted was to get a decent wage and to be able to work. For me, their dilemma was humanizing. All these years I had hated people who would even think of crossing a picket line. But here I really understood what they were going through. And it's not their fault if it's a systemic problem.

Q: You were with those people—the ones who decided to return to their jobs at the plant—as they prepared to cross the picket line.
Kopple: Yes, but I didn't cross the picket line. I could have, but I didn't. We stopped. There were pickets all the way down the road. I went with them down that road, but when they got to the actual entrance to the plant gate, I got out.

Q: Why?
Kopple: I don't know what went on in my mind. I could have gone right through with them, which would have been visually incredible. But I didn't. I just got out and let them go.

Q: You personally couldn't bring yourself to do it?
Kopple: I don't know why. I just didn't do it. But what I do is of no consequence. What's important is what they did.

Q: When you embark upon a film like *Harlan County, U.S.A.* or *American Dream*, surely you have preconceived ideas as to what you hope to communicate and where you see the film heading. How do you keep your biases from getting in the way of the story unfolding?

Kopple: I let my biases get in the way. I'm not objective at all in my filmmaking. With *American Dream*, I figured that if you're going to be out filming in weather that's sixty-below with the wind-chill factor, you'd better care about something. Something's got to keep you warm inside. I just hope that I'm responsible to the people I'm filming.

Q: Did you find some of your own ideas challenged as the filming of *American Dream* progressed?

Kopple: I don't know. Jumping from filming the national union to the local, for example, in my heart of hearts, I wanted the national to be there for the local. But then I started to hear what the national union was saying—that if every local decides that its cause is the best, and every local goes on strike, the whole union would be dissolved. I figured I didn't know enough about this. So I made a conscious decision to tell the story as truthfully as I possibly could by getting as close to these people as they would let me. Sure, I'd get swept up in things; when I was in one area, I'd feel a certain way, and when I was in another, I'd feel differently.

Q: How difficult was it to get access to all these people? You even had access to the company.

Kopple: I was the only one who got into the plant. I think they did it because I wasn't from the local television news and they knew they wouldn't see what I filmed that night at ten or eleven o'clock. And I think, because I lived in the community for so long, people generally saw that I wasn't just there for a cheap shot, that I was really there for the long term.

Q: You were there, off and on, for how long?

Kopple: Three years. I also think being a woman helps, because you can be a lot more intimate. People aren't as intimidated by you and you can ask things that maybe a male would have a tougher time doing. Plus, I'm persistent. I can be a real pain in the neck. So it's easier for them to let me in. But sometimes it was hard. With the national union there were times I had to give speeches about why I should be allowed into their meetings, since they saw them as sacred and didn't think I should be there.

Q: Whether it's Harlan County, Kentucky, or Austin, Minnesota, you

are often on location for years at a time. This must be an exhilarating, though emotionally draining, experience. How do you cope?
Kopple: A part of me really loves small towns. I like the fact that people know me and they talk to me and invite me over for dinner or for picnics, so for a moment in time I feel as if I'm part of the community.

But it also takes a tremendous toll on me, because I'm not in my own home. In Austin I was living in a motel. So I would always come back to New York. But even that could be difficult. Having to raise money for every roll of film and go deep into debt, coming home to sometimes find your electricity turned off or creditors and collection agencies after you, it's tough.

Q: But I'd have thought that after winning an Academy Award for *Harlan County*, you would have gained a certain amount of credibility, if you will, that would have made it easier for you to obtain financing for *American Dream*.
Kopple: No. Not at all. Getting financing isn't easy. It's really hard. With *American Dream*, a lot of people didn't want to invest in a film about meatpacking and economic crisis in the Middle West. It just wasn't a hot, sexy subject.

Besides, applying to churches and foundations for money, people think, "Oh, Barbara Kopple, she got an Academy Award. Let's give someone else a chance." And I understand that. But I need money, too.

Doing *American Dream* was really hard. For quite a while, I couldn't even find a lab to give me credit to develop my film. So I had the film stacked up until I could get enough money to buy a bunch of used refrigerators so I could store the film. I filled my whole office with used refrigerators, putting the film in the freezers, because at that point the lab wouldn't even develop the film unless I paid for half of it up front. And I had nothing. No money at all.

Q: What keeps you going?
Kopple: I think a lot of the love I've gotten from my family has enabled me to take risks in my life and do the things that are important to me. I grew up in Scarsdale, in a very stable, wonderful family with incredibly supportive parents. When I was about nineteen, I worked with a group of people on a film called *Winter Soldier*, about Vietnam veterans giving testimony on war crimes. We had a fundraising screening and my parents came to it. And nobody knew they were my parents. At the end of the film, my father stood up and said, "I think what these kids have done

is great, and here is my check for five hundred dollars." And he slapped it on the table and said, "I hope everybody in this room does the same." Then he and my mother walked out, and I thought, "Yes, those are my parents." I was just so proud.

Also, knowing that I'm going to show a film later, that's part of what gets me through it all. Seeing a film in a darkened room on a big screen. It has such power.

Q: I understand that *American Dream* has been shown in Austin. Tell me about the response.
Kopple: The P-9 women's support network, which is still functional, showed the film last year on Memorial Day weekend at the local high school, where a lot of the P-9 meetings had taken place. The showing was only for those people who didn't cross the picket line and had supported the strike. About 1,200 to 1,500 people showed up.

I hadn't seen them since the film was finished and had won an Academy Award a month or so before. And so going back there was very scary for me. I kept thinking, "What if they hate the film?" I just didn't know, because the film does have so many layers, and I guess depending upon how you look at it or who you are, there are a lot of different things you can take from it.

During the showing, it was pretty incredible, because there was dead silence. I mean, you could hear a pin drop, that's how silent and tense it was in that room. Then, at the end of the film, as the credits rolled, people stood up and applauded. And that was a great relief. One woman came over to me and put her arms around me and said, "How could you think we wouldn't like it? I loved it." Another woman said, "Now my kid's going to know where I was and what I was doing." And somebody else said, "This is going to start the healing process again. Thank you." It was wonderful. I'll never forget it.

Q: What about the response from people who crossed the picket line, or others in Austin? I understand the film was shown at the local movie theater there earlier this year.
Kopple: I talked to John Morrison, who was one of the people who ultimately didn't believe in what P-9 was doing so he went with the parent union and finally crossed the picket line. He said he came out of the film and was stunned. He told me, with tears in his eyes, that he was glad he had trusted me. He thought the film accurately portrayed what happened as he saw it.

Q: The ultimate compliment.
Kopple: Yeah. But the company gave it a "C." They said they thought the film that should have been made was how much better it is in the plant right now. And the mayor of Austin wouldn't even see it. He said he thought it was absolutely obscene that it was coming to Austin. He claimed it was going to tear people up after he had worked so hard to heal the wounds.

Q: The nationwide distribution of *American Dream* was delayed for almost a year after you won the Oscar. Does that bother you?
Kopple: You know what? It's okay, because I think the film is more valuable now than it would have been had it come out right after the Academy Awards last year. We're smack in the middle of an election year. And what people are dealing with now—and in the film—are these sorts of meat-and-potato issues, issues about the economy and jobs and bringing back the whole essence of the American dream.

Q: Women played a vital role in the organizing efforts portrayed in both *Harlan County* and *American Dream*. With more and more women entering the work force, do you think it's likely that they will become the vanguard of the labor movement?
Kopple: I don't know, but I hope it's true. I'd like to see more women in union leadership positions. I think we can be much more humane. I think if women were in charge, many national unions would be more responsive to their rank and file. But women also can be very tough. I pity any corporation that crosses them.

Q: While making a film, you walk into people's lives, become totally immersed in their struggles, but then ultimately move on. What do you take with you, and how would you say you've been changed by these experiences?
Kopple: I've learned the important thing is to always stand up for what you believe in, because the only way you'll really be defeated is if you don't. These experiences affect me profoundly. They've made me understand what the human spirit is about and have made me an optimist in my life. I believe there's nothing that people can't do.

Filmmaker's Knockout Punch

Harlan Jacobson / 1993

From the *Washington Post*, February 12, 1993, C2. Reprinted with permission.

When *Fallen Champ: The Untold Story of Mike Tyson* airs tonight on NBC, director Barbara Kopple will reach a greater audience than she did with her two Oscar-winning documentaries, *Harlan County, U.S.A.* (1976) and *American Dream* (1990), combined and multiplied by ten. It's an irony that's not lost on the forty-year-old New York independent filmmaker, whose works have won widespread critical acclaim but, like virtually all documentaries, never reached blockbuster audiences.

"The D-word," Kopple said with a sigh before a high-powered preview crowd Sunday night, referring to the networks' well-known aversion to "real" documentaries. "I'm not allowed to say that word; I'm supposed to say 'reality-based film.'"

"NBC didn't quite know how to deal with me," Kopple continues. "I was like this alien from outer space. There was no script, and when they asked to see dailies, I said, 'Sure, but they won't help.'"

It's no wonder. While TV producers are known for the speed with which they can turn scandals-of-the-week into movies-of-the-week, Kopple is known for the time she invests in her films, often living with her subjects until she has infiltrated their lives. She spent four years making *Harlan County* and five on *American Dream*; both tell the story of labor strikes. "Documentaries are incredible, cerebral puzzles," Kopple says. "They need a lot of analysis and thought."

On most of her films, Kopple says, "I'm so riveted that I can't leave. I want to know who these people are, what they're doing, and what they're going through. It ends up being part of something I'll never, ever forget, even if the film never comes out."

It's that "never, ever" that beguiles you about Kopple: It's the voice of the girl who sat next to you in sixth grade coming out of an adult who won't leave the premises until she's forced you to tell the truth. "I really care about truthfulness. I really struggle to get underneath, somewhere in there deep, and try to figure out what's going on. In this one particularly, because it was a departure for me."

Start to finish, *Fallen Champ* took Kopple seven months, working around the clock, to make; it was shot on film and edited on video. "It's the only way we could do it," she says, "and bring it in on time and under budget," which, she adds, was "the same as a TV movie of the week—on the low side."

For Kopple, raising money for her own documentaries has often been as difficult as—if not more difficult than—the filmmaking process itself. This time, the network gave her the money up front. "It felt like a hundred pounds had been lifted from my shoulders," she says. "All I had to do was concentrate on the film." But the downside of working for television, she says, was the speedy timetable: "I had to ask people to spill their guts and trust me. If they said no, I could not spend more time with them. I had to take the no and move on."

To Kopple, *Fallen Champ* "is not just a story about date rape. It's as much about who Mike Tyson is as we could do in ninety-two minutes. . . . It's not about a movement; it's about an individual."

Kopple says she sees Tyson as a black kid in whom few wanted to invest time, attention, or money until he made himself a vehicle for other people's glory or profits. When it all clicked in, Tyson was deluged.

"It happens to so many athletes. You get money and cars and clothes and homes and all these women who throw themselves at you. I think he just didn't know or understand what 'no' meant. He just thought, 'I've earned this.' He didn't think that if a woman said no, she meant it. Or that it applied to him. . . .

"But there's some hope for Mike Tyson. He needs to do some deep thinking. He's only twenty-six years old. If he can get around the right people, there's a lot he could add to society."

For *Fallen Champ*, Kopple shot eighty-odd interviews, of which "fifty-two made the film," she says proudly. "The only way you can learn is by being able to hear a lot of sides. Too often we're just duped by one particular person's line of thought."

She never met Tyson, though. "[Boxing promoter] Don King wouldn't let me near him. Alan Dershowitz [Tyson's lawyer] really tried to get me in," she remembers, but no go. "King came over to me in Indianapolis at the Black Expo and said"—Kopple does her best imitation of King's rasp—"'If I were payin' for this [film], little sister, you could see Mike.

And I'd let you have your artistic freedom—don't worry 'bout that. But I'm not.'"

After shooting footage of Louis Farrakhan at a Free Mike Tyson Rally in Indianapolis, Kopple canceled her interview with the Nation of Islam leader. "I didn't think I needed it," she explains. *Fallen Champ* catches Farrakhan in a vitriolic tirade, denouncing women for "the deceitful games you play."

"There's a tremendous anger and hatred of women" in Farrakhan, says Kopple. "And there's lots more [footage] where that came from. He just really went off on women and Desiree Washington . . . almost as if she was a piece of bait that somebody had let out. I was shocked listening to it, and it takes a lot to shock me. I usually go with the punches of almost anything and try to figure out where it came from and why. This just stopped me in my tracks."

Finally, does Kopple believe that Tyson is guilty?

Kopple says Tyson's appeal, led by Dershowitz, will begin Monday in Indianapolis, and there are intimations that it will have a twist. So, she says, "I have a lot of opinions but I'm reluctant to get into it, because real-life events are forging forward."

Stand Up and Do Something: Barbara Kopple Speaks with Lisa Lincoln

Lisa Lincoln / 1998

From *Why* magazine, Winter 1998, 3–6. Reprinted by permission of WhyHunger.

Lisa Lincoln: How did you start to make the sort of films that you make?
Barbara Kopple: It started with *Winter Soldier*. And that was a group of us, a collective, getting together, to try to do something about the war in Vietnam. We were very new filmmakers, and very young. Jane Fonda and Donald Sutherland got a little bit of money together to help us. But everybody worked for free. And Lucy Jarvis, who used to work at one of the networks, got us tapes. A group of us went to Detroit and we filmed Vietnam veterans giving testimony about war crimes that they had committed. It made us feel not so powerless. It was an amazing, wonderful learning experience. Plus it was so wonderful for the veterans who testified. It was the first time anything like that had ever happened.

There were incredible stories. Like this guy, Evan Haney, who was a Native American. He stood up and he said, "The Vietnamese are so much like us." He said, "We pray in the same way." He said, "We have a treaty that says 'For as long as the rivers shall flow, and for as long as the trees shall grow....'" He said, "The way things are going and how we're acting as this country, the rivers aren't going to flow anymore, and the trees aren't going to grow." And then he just broke down in tears. Just one after another told their stories, and they would have someone sitting next to them, who had been there, who would say that everything that that person said was true. And there were informal groups of veterans in the halls that talked about racism and other things.

And to be really true to these veterans, we all edited the film, as well as shot it.... We lived with the veterans during this process... they would look at different pieces of footage that we were putting together, and they would say, "Yes, this is very real." And in the morning, we would wake up to start work, and sometimes the veterans would still feel that they had the rifles in their hands, and they would jump. That kind of thing. We all ate together, and we all lived together until the film was finished.

It was shown at the Cannes Film Festival, and it won the Critics Choice, but it only showed on one WNET station, and everywhere else the film was censored.

LL: You couldn't get it distributed?
BK: No, a lot of people wanted to distribute it, but places wouldn't show it. But Vietnam veterans took it everywhere with them—they tried to heal other veterans—to universities and other places to talk about the war. They would show excerpts from it. So that was a way of starting.

Then I started *Harlan County*. I started my own little company and that was the first film that I did. . . . Once again there was no money whatsoever, except for a few little grants. Everybody worked for free on it, except the editors, and, of course, the mix and all the technical stuff at the end. . . . I learned what life and death were all about. Because we had guns pointed at us, and I was told if I was ever caught alone at night, I'd be killed. We were machine gunned with semi-automatic carbines with tracer bullets on the picket line. You can hear me screaming in the film, "Don't shoot!" at the top of my lungs. I was very young, so I thought, "Ah, ah, I'll just live forever"—not really that afraid, but pretty afraid. We lived with the coal miners, and at night, the gun thugs would shoot up their homes, so it was pretty scary.

American Dream, another film, really showed the economic crisis in the Midwest. It was more complicated because it was a local union fighting against its parent union. And it was also both of them fighting against the company. Of course, we would pick a Minnesota winter to go out on the picket lines. It was sixty degrees below with wind-chill factor. And we would sometimes just pray that the equipment, the batteries, would be dying down so that we would have an excuse to sit in a warm car for a few minutes. Lots of times we were freezing. The material we got was really poignant. There's one scene where these Midwestern men just didn't know what to do anymore. They weren't working, they weren't supporting their families. They just broke down and cried. They had been taught since they were children that you just never cross a picket line, and these guys did. So that's a start.

LL: Looking through this list of your projects, I see some major themes: workers' rights, civil rights, women's rights, the empowerment of people. . . .

BK: When I was doing the films, I didn't categorize them in any way. I went because I really want to tell gripping stories about people in crisis, and show that sometimes people, that you never hear of unless somebody's there to tell their story, are the people who probably have the most important things to say. When I made *American Dream*, I just wanted those people to know that their struggles were important and to lend them a voice. So that was a big reason why I went and filmed them. And also in Harlan County, if we hadn't been there, there probably would have been a lot more people killed. When we were on the picket line, sometimes we wouldn't even have film in our camera, and we would be there just to try to keep the violence down. We would pretend we would have film in our camera because nobody wanted to commit murder in living color. . . .

LL: Do you see your role as filmmaker and artist as someone who documents?
BK: I think what I like to do is to tell compelling stories, to allow you inside of why people make decisions, and how average flesh and blood people rise to occasions, and are really strong, and just overcome so much. To let you see, as if you're not watching a film, but almost as if you're experiencing what they're going through. I like to film through different peoples' points of view, so you really feel like you're there.

LL: Your connection to your viewer is very strong.
BK: Well, my connection to my viewer is really strong, but the connection to people who are the subjects of the films is very, very strong. I like to do things where what they have to say and who they are is portrayed in a very honest, open way. I feel honored and fortunate to be given so much access in so many of these cases. If you're given total access to do things, that's when you can really see everything, and really feel everything.

LL: It seems to me that your work shows over and over again just how courageous people are.
BK: That's definitely what I feel. I also feel that there is no reason in the world why you can't stand up and do something. . . . And if you stand

up and you're able do something, other people will stand up with you. Fighting for, and believing in what you think is right, is very important. . . .

LL: Tell me about other films that you've done.
BK: There's a piece we did about immigration for the Alliance for Justice. One of the characters in it, Jesus Collado, had lived in this country for something like twenty-five years, and twenty-three years ago he had a girlfriend who was fifteen and he was nineteen and he had sex with her. From where he comes from, in the Dominican Republic, people marry when they're sixteen. She was very willing, but the mother got upset and wanted to break it off. So she went to the police and complained, "This guy is seeing my daughter and she's fifteen." So he got a misdemeanor charge and he promised he wouldn't see her any more. And then twenty-three years later he's doing some work for his mother back in the DR. He's married, he has three children. All his brothers and sisters are here, and his mother, everybody. And he came back into the country, and because of the new immigration laws he was imprisoned because of this misdemeanor twenty-three years ago, and there was no way of getting him out. And he sat in there for six or seven months in tears, and all his family were in tears. It was horrible. The only way he could get out of prison was to say that they could deport him. He had been a great citizen, all his family were citizens. He managed his own restaurant. The whole family was so close to each other.

We started showing the film around before we finished it, and we got Anthony Lewis interested in it, and Juan Gonzalez. And then we showed at First Monday, which [involves] law students all over the country. Collado got out a couple of weeks after we started showing it to the law students. The INS got really frightened because they really had no right to hold him . . . the film just added a lot of publicity . . . that was such a wonderful victory! Now he's having his hearing. Many, many people have seen [the film], and many people have come to his aid. . . .

We also did another film called *Defending Our Daughters*, which we filmed in Pakistan and Egypt and the U.S. and Sarajevo. It's all about women being activists and overcoming horrible things, like female genital mutilation. It tells about girls who can be sold by their fathers in Pakistan. The film tells how one of them ran away and married someone that she loved, and now has to be in hiding because her father can kill her if he wants. . . . Also in Pakistan, women who are raped, unless there are four witnesses, then it is the woman's fault. In Sarajevo, rape was used as a weapon of war, and nobody's been prosecuted for rape. . . .

The films tell the stories of people. You're really with these people and you really see the risks that they have to take. Like the young girl in Pakistan having to lie down in a van, to show the filmmakers the way to her village, because she knows that she could be taken out and beaten or killed by her father if anyone knows she's in there. The kind of risks that women take, and how proactive they are. Like these two women lawyers, also in Pakistan, who put together this shelter for battered women, and take these kinds of risks. They've been told that their kids could be killed, and they could be killed, because what they are doing is totally against the culture of that country.

The kind of films that I make are about people taking risks for things that they believe in . . . it's stories, it's storytelling, it's looking underneath, and looking at what we're made of as human beings when it comes to our survival, or the survival of others.

LL: What about the artist's role in society?
BK: Because we're able to do things that people can see or know about, I just think that we have to do things in our lives that are very accurate, and make them so that audiences can feel them and understand them. Whether you use the perseverance of people, or you use comedy, or any device that you have to get the audience to want to see, and feel and hear what's going on. And maybe the audience can do something in their lives. It's not that the films change anybody, but they can encourage you to stand up for something you believe in your own life. They can affirm that if you've seen injustice . . . still you can do something.

LL: Were you drawn to filmmaking by a film that you saw?
BK: Well, one of the films that got me into filmmaking was called *The Battle of Algiers*. . . . I liked the style of it because it really made me feel as if I was experiencing it. It was shot in black and white, in a real kind of style, so it wasn't just beautiful shots. I could really feel the agony of the people, and the courage of the people. So that film really influenced me at a very young age.

LL: We are asking people whether there was a particular experience in their lives that influenced their careers. . . .
BK: Well, I grew up in a time when women were really starting to express

themselves. I knew from a very early age that I wanted to do something in my life, not just be a housewife. I think that I was most stirred when I was thirteen and my house burned down. I was supposed to have memorized a poem or something for the next day. So I just had my mother write me a note—"Sorry, but we had a personal tragedy." I brought it in to my teacher, and he didn't believe that it was a real note, because my mother had signed her name, "Mrs. Marjorie Kopple," not "Mrs. Alfred Kopple." I went home, and I said, "Mom, he didn't believe that you wrote this note. I don't understand." And I said, "Does this mean that when you're married you're no longer you, that you're part of my father?" Not that I had anything against my father, but I was very concerned at that age—and I was pretty young—with identity. And so that small lesson is something I never forgot. I knew that I was not going to let that happen to me.

Woody Captured on the Spot, without a Script

Michel Ciment / 1998

From *Positif*, February 1998, 37–39. Translated from French by Holly Prall. Reprinted by permission.

Michel Ciment: How did you come up with the idea to devote a film to Woody Allen after all the great social and political documentaries like *Harlan County, U.S.A.* and *American Dream*?

Barbara Kopple: One of my friends from Chicago, Jim Stern, a theatrical producer who made the show *Bunny Bunny* after the life of Gilda Radner (one of the *Saturday Night Live* actors who died from cancer), telephoned me one day to ask me if I was interested in following Woody Allen during the first tour of his life. He was going to Europe for twenty-three days and to eighteen different cities. I didn't think for more than ten minutes before I agreed! Then I went to his house, and we talked together for half an hour, which is a lot for Woody Allen! At the end of our conversation, he accompanied me to the door and told me that he did not want to go! He had liked the idea from a distance, but, now that it was approaching, it seemed like it was too imposing. As I left, I thought that this would be a very special film and I wished I'd had my camera with me to film that moment. There were no conditions that he posed, and the only thing that I asked from him, was that he give me access to everything wherever he went. He agreed. And, in fact, I could do whatever I wanted.

Ciment: It's well known that Woody Allen likes to protect his private life and that he's very timid. He was going to, during this trip, expose himself not only to ridicule, but also to your objective eye.

Kopple: Our team was made up of four people. Most of the time, I was busy with sound for the part of the documentary on Woody Allen himself, because my sound engineer, Peter Miller, put in place a system for recording the concerts that had him almost every day in a different city. My style of film has always been very intimate, and I made sure that the camera wasn't too present, so that people weren't aware of it. The people that I film can just live their lives and forget that we're there. We can be like a sofa or a lamp! That's what we did. I was with Woody between sixteen and eighteen hours a day. We traveled in the same airplane, and I spent with him all the time that he was awake, and sometimes when he wasn't! I could go and come as I wanted. He said that we could always be there during the day without asking permission. He conducted himself as a perfect gentleman, always agreeable, and it was a pleasure to travel with him.

Ciment: I know that children forget easily that they are in front of a camera, like adults who are not in the habit of being filmed, but this absence of consciousness is unexpected in a film comedian!
Kopple: It's possible that in his mind it was a home movie (a family film) and not something that would interest the whole world. The idea of a documentary is very different than that of a fictional work. I believe also that he had confidence in me, that he believed me to be someone responsible, and that I was not going to do something foolish. And he waited to see what would come of this experience. I never asked him why he agreed to the idea of this film portrait, and, in fact, it's not my problem. During the tour, he showed his love of music, which he played with sheer abandon, like he was searching his deepest soul to express himself by the clarinet. He behaved in all these strange villages like in his New York club: he played his instrument, shook his head and tapped his foot. Except that here he sent kisses to the audience, shook hands, and did a comic number on stage in front of auditoriums of fifteen hundred to eighteen hundred people. He couldn't have been more happy, allowing himself to be photographed by the paparazzi, and not refusing contact with the public. That's explained maybe in part by the presence of Soon-Yi Previn at his side, who gave him a youthfulness of spirit and behavior.

Ciment: What is striking is how the women who accompany him, his sister Letty Aronson and his companion Soon-Yi, do not hesitate to criticize him and make negative comments to him even if it is affectionately.
Kopple: The problem with celebrities like Woody Allen is that they are surrounded by people who want to please them and always tell them yes. And I believe that he needs—like a measure of moral hygiene—to have

near him people who will hold him to the truth, to the reality of things. He allows Letty and Soon-Yi to tell him that, if his orchestra played well, he should compliment them. In his work and his inner world, he is like a tower of steel, but, in his ordinary life that he shares with common mortals, he is very fragile and obsessive. At some point he needs to be saved from his occupation with himself!

Ciment: What is the relationship between what you shot and what you kept in the final film?
Kopple: I shot around fifty hours during the eighteen concerts, for 140 minutes of film. The concerts represent 25 percent of the film and the rest is a documentary about Woody. Everything was shot on 16 mm. Since making *Harlan County, U.S.A.*, I do much of the camerawork handheld. The equipment is lighter today. But the nagra to record the sound is still heavy. However, when you know you're getting a good sound environment, you do not feel the weight, you feel like you're flying. However, once you stop, you feel it in your muscles. From this point of view, the trip was exhausting and these sixteen to eighteen hours a day filming, I really experienced physically. But as soon as I arrived in the editing room, I forgot all these sufferings. What we filmed literally jumped from the screen. The first cut lasted nine hours, the second six and a half, the third three and a half. That was when Woody and Soon-Yi came into the editing room; they were like two kids. They sat, she surrounded in his arms, he was leaning over her and they giggled like crazy nonstop locked in their intimate cocoon. The only thing he said to me was this: "How are you going to edit it down?" And I told him that it was my problem. He then replied, "I'm glad!" and he left.

Ciment: Unlike other directors like Scorsese, Wenders, or Tavernier, the world of the documentary is totally alien. Has he talked to you about that?
Kopple: Never. What happened is that he became the subject and I the director. I was filming and he couldn't talk to me about anything: he had to live his life. If I wanted to know something, I asked him a question and he answered. Woody is twofold. If you are asking about his music, his films, his philosophy of life, he is very serious in his responses. But in his everyday life with his family and his loved ones, he doesn't stop joking, telling stories, revealing his lack of assurance. He's a normal person, with as he says, his chronic dissatisfaction, his claustrophobia, his hypochondria.

Ciment: In Bologna, you showed visually, in filming the houses and the streets, the sense of confinement he confesses experiencing.
Barbara Kopple: The scenes in Bologna are in fact some of my favorites. When he looked through the window and he saw the thousands of people waiting for him, you could read the fear on his face. It was a real feeling, as if he received a blow to the chest. Woody was totally honest during the trip. When a woman, trying to be polite, said to him, "You like Bologna, you couldn't wait to come here," he responded: "Not at all, I was very scared to come to Bologna, because I like open spaces." And when Soon-Yi told him that he shouldn't have said that, he added, "With Valium, I can learn to like your city." This candor is marvelous. It was also the first time that he'd performed in this way in public and it was a shock for him to see that all the tickets were sold for each concert. That gave him immense pleasure. Europe, in a sense, allowed him to flourish. Why he wanted to start his tour by stopping first in Paris is that it is a city where he feels safe. It feels like home. So we had to make a detour before he gave his first concert in Madrid.

Ciment: The idea of the visit to his parents at the end of the film didn't make him apprehensive?
Kopple: It was important for me that this scene takes place. The return home, it is like closing the loop. We arrived with gifts, because he always brings to his parents what he collects in his travels. I wanted to show the environment from which he came, and I knew it would be a surprise to the public. There is something universal in this family reunion thing. Whoever we are, we become children again around our parents. Here is this writer, this movie director, this world-famous comedian who's looking for the approval of his father and mother, like he was twelve years old, and then his father says that he should have been a pharmacist. Everything was spontaneous in that sequence, no one paid attention to us and they had their regular family meals.

Ciment: Woody Allen was not embarrassed that his mother is filmed saying he should not have married an Oriental but a good Jewish girl?
Kopple: Not in the least. He didn't think about it that way. What you need to understand is that Woody doesn't think about exterior things, but only about interior things. For him, it was a very funny scene that made him laugh and that he saw from a different perspective than us.

Ciment: In a sense, it's informative that he's agreed for the first time to

be filmed this way and then that he shot *Deconstructing Harry*, his work maybe the most directly addressing his intimate and artistic problems.
Kopple: But *Harry* . . . nevertheless is a fiction film written in advance, played by actors. It is not a documentary, which shows his real life. Whatever the autobiographical elements in *Deconstructing Harry*, we know that it is a product of his imagination. While my *Wild Man Blues* is captured on the spot, without a script. I'm not sure that Woody Allen knows exactly what I grabbed with my camera. I believe that for people, the makers of documentaries are aliens, strangers who come from another planet. And this is no different for a filmmaker of fiction. He knows about a script, an actor, a partition, a comic effect, but he ignores what can be documentary material.

Ciment: Were there moments that you wanted to keep in the final cut?
Kopple: I think that the film has a length and a pace that works. But I really liked a scene where he had lunch with Gianni Versace, and another with a fashion show which Soon-Yi wanted to go to, but where she was jealous to see all these great-looking models. I wanted every scene to be different and to construct little by a little a portrait that surprises with new elements. This film was like a road movie, much simpler than those I shot before, with their multiple themes, their greater complexity and the regular appearance of new characters. It was physically hard, but more linear than usual. We worked with a single camera, except in London, where we added another, because I wanted a coda with more energy.

Ciment: Between shots did you have conversations with him?
Kopple: Practically none, because we were dead tired. Woody was always busy—walking in the street, visiting with the mayor, preparing for the concert—and undoubtedly that was the reason why he is so very "open." When we parted, it was two in the morning and he had to get up early. This left little time to chat!

Woody Allen's "Wild" Concerts: Filmmaker Blows Own Horn on His European Jazz Tour

Gary Arnold / 1998

From the *Washington Times*, May 8, 1998, C12. Copyright © 1998 The Washington Times LLC. This reprint does not constitute or imply any endorsement or sponsorship of any product, service, company, or organization. License # 38248.

"It's a window onto Woody, that's all it is," director Barbara Kopple says of her newest documentary feature, *Wild Man Blues*.

This disarming, entertaining, and ultimately invaluable digest of a European jazz concert tour headlined by Woody Allen was shown during Filmfest DC and begins an exclusive commercial engagement today at the Cineplex Odeon Inner Circle.

Wild Man derives its mischievous title from a Louis Armstrong–Jelly Roll Morton composition, one of thirteen jazz selections excerpted in the course of the movie, which summarizes a whirlwind excursion in March 1996.

The subject, famous as a comedian and filmmaker but also a devoted amateur jazz clarinetist since his teens, had agreed to perform in eighteen cities in twenty-three days. The itinerary began in Paris and concluded in London. Several bookings were in Italy, including a charity date in Venice to help raise funds for a venerable theater damaged by fire.

Miss Kopple and her crew (customarily the director, cameraman Tom Hurwitz, soundman Peter Miller, and a camera assistant) were invited to tag along and immortalize the gig, which had been contemplated for years and then suddenly mushroomed.

"Originally, Woody thought there would be two or three cities," Miss Kopple says. "He and Eddy Davis, the banjo player and band leader with the group Woody played with for years, at Michael's Pub in New York, had talked about a tour. Other cities got wind of the fact that a modest little tour was in the works and began to clamor for consideration. It went totally out of proportion. Kind of like throwing a party. You know, you think it would be nice to have a few people over. Then before you know it, the guest list is up to fifty and you need to rent a hall and hire a caterer."

The Kopple crew proved such unobtrusive baggage that a bonus excursion was added back home in New York City: a visit to Martin and Nettie Konigsberg, the elderly parents of Woody Allen, who was born Alan Stewart Konigsberg in Brooklyn on December 1, 1935.

"I believe his father is now ninety-eight and his mother ninety-five," Miss Kopple says, during a conversation at the Henley Park Hotel. "I always had a wireless microphone on Woody while we were shooting, so I knew everything he was doing."

The idea of filming the tour may have originated with Jean Doumanian, a friend and business associate of Woody Allen's for many years. A fleeting, unidentified presence in the movie, she manages the production company, Sweetland, that negotiates his movie projects and other professional obligations. Letty Aronson, eight years her brother's junior, is also a partner in Sweetland.

Barbara Kopple is probably best known for Academy Award–winning documentary features that reflected labor troubles and disillusions in the heartland: *Harlan County, U.S.A.* in 1977 and *American Dream* in 1991.

In recent years she has branched out thematically and done notable TV profiles of Mike Tyson and Len Dykstra, among other subjects. Her *Fallen Champ: The Untold Story of Mike Tyson*, in 1993, was the first documentary project shown as an NBC *Movie of the Week*.

Miss Kopple was approached indirectly about the Woody Allen venture. "A friend named Jim Stern, a theater director in Chicago, just called up one day," she says. "Out of the blue he asks, 'How would you like to go on tour with Woody Allen?'"

Her immediate response: "Yeah, right."

The intermediary insisted it was a legitimate proposition and evidently relayed Miss Kopple's interest to Letty Aronson, who called and made arrangements for a meeting with her brother.

"I went over to his apartment, and we sat and talked," Miss Kopple recalls. "Talked about everything except the tour. We talked a lot about a mutual friend, a magician named David Blaine. Talked about movies.

Probably the weather. Time was passing. Finally, I thought I should say something about the tour. I asked if he was looking forward to it."

He wasn't. Mr. Allen confessed that he would rather not go. "Too many cities," she explains, "including several he'd never been to before. He wasn't thrilled about that."

This trepidation proved music to her ears. "At that point I became really excited," Miss Kopple says. "My antenna went way up."

At the prospect of sharing eighteen days of enforced intimacy with a grumpy, apprehensive Woody Allen?

Not exactly. "I just realized," she says, "that this thing could go in interesting directions. It's a first. And maybe a last.

"Woody Allen never tours. He probably never will again. But he's doing it this time, basically out of his love for jazz and because he believes that New Orleans–style jazz deserves a special showcase. It's not the most popular of the jazz traditions, but he and his group have been playing it together for years. Clearly, it's a unique opportunity for a filmmaker: Let's see what Woody Allen is like during this brief period of time."

The Kopple crew traveled in charter planes with Mr. Allen, Miss Aronson, and Miss Previn. The other band members went in separate flights. Miss Kopple shot get-acquainted interludes with this sextet in addition to the concert highlights, but only a sustained passage with Eddy Davis survives the final cut.

About fifty hours of film was exposed, and the first rough cut came in at eleven and a half hours. The filmmaker confirms that a lot of amusing stuff ended up on the cutting room floor. She does not envision an expanded or "restored" version, even if the Allen public is receptive enough to beg and plead.

"I knew this was [going to be] an incredibly funny piece when we started filming," Miss Kopple says. "I would often double over in laughter while we were in planes or hotel rooms or reception rooms or whatever. I hoped my voice would be muffled enough to stay off the soundtrack.

"Woody went about the business of living his life and making these concert dates. He acted naturally, and we concentrated on capturing as many of the moments of his waking hours as we could. It was physically grueling to do that for sixteen hours a day. We didn't get much sleep or nourishment, but that's the way nonfiction shooting works. Once we got into the editing room, it was bliss. The footage was so wonderful that people would often wander in when they needed a pick-me-up."

Miss Kopple insists there were "no rules" about her access to Mr. Allen.

However, an understanding prevailed about her own lack of interest in pursuing lines of inquiry that would lead directly to the subject of the scandal that surrounded the subject, Mia Farrow and Soon-Yi Previn a few years ago.

"That wasn't what I was after," Miss Kopple remarks. "I don't operate like a *Hard Copy* sort of journalist. I'm content to observe and record and let the life right in front of us unfold. If the touchy subjects came up, they would be pursued. But the instigation wouldn't come from us. Woody or Soon-Yi or Letty or someone who crossed their path during the tour would have to bring up the unpleasant stuff. All I'm thinking about is how to remain unobtrusive and keep the subjects relaxed enough to behave as they would if camera and sound equipment weren't there."

Any secrets to keeping Woody Allen relaxed? "We gave him a lot of Valium," Miss Kopple says. Instantly, she explains, "I'm kidding. A total joke."

But seriously, she does believe that the crew was a reassuring aspect of the trip for Mr. Allen. "What we did was familiar to him and non-threatening," she says. "And the situations he was thrown into were the threats. He didn't care what we were doing. He did care about getting from point A to point B in one piece while fans and audiences were waiting for him. We were more like the friendly neighborhood bartender."

Born in New York City in 1946 and raised in suburban Scarsdale, New York, Barbara Kopple was an undergraduate at Northeastern University in Boston when "cinéma-vérité" became a fashionable catch phrase for several approaches to documentary filmmaking in the mid-1960s.

She began shooting footage to supplement class studies while majoring in psychology. She has branched out into fictional projects, directing two episodes of *Homicide: Life on the Streets*. She is nearing completion of a major documentary project called "Generations" and hopes to film back-to-back fictional projects, a belated movie version of the David Rabe play *In the Boom Boom Room* and a love story titled *Joe Glory*, set against an explosive political backdrop, the 1949 riots in Peekskill, New York, during a Paul Robeson concert.

"I'm a filmmaker," Miss Kopple remarks. "I make all kinds of films. . . . But coming from nonfiction films gives you a good grounding with actors who are interested in getting at authentic kinds of behavior. The thing that keeps any movie in balance, whether it's fictional or nonfiction, is having a story line.

"You try to take people on a journey and help them forget that any artifice could be a stumbling block. You live a short lifetime with the people you're filming and want to make it count. I think the audience feels the same way when they look through the window you've tried to open."

Scene One: Something about Barbara

Bill Kirtz / 1999

From "Huskies in Hollywood: Stars Behind the Screen," *Northeastern Magazine Online*, January 1999. Reprinted by permission.

Two Academy Awards. A shooting schedule crammed with TV series and feature films. And with *Wild Man Blues*, a rare nonfiction breakthrough into box office black ink.

Still, Barbara Kopple doesn't "see myself as really successful. I've got a long way to go."

The way started at Northeastern in 1967, when the product of Scarsdale, New York, affluence fell into filmmaking with a look at Medfield (Massachusetts) State Hospital lobotomy patients. Anxious to "do something entirely different from my previous experience," she'd first enrolled at West Virginia's University of Charleston. Drawn to Boston by the Vietnam protest movement, Kopple came here to study social organizations and social welfare.

In late 1968, she moved on to New York's New School. After she took only a couple of classes in cinéma vérité—the cinema of truth—the masters of that genre, Albert and David Maysles, hired her as a general assistant. She helped light and shoot their exploration of door-to-door Bible sellers' bleak lives (*Salesman*) and riveting account—including an on-camera killing—of the Rolling Stones' 1969 American tour, *Gimme Shelter*.

Kopple has credited the Maysles brothers with teaching her everything about filmmaking, from the ground up. But at some point, she says, every filmmaker must develop his or her own skills. Hers are an anthropological approach and what Woody Allen has termed the knack for being unobtrusive.

She doesn't scorn academic training, however. She has taught at New York University's well-regarded film school, and thinks such programs are useful because students "have people rooting for you and pushing you."

To make her breakthrough film, the gritty, violent *Harlan County, U.S.A.* (produced for a piddling $350,000), Kopple immersed herself in a Kentucky coal-mining community. It earned her a VW van trip to Los Angeles and a 1976 Oscar she accepted in a borrowed dress.

Her second Academy Award came for *American Dream* in 1990. She earned it by spending five years detailing a bitter strike at a Minnesota meatpacking plant. She shot during sixty-degree-below-zero wind-chill days, talked her way into previously closed union negotiations, formed friendships with scabs and strikers' wives. Financing came no easier than filmmaking. Rock icon Bruce Springsteen rescued the project with $25,000 just before her original backers pulled the plug. Money problems delayed commercial release for a year, and she's figured she's taken a six-figure bath on the whole thing.

Kopple's more recent work has been better financed but no less rough-edged, including a South African Videovision study of Nelson Mandela's Robben Island prison, a Lifetime cable TV indictment (*Defending Our Daughters*) of crimes against women throughout the world, and a nuanced NBC profile of boxer Mike Tyson.

And then came Woody.

Crumb director Terry Zwigoff was first hired to document Allen's 1996 European tour with his Dixieland band. Zwigoff left the project—some say because Allen was uncomfortable with his attempts to probe his psyche, some because Zwigoff wasn't promised final cut, the absolute right to decide what to include. Then Allen's longtime friend and producer Jean Doumanian asked Kopple to film the twenty-three-day jaunt.

Glad of the chance to finally work without budget constraints, Kopple accepted Doumanian as her producer, but insisted on total artistic control and complete access to Allen and future wife Soon-Yi Previn.

Wild Man Blues has been a rare documentary commercial success and earned generally favorable reviews. Still, a few dismiss it as a soft feature—as Allen's carefully orchestrated route to rehabilitation after his much-condemned wooing of the young adopted daughter of his former companion, Mia Farrow.

Whatever Allen's intent, the film shows him as twitchy and self-absorbed off-screen as on, alternately dominating and dominated by Previn, eternally dismissed by his nonagenarian parents. A press release it isn't. Kopple catches Allen telling bystanders Previn grew up eating out of Korean garbage cans and dismissing his infinitely more talented musical colleagues. And the final scene in his parents' Brooklyn apartment, where they tell him he should have been a pharmacist already, shows something about Woody that his own mock-autobiographical movies haven't.

Kopple, whose four-person crew shot fifty hours of film during their sixteen to eighteen hours of daily access to Allen and Previn, shrugs at the carpers. She says, "The hard thing is to beg critics to just lie back and look at the film for entertainment: 'Is it done well? Do you forget the camera is there?'"

In any event, she's had little time to brood, plunging into three episodes of the NBC drama *Homicide*. "The *Homicides* were really fun," she says. "The cast and crew were great. It was very quick and very real. It's much easier than nonfiction. It has a script, and you can do as many takes as you want. Real life doesn't repeat itself."

For the fifty-two-year-old Kopple, real life has sometimes meant altering reality. For a long time, she claimed an NU psychology degree and shaved six years off her age. Still, as she's said, she's no journalist and never claimed objectivity.

Objectivity won't be necessary for her next two projects, both feature films. The first, *Joe Glory*, is a politics-based love story in which she plans to cast Natalie (*Beautiful Girls*) Portman. The second is the screen version of David Rabe's play about the rape of a go-go dancer, *In the Boom Boom Room*, with Patricia Arquette.

Then, Kopple says she'll return to the financially challenged world of nonfiction filmmaking. At the top of her wish list is finishing "Woodstock Two," which will compare the 1994 festival with the famous original. She began what she calls this "passionate and important project" five years ago, but money problems have delayed completion.

Difficulty getting backers, who almost certainly won't recoup their investment, is a common headache for even the most celebrated documentarians. Take Errol Morris's *The Thin Blue Line*, the 1988 stunner that freed an innocent drifter from death row and drew more attention for not winning an Oscar than most documentary winners receive for getting one. It's grossed only $1.2 million, less than Marlon Brando's daily fee and about the cost of Kopple's *American Dream*.

Kopple seems resigned to it all. "Financial problems are always really difficult. No matter who you are and what you've done, it's never easy. But I don't measure success by money but by what you're able to give people. Documentaries are much more important than any fiction film. They'll continue to live on."

Living for the City: Barbara Kopple

Steve Chagollan / 2000

From *Variety*, suppl. *New York Entertainment Town*, October 30–November 5, 2000, 3. Copyright © 2000 Reed Business Information, a division of Reed Elsevier, Inc. Reprinted by permission.

BARBARA KOPPLE: Two-time Oscar-winning documentary filmmaker. Her *My Generation*, about two generations of Woodstock festivals, played at Sundance and Venice.

ORIGINS: Westchester. "But I've been living in New York now for eighteen years, maybe twenty years. Isn't that outrageous?"

HOME TURF: Soho

N.Y. AS STIMULUS: "I like being around a community of people who really want you to succeed. I just love the people that are here; they're extremely smart. You don't just have friends who are in the film community, you have friends that do a lot of other things. And that's what makes it exciting. Everything is so close by and you can do everything, from listening to fabulous music that you love or going to theater or seeing films. And bars and restaurants are open till three, four in the morning. You don't have to drive long distances to get to them. And you can just leave the city and go out into the beautiful countryside. So it's just all within your grasp."

DOWN TIME: "I have a family place in Yorktown Heights that I go to. And when I can, I try to go on a little vacation. But the family place is beautiful. It has rolling hills. In the winter, you can go tobogganing or ice skating. In the summer, you can garden, pick flowers, and lounge about."

AT PLAY: "I have a friend who's an incredible theater critic and so he brings me to all the sort of newest, hottest plays that he thinks I would enjoy. I sit there but I'm not allowed to do anything because all the critics are writing things down. I play a lot of tennis. Different friends who are singers will invite me to go and listen to them. There's everything here that you could possibly want to do in your wildest dreams."

GOOD EATS: "I love the River Cafe. And I like to try to go there on the Fourth of July because it's right under the (Brooklyn) Bridge and you can just see all the fireworks. It's on a barge and it's just fabulous. I like Barolo, which is a neighborhood Italian place and they have a beautiful garden. Also, it's all open. So even in the winter time or if it's pouring rain, you can just feel the rain sort of a few feet away from you and it's just very beautiful."

Free Love, Commercialism, and Violence: Oscar-Winning Documentarian Barbara Kopple Explores Three Generations of Woodstock

Jennifer M. Wood / 2001

From *MovieMaker Magazine*, no. 43 (Summer 2001): 32–33. Reprinted courtesy of *MovieMaker Magazine*.

She's lived amongst the coal miners in rural Harlan County, Kentucky; stood by the underpaid and overworked meatpackers who took a stand against corporate America in Austin, Minnesota; delved deeper into the JFK conspiracy than most others have dared go. . . . She's also gone several rounds with a side of Mike Tyson few know about and discovered the wild side of Woody Allen.

Documentarian (or "nonfiction filmmaker," the term she prefers) Barbara Kopple has spent the last quarter century probing the hearts, minds, and intentions of the American public, providing nonfiction moviegoers with a personal experience they're not likely to find elsewhere. Her ability to turn plebian America heroic and to make accessible some of the world's most famous personalities has made Kopple one of the most celebrated women in film—and she has two Oscars to prove it. *My Generation*, Kopple's latest film, about the three generations of Woodstock, examines just how much the famed music festival's audience has changed.

Like most of Kopple's other films, the road to completion on *My Generation* was not without its detours. Though it was the organizers of the festival itself who enlisted Kopple's help, it was the festival's financial backers who almost made *My Generation* a film that never was.

In January of 1994, Propaganda Films' Joni Sighvatsson and original Woodstock producer Michael Lang made Barbara Kopple an offer she wouldn't refuse: they asked her to film the making—and final result—of their latest brainchild, Woodstock '94. The film, like the concert, would be supported by the generous contribution of then music giant PolyGram. Just one month after extending the invitation, filming on the project began. Says Kopple, "I started filming the behind-the-scenes stuff—PolyGram discussing very important issues like 'How many condoms do you think will be sold' and why 'Ben & Jerry's is out and Häagen Daz is in.'"

Though PolyGram had quickly come on board as the main sponsor of the resurrected music festival, as the concert neared, they "started getting cold feet." Though their primary concerns were with the could-be detrimental repercussions associated with such a gigantic undertaking—including audience safety issues and the financial risk that PolyGram was taking if the concert did not run smoothly—the contract between PolyGram and Woodstock Ventures was ironclad; there was no turning back. The one aspect the company *could* annul was Kopple's project. "They had to go along with the concert but the one thing they could stop was the film—and so they just stopped," Kopple said.

Unaware of the indefatigable personality they were dealing with, PolyGram informed Kopple that, due to financial reasons, they could no longer foot the bill for her film. Had it been any other director, the motion picture record of Woodstock '94 probably would have been aborted right there, but according to Kopple "I wasn't going to let money stop me from doing it, so I just kept going."

Though "stuck with all this footage and not a penny to my name," Kopple persisted, "throwing whatever money I had into having the film edited." Just about the time she finished editing her Woodstock '94 footage into a comfortable mix between the '69 and '94 events, another wrench arose in the form of Woodstock '99. "I took a deep breath and went and did '99 with a *really* small crew—one 16mm camera and two DV cameras. I then had to reopen the film again and begin the editing process all over. But I was glad that happened because, in a way, it just came around full circle."

Though the majority of *My Generation* focuses on the '94 concert—perhaps as a symbol of its milestone meaning, bridging the generation gap between the crowds that flocked before and after—Kopple refuses to take the easy way out and give the audience the viewpoint of just one group. She doesn't simply focus on the audience, the organizers, the locals whose towns were invaded by Woodstock, or the corporations behind the latter two events. Rather, Kopple honestly depicts how each of these groups interacts with the other. While Michael Lang is anxious to "see what people will make of [Woodstock], and whether they'll carry that traditional spirit," the people of Saugerties, New York, worry about what will happen if some of the attendees decide to break into their homes and kill them. The financial backers and vendors, predictably, are only concerned with financial gain and product sell-through (going back to the lurking condom question, the eighty thousand people who *did* decide to "Rock 'n' Roll Them On" was a pleasant surprise to those who only anticipated ten to fifty thousand). And though the social and political climate surrounding each concert is certainly as different as the music, the one group that does seem united is the audience.

For Kopple, the biggest difference between the audiences was the level of honesty: "Some of the guys were very honest in '99 and said that they came to 'get laid, listen to music, and get stoned,' or whatever. It was probably the same in '69; it was probably the same in '94," says Kopple of the festival attendees. And while each of the concerts is remembered in a distinctive way—'69 as a representation of the free-love generation; '94 for the commercialism and excessive merchandising; '99 for the violent acts that were broadcast on television sets across the world—each generation is essentially the same.

When questioned as to the seeming cynicism that exists in the minds of the audience members of the latter two concerts—particularly the '99 event—Kopple is quick to construe this seeming animosity in a completely different way. "My feeling is that all of us—no matter who we are—want to get together and be part of a community and have a sense of ritual and be with people that we like and then listen to music that we love, no matter what that music is. In 1969, people had something to hang their hat on because it was the women's movement and the war in Vietnam. In '94 and '99, there were all sorts of other problems: everything from AIDS, so you can't even be intimate with people, to environmental issues to sort of 'the corporate takeover' as they say in the film, of the music industry." Kopple goes on to point out that, contrary to popular perception, even the 1969 event was not *completely* peaceful. "In '69, they burned down hamburger stands; in '99 they burned from within. Even though this wasn't part of the film, women were reported to have been raped in 1969 and also in 1999. So I think we're all the same—no matter what generation we come from.... I think it's all of as just trying to find ourselves in our own skin, no matter who we are and no matter how old we are."

Documentary Filmmaker Barbara Kopple Discusses Summer in the Hamptons, as Shown in Her New Miniseries for ABC

Charles Gibson / 2002

From *Good Morning America*, May 28, 2002. © 2002 American Broadcasting Companies, Inc. Reprinted by permission.

Charles Gibson, co-host: The Hamptons, the American Riviera on Long Island's east coast, the playground of the rich and the richer. But what makes it interesting to us is that it's the topic of a new ABC reality miniseries, they're calling it, from a surprising source, Barbara Kopple, the documentarian who has won Oscars for her movies about coal miners and meatpackers. But she went out to this area of a few tiny towns that have become the summer home for socialite celebrities from Jerry Seinfeld to Sean Combs, and she shot three hundred hours of documentary footage about the rich, the richer, and the folks who work for them out there, and it really is a fascinating result that she's come up with.

And nice to have you with us.
Barbara Kopple: Thank you. It's a pleasure to be here.

Gibson: Now people not from New York may not know what the Hamptons are. But these are tiny little towns out in the eastern part of Long Island. Everybody heads out there. Just to give some people an idea of what it's like, what are some of the rents out there?
Kopple: Oh, people can pay rents anywhere from a couple hundred thousand dollars for the summer to . . .

Gibson: A couple of hundred thousand dollars for the summer.

Kopple: Sure.

Gibson: Does that get you beach front?
Kopple: That gets you beach front.

Gibson: OK.
Kopple: Or fifty thousand dollars for a month.

Gibson: Fifty thousand dollars for a month.
Kopple: Right.

Gibson: Now there's one group of thirty kids who come out—I say kids, young people. Actually sort of yuppie, young . . .
Kopple: They call themselves singles and professionals.

Gibson: Right. Thirty kids who take a house. What did they pay for that summer, do you know?
Kopple: Somebody owned the house and it's a big thing in the Hamptons. It's called share housing. And they pay three thousand dollars every other weekend to live in a room with four or five other people. But they love every second of it. For them, it's about finding a sense of community and finding people in a city that's sometimes very lonely.

Gibson: Well, yes. New York, even though for all its people, can—for all the people here, can be lonely, as these young people say. But you go out there and from watching what you've put together, you get some sense that it's some sort of meat market for these young people.
Kopple: I think that people's hormones are raging. It's the summer. There's hot dancing, there's clubs. But it's also about friendships. And many people who have done this all their lives have made their most incredible friendships while they've been there.

Gibson: Well, you're very nice to them, but as I watch your documentary, I get the sense that these are incredibly self-absorbed people who think that the social scene out there is incredibly important.
Kopple: Well, the social scene, to many, is very important out there. It's about being seen. And also for the locals, the fishermen and the farmers and others, it's very important too, because that's how they make their money during the course of the summer.

Gibson: You documented the summer of 2001.
Kopple: Yeah.

Gibson: And there was a young woman who you show in this documentary named—I'm not quite sure of her name, Lizzie Grubman is her name?
Kopple: Lizzie Grubman.

Gibson: She's a well-known publicist here in New York.
Kopple: Yes.

Gibson: And she represents a couple of the clubs out there. And during the summer, she was arrested for backing her Mercedes SUV over a bunch of people. I mean, there were twelve or fourteen people badly hurt by this outside of a nightclub. It was very controversial out there. And you document some of it. Let's take a look at what you shot.

Clip from *The Hamptons*:

> **Lizzie Grubman (Publicist):** From Memorial Day to Labor Day, I work 24/7. But July Fourth is really when I feel the summer kicks off. It's—everyone's like, the summer should be easy. The summer's the hardest part of my life.
> **Unidentified Man #1:** Are you not with this table?
> **Unidentified Man #2:** I'm with the table, but . . .
> **Man #1:** All right. Well, everybody's waiting anyway, man, so it doesn't matter. Everybody's a celebrity. Everybody's special. You know what? Everybody can wait.
> **Unidentified Man #3:** Thank you, man.
> **Marklen Kennedy** (Head of Security, Conscience Point Club): Thanks.
> **Man #3:** We'll see you later.
> **Kennedy:** OK.
>   I have no idea who he is. Somehow, you play this PR game where you act like you know people. I guarantee he'd never know who I was anywhere that we walked down the street.
>   I was inside, I had a walkie-talkie. I see the black Mercedes that's out there, which is Lizzie Grubman's. And you look up and you're seeing a car coming backwards. You can't get there fast enough, words can't come out of your mouth to try to tell the people to move. And I sit there and I watch as

these people are hit. There's people that are unconscious that are laying all over the place. There are broken limbs. You could see arm—arms staying to the side, there was legs that were like that and just a lot of blood. It was really quiet for the first ten seconds afterwards and then all of a sudden, people realized, and they just started screaming.

Steve Gaines (Writer): "Assault with an SUV." "It was no accident." I just think that, you know, she's blonde and she's kind of pretty and her father was powerful and rich, and this terrible tragedy happened.

Grubman: I feel very sorry about the people that were hurt in the accident. This was an accident. I did not intend to hurt anyone nor did I intend to leave the scene of the accident. There's a lot of details that I wish I could discuss with all of you, but unfortunately, my lawyer has advised me not to. Once again, I'm sorry and I am wishing and hoping that all the people that got hurt get better quickly.

Gibson: Now, this case sort of gal—I mean, everybody was paying attention to this in New York, which shows how important the Hamptons are, and yet this is somebody, basically, nobody's ever heard of. Is this a microcosm of what the Hamptons are about?

Kopple: Well, not really. I think Richard Johnson, who's one of the people that we interviewed, put it very well. He said if John Kennedy's plane had gone down or Princess Diana had been killed, none of this would have been out there. But this was a quiet summer. And also, the Hamptons is small-town America. Everybody knows what everybody else is doing. And the minute something happens, it's a gossip rumor mill.

Gibson: You mentioned the locals, the people that grow the vegetables and the fruit and who work the stores and whatever out there. What do they think of all this influx of these rich people that come out every summer?

Kopple: Well, I think that they actually love it and hate it. It's important to them because those are the people they sell the vegetables to or those are the people who buy their fish.

Gibson: Well, they make their money off them. But what do they think of them?

Kopple: Different people feel different ways. It depends who you talk to. Some people feel, oh, they're just ruining the environment. And other people are more curious. In the winter, it's sort of very dull out there, so a lot of people like the excitement and like to meet new people.

Gibson: Well, it's a very peculiar way of life that exists out there during the summer. Well documented by Barbara Kopple in this reality miniseries, as we're calling it. And you can see *The Hamptons* on ABC next Sunday and Monday at 9:00 p.m. Eastern time. And I guarantee, if you watch it, you'll get very absorbed in what she has been able to find with her cameras.

Thanks very much and good to have you with us, Barbara.

Kopple: Thank you.

Kopple on Audience Appreciation

Mary Sampson / 2002

From "Minding Their Own Business: Reflections on the Documentary Marketplace," *Independent Film and Video Monthly* 25 (October 2002): 54. Now the *Independent* online at www.independent-magazine.org. Reprinted by permission.

For Barbara Kopple, the increase in audience awareness and acceptance of the documentary form of storytelling is the noteworthy thing in the world of filmmaking today.

Certainly, some of this change in the audience's attitude is due to the rise of reality programming on television networks and cable outlets. But Kopple, who in 1977 won the first of her two Academy Awards for documentary film, saw the seeds of this audience growth planted in the theaters a long time ago. "Peter Davis's *Hearts and Minds* did very well at the box office," says Kopple. "And then, little by little, more and more nonfiction films started showing up in theaters." The result is that now there are nonfiction films in theaters that rival fiction stories in their beauty, their narrative storytelling ability, their humanness, and their clear point of view. "And what makes them even more wonderful than fiction is that nonfiction films are real," she says. (Just about the only creative tool Kopple does not see in use by documentarians today is manipulation of reality, which would, in her opinion, tip them over into the reality programming genre.)

Kopple sees both the increase in television documentaries and the theatrical release of films produced by networks as encouraging signs for independent theatrical documentaries and their makers. "It's always hard to make a film," she notes. "Places like HBO have allowed more and more filmmakers to get work done and get it shown." Nor is she troubled by the possibility of television documentaries taking the audience away from theatrical releases. She compares this situation to when video stores first came into existence and the unfounded fear that they would take business away from movie theaters. It's two different things. "A film won't be seen on cable for a long time if it first goes theatrical," Kopple points out. "And you aren't going to see the beautiful quality of a documentary film on a small screen. The theater is mesmerizing."

Taking a broad view of the history of marketing many different types of media, Kopple notes a potential downside to digital technology and documentaries. "I understand there are going to be films shown on the Internet," Kopple notes, "and that has the film industry in general a little nervous because people are afraid that what happened in the music industry is also going to happen in the film industry."

Another thing documentary filmmakers should concern themselves with, according to Kopple, is the marketing of their films. "*Hoop Dreams* was successful early on because Fine Line did a good job marketing it. And *Buena Vista Social Club* owes a lot of its success to the soundtrack." Kopple recommends a documentary filmmaker decide where she wants to go with her film right off. "If you go to television," she says, "you know it will appear on television. But you also may have to forego getting both a theatrical and a broadcast release." Networks like HBO, according to Kopple, are giving documentary filmmakers more opportunity to have both a network and a theatrical release by giving some documentaries up to a six-month theatrical before broadcasting the film.

She also believes in making documentaries for a general audience and letting the people find their way to a film through their interest in the subject matter. "Some people are going to be interested in the subject matter of *Wild Man Blues*," she thinks. "And some are going to go more for *Harlan County, U.S.A.*"

Kopple looks with pleasure on the vastly wider options available to someone just entering the field of documentaries now, as opposed to in the seventies. "There are a lot of different routes you could take now," she says. "You can do something for A&E or the History Channel to get your feet wet. Or you could go and do something you feel incredibly passionate about and try to do it as a theatrical film." She doesn't try to predict the future of documentaries, but she does voice some hopes for it. "I hope there will be more and more nonfiction theatrical films that succeed so that there will one day be nonfiction films in theaters all over the world."

Barbara Kopple

Alison Sloane Gaylin / 2004

From *Shoot Online*, October 15, 2004. Reprinted by permission.

Barbara Kopple, who directs commercials via bicoastal nonfiction spots, spent a lot of time laughing while helming a humor-driven Sprint campaign out of Publicis & Hal Riney, San Francisco. The ads feature school kids whose activities are timed—and billed—like cell phone minutes, and their performances delighted her. Kopple, a noted documentary filmmaker who won Oscars for *Harlan County, U.S.A.* (1976) and *American Dream* ('91), loved working on the Sprint project's first round of ads, "Red Ball," "Soccer," "New Kid," and "Macaroni Minutes."

"Mark Sweeney was the creative director, and I've never had more fun with anybody," says Kopple. "We had a blast. The two of us were at the monitor watching, and sometimes we would be doubled over in laughter. Everybody was so real and hilariously funny that we could hardly contain ourselves."

"Red Ball" shows a group of elementary school kids, each holding a ball. They're sitting outside with their teacher, who says, "What I need now is for you to tell me how many minutes you're going to use this ball every month for the next two years."

We then see reaction shots of the totally perplexed kids. The teacher continues, "And remember, if you guess too few and go over, there's an overage charge. And if you guess too many—well, that's just a waste, isn't it?" Now the kids are really baffled. Supered text asks, "How does your wireless company make you feel?" After a voiceover explains the advantages of using the Sprint PCS Fair & Flexible Plan, we hear a kid say, "If you don't have to guess, it's good."

Laura House, who plays the teacher in the spot (as well as the instructor in "New Kid"), is a stand-up comic and a former teacher, and her experience prepared her perfectly for the roles. "She was right on target all the time," says Kopple.

The children that appeared in the ads were real kids, not child actors. "What was cool about working with them is that they were so honest and they just went right along with things," says Kopple. "Some of what happened was not what they expected so they would look really confused and uncomfortable with certain things."

Kopple reveals one of the techniques she used to get the priceless responses she captured: "They didn't know they were performers," she says. "They thought this was real—a real soccer class, a real art class, a real cafeteria. What I would do is put a little earpiece in the actor/teacher's ear and say things for them to ask the students to get a reaction."

Kopple also directed the second round of the campaign, which aired during the telecast of the Summer Olympic Games from Athens. "Synch Swim," "Floor Exercise," and "Greco Roman Wrestling" feature Olympic gymnast Mary Lou Retton, and "New Swimmer" features Olympic swimmer Mark Spitz.

In addition to the Sprint work, Kopple recently completed a campaign for Target and the Tiger Woods Foundation's "Start Something" program, out of Target Direct. The director has a number of non-spot projects on her plate as well. For starters, she's finishing up an independent feature, *Havoc*, starring Anne Hathaway and Bijou Phillips. In addition, she's wrapping up *Bearing Witness*, a full-length documentary about women war journalists, for A&E.

Havoc marks her theatrical feature debut, but Kopple has directed episodes of such series as *Oz* and *Homicide: Life on the Street*. She has also executive produced and directed *I Married . . .* , a VH1 series that looks at the lives of people who are married to celebrities. The show has profiled the spouses of figures such as MC Hammer, Darius Rucker (front man for Hootie & the Blowfish), Carnie Wilson, and Omarosa Manigault-Stallworth, from the first season of *The Apprentice*.

Reel Life

Kopple notes that having a strong nonfiction background has helped in her commercial endeavors, particularly with real-people work. "Doing documentary work, you're always looking for things that are real and for characters that can really spring out on the screen and be able to tell a story," says Kopple. "That helps a lot with doing [work like the Sprint spots].

"What's fun about doing spots is that you have to do an entire story in thirty seconds," she continues. "In longer formats, you have some time to get to that place you need to get to. Here, if you're not able to do it in thirty or sixty seconds, it's not going to say it. You have to watch for all sorts of different elements as you're doing it."

Kopple joined nonfiction in '96, long before the reality TV phenomenon and the popularity of theatrically released documentaries. "Many years ago, [the executives at nonfiction] came to me and Peter Gilbert [who produced *Hoop Dreams* and also directs spots out of nonfiction] and said, 'We really think documentary filmmakers should be making spots,'" recalls Kopple. "It was when people weren't thinking much about documentaries, and real people spots weren't happening. They were the leaders of doing that, and at the beginning, it was tough. Now, nonfiction has a roster and it's getting much easier. We were their guineas pigs and I'm glad."

Tales from the Front: A Conversation with Documentarian Barbara Kopple

Katrina Onstad / 2005

From CBC.ca, April 27, 2005. Reprinted by permission of the Canadian Broadcasting Corporation (CBC).

When searching "Barbara Kopple" in various newspaper databases, the American documentary director-producer's name often comes up as a synonym for serious-minded filmmaking. Industry types make statements like (to paraphrase): "We're not trying to be Barbara Kopple here—*Real World: Stockholm* is entertainment!"

Kopple's reputation is not entirely unwarranted; she did start her career working with cinéma-vérité pioneers the Maysles Brothers (*Gimme Shelter*), and is perhaps best known for the Oscar-winning 1976 film *Harlan County, U.S.A.* which she shot while living among striking coal miners in Kentucky. Thirteen years later, *American Dream*, about labor disputes in a Minnesota meatpackers plant, earned her a second Oscar for best documentary film.

But on the phone from her production office in New York City, Kopple, though warm and almost girlish at fifty-eight years old, sounds a little annoyed when the "earnest" moniker is brought up.

"I think they just latch onto a name," she says with a sigh. "They do that with Ken Burns, too."

Kopple's irritation is not entirely unwarranted, either; over the course of her prolific career, she has made many entertaining films that don't involve striking workers ("I like to laugh," she swears). She followed Woody Allen on a jazz-and-neuroses tour of Europe in *Wild Man Blues*, and just completed a series about rock-star spouses for VH1. In fact, Kopple's strength is that she is all things: her seemingly frivolous work, like a TV miniseries on the rich and gaudy citizens of the Hamptons, is marked by a subtle, smart political perspective, and her more earnest films are as accessible as any good drama.

This week, the Toronto film festival Hot Docs will screen *Bearing Witness*, a collaborative effort that is being billed as a "Barbara Kopple" film, presumably because of all that the name implies.

In *Bearing Witness*, Kopple and her co-filmmakers Bob Eisenhardt and Marijana Wotton tell a multitude of harrowing stories from the perspective of five women journalists: how veteran *London Times* reporter Marie Colvin lost her eye to a grenade in Sri Lanka; how freelance photographer Molly Bingham was kidnapped and held in Abu Ghraib prison at the start of the Iraq war. These experiences are harrowing but perhaps universal in tone, if not detail, among reporters on foreign assignments. *Bearing Witness* is more fascinating when the subjects reveal a different form of sacrifice, one that perhaps only female reporters truly understand. Talking from a variety of locations including Iraq, Palestine, and London, these women reject the macho posturing that characterizes fictional depictions of their work (think of the one-upping, weathered journalists in *The Year of Living Dangerously*). They speak frankly, sometimes with distressing poignancy, about personal sacrifices made in the quest to become top professionals. We talked with Kopple about the same.

Q: *Bearing Witness*'s original title was "In Harm's Way," which makes these women sound much more vulnerable than they appear on screen. Can you talk about the name change?
A: It was a working title that A&E [the channel that funded the film] gave it. Our title was *Bearing Witness* because it's about being a survivor, an onlooker, someone who is really trying to expose the different costs of war, or the hidden costs of war. It's also about bearing witness to the causes behind atrocities, tortures, war crimes, or genocide. The women we covered included a still photographer, a CNN camerawoman, an American woman who was working for Al-Jazeera, and two incredible veterans who work for the *London Times*. They are sensational women and witnesses.

Q: Did you go to any of these war-torn locations yourself?
A: No, [director-producer] Marijana Wotton was in Iraq and I was on some shoots in America. It took a lot of people to make this film happen. Our editor, Bob Eisenhardt, had 350 hours of footage and he really had to shape it and put together the storylines. When you have five different

characters, you don't want to get lost. It took a lot of finessing. Some of the footage was stock and many of the women had their own photos or their own home movies. When [*London Times* reporter] Marie Colvin [visits mass graves in Iraq], that was something that had already happened quite a few years before. Molly [Bingham, photographer] had already been out of Abu Ghraib prison, but we were with her when she went back to shoot the women who [were imprisoned] there.

Q: I think audiences still have an idea, probably a naïve one, of auteur filmmaking. We expect a director to be in the middle of the action. Is there something misleading about *Bearing Witness* being billed as a Barbara Kopple film?
A: I think there are no rules of how to work. Films aren't made by one person, ever; they are made by a lot of different people working together making things happen. You'd be amazed. For Michael Moore's film *Fahrenheit 9/11*, he had people that he hired to film the soldiers in Iraq, and tons of other stuff. Somebody has to be at the center of it to make sure everything works, but you have to have tentacles everywhere.

Q: What do you make of the rise of guerilla doc filmmaking, from semi-celebrity directors like Moore and Nick Broomfield? Do subjects lose out when the directors themselves become part of the narrative?
A: I think there are so many different brands of documentary filmmaking and the wonder of doing it is that there is no one way to do it. It just depends what your story is, and the best way you feel you can tell it. I'm in favor of anything that tells a wonderful story.

Q: And yet you're nowhere to be seen in your work.
A: No. That's a personal choice. I like to pretend to be invisible. But that doesn't mean I wouldn't do it at some other point. You just have to be open. Fiction directors do films that are sometimes comedies, sometimes serious drama. It's the same with nonfiction filmmakers. We don't want to be put in a box. We want to be free to breathe and to try all different kinds of methods in our work.

Q: And you have a fiction film, *Havoc* [about wealthy L.A. teens colliding with Latino gangster culture], coming out this year. What's that jump like for a documentary maker?
A: Wonderful. It's like opening your wings and flying. It maybe wasn't that different [from documentaries] because we shot it in a very real and

gritty way. All my life, I've been struggling to find some sense of truthfulness and that's the same kind of thing that you strive for when getting an actor to portray a character. We're doing a Jack Kevorkian piece that's going to be fiction, too.

I think whatever way you can express yourself is something you should buy into. Anything that sharpens your craft. But documentaries are my favorite and if I never got to make another fiction film that would be fine as long as I could keep making documentaries. They're so alive, so in the moment, you never know what corner you're going to go around.

Q: In a way, *Bearing Witness* is quite bleak, despite the professional strength of these women. Janine DiGiovanni, a *London Times* correspondent, is the only one who seems personally fulfilled, but she takes such a surprisingly conventional route to fulfillment: we see her getting married in a white dress, having a baby, and basically leaving her profession. Is there no way to strike that elusive work-life balance?
A: Janine has done it. She has thirteen-month-old Luca and a wonderful husband. She has done it.

Q: But it looks like she bails on her career.
A: Don't count her out. She's written a book, a memoir of war, and since Luca has been born she's gone to refugee camps [in Israel]. She has to think twice about it now, but compare her with Mary Rogers [CNN camerawoman] in the film who says: "When I was twenty, I met this guy and really liked him and he was my best friend [and we could have been married], but I wanted to continue the work. And now I go home and there's no one there. There's just me." Those are decisions that we all make in our lives, about family and kids, in particular if you're a woman because you have that ticking clock.

Q: You won your first Oscar when you were twenty-one, and you've had a very high-profile, very successful professional life. Have you confronted these issues yourself?
A: I have a son. He's now twenty-three. It was very hard, but I took him a lot of places, nowhere dangerous, but he came on a lot of shoots. I remember I took him to Minnesota [during the filming of *American Dream*], and we had an apartment there. He played with other little kids who were around, but then we left, and it was hard. Do I regret it? I don't think so. I think that we love each other so much. I'm proud of him; he's going for a medical degree. But I don't think I could have gotten through

my life without having a child. I think having children, at least for me, or at least being lucky enough to have him, was something that was really important and gave me balance.

Q: Is it a good time in documentary film? There have been a rash of surprise box-office documentary successes over the past couple of years, but at the same time, the rise of reality TV almost seems like an abuse of documentary techniques, just loathsome, puerile voyeurism.
A: Oh, it's a much better time to make films. There's more funding. Not only are there now films that can say something deeply, they are also done in a way that makes larger audiences want to see them. If reality series have raised the temperature for understanding docs, that's great, that allows us to do the kind of work that we want. I mean, it's always hard, you're always struggling, you're always trying to figure out how you can make a particular film or how to finish a film you've started, but people want to see them these days. They want that sense of communication. For once we're being appreciated.

Q: Why do you think that is?
A: Because look at the world right now. We need to hear the world's stories. It's a time when we need to reflect.

Q: So now you sound like Barbara Kopple, serious filmmaker.
A: [Laughs] I never consider my reputation. I just think that I'm a filmmaker. I don't think that I'm a serious filmmaker. Social issues are important to me, but during the Woody Allen film, I couldn't stop laughing. I remember, I think he was in Turin, and there were zillions of people outside in the streets, and he parted the hotel curtain and he looked out and he got really scared and didn't want to go out. Soon-Yi [Previn, Allen's wife] said: "Why don't you go to the door and wave?" And he said: "What if they're not here for me?" And I would hear that and double over with laughter and just hope that my voice wasn't getting on the mic.

Women Who Witness War: Female Correspondents in Iraq Are Subject of Documentary

Michael Lisi / 2005

From *Times Union*, Albany, NY, October 20, 2005. Reprinted by permission.

May Ying Welsh was an American journalist reporting on the war in Iraq for Al-Jazeera, the Arab world's premier news organization. Her coworkers warned her to leave the country or risk being shot in the street.

Janine DiGiovanni, a reporter for the *Times* of London, was so dedicated—or addicted—to her job that she covered the war from the Gaza Strip while she was eight months pregnant. Another *Times* writer, Marie Colvin, lost an eye to grenade shrapnel while covering the fighting in Sri Lanka. Now she wears an eye patch. The twice-divorced chain smoker suffers from post-traumatic stress syndrome caused by the horrible combat she's witnessed.

The stories of these women, along with those of two other female war correspondents who covered the first year of the war, captivated Academy Award–winning documentary filmmaker Barbara Kopple. They would become the subjects of *Bearing Witness*, a film by Kopple, co-director/producer Marijana Wotton, and editor Bob Eisenhardt that tells the story of women journalists who daily risked their lives to tell the untold stories of the war in Iraq.

"It seemed like an important time for filmmakers to answer critical questions about the war: What the causes of war are, who are the victims, what are the hidden costs of war and what actually happens in a war on a day-to-day basis," explained Kopple in a phone interview from her New York City office. "This is a story about women covering a war, showing how they keep their lives in balance, and the things they sacrifice because of it."

"I think the people who see this story will have a lot to empathize with," said Eisenhardt, an Emmy-winning editor who pieced together *Witness* from more than three hundred hours of footage. "You see these women as individuals trying to do a very difficult job, and sacrificing a lot to do it."

The film, set to show at noon on Sunday at Chatham's Crandell Theatre as part of the 2005 FilmColumbia film festival, came together shortly after U.S. forces bombed Iraq in March 2003. It was actress Maryam d'Abo, a Bond girl in 1987's *The Living Daylights* and a friend of Kopple's, who called with the idea for *Bearing Witness*. Kopple loved the possibility of profiling female reporters who weren't embedded with U.S. troops—which gave them more freedom to cover stories but made their jobs very dangerous. The pair pitched the movie to the A&E network, where the film aired in May. It wasn't too tough to find the reporters to spotlight.

Kopple knew Welsh since she was a child and is a good friend of her family. D'Abo knew DiGiovanni and CNN's Cairo bureau videographer Mary Rogers. Wotton, who twice traveled to Iraq to shoot footage for the film, and Kopple met freelance photographer Molly Bingham in New York. Bingham made world headlines after Saddam Hussein's secret police jailed her in the infamous Abu Ghraib prison for a week at the start of the Iraq war.

"These are women who run toward danger," Eisenhardt said. "Marie (Colvin) said that the gunfire is scary, but that's usually where the story is."

And that's an exciting prospect for these women in *Witness*—especially DiGiovanni, a self-described war correspondence addict who eventually realized that being on the front lines of a war wasn't where she wanted to be as a newlywed with a newborn son. "*Bearing Witness* is, for me, the story of these women who try to bring these (war) truths to light and keep their stories really strong, while facing their own personal conflicts," Kopple said. Such as Welsh, who found it as fascinating as it was difficult to report on the war as a correspondent for Al-Jazeera. Welsh, who speaks fluent Iraqi Arabic and was in Iraq during the initial U.S. bombings, struggles in the film as she strives to gain the trust of the American soldiers she's trying to cover and her Al-Jazeera colleagues.

"She always felt like she wasn't comfortable in her own skin," said Kopple of Welsh. Especially as the war progressed and reporters—most definitely American reporters—became real targets of Iraqi insurgents. Welsh, who describes herself in the film as an "American in love with

Iraq" ends up being detested by the Iraqis. Her co-workers at Al-Jazeera urge her to leave or be killed by angry Iraqis.

"There was considerable danger for May, because people on the streets knew who she was," said Eisenhardt. "That's why her friends at Al-Jazeera told her that she couldn't stay." Kopple knows what it's like to be a reporter in the line of fire. She was shot at while filming a picket line for her Oscar-winning documentary *Harlan County, U.S.A.*; the 1976 documentary chronicles a bitter strike by Kentucky coal miners and their attempt to unionize.

"You always knew that reporters, for a long time, were totally game," she said. "When I was doing *Harlan County*, (company thugs) opened up with tracer bullets out of semiautomatic carbines. If they got us, there would be no one there to cover what was going on in eastern Kentucky."

Which is one reason why Kopple could relate to the women of *Witness*. But she was hard-pressed when asked which one was the most interesting to cover.

"I loved May for her truthfulness and her youth, and I loved Janine for wanting to have it all (a career and a family) and getting it," she said. "I loved Marie's courage and what Molly went through at Abu Ghraib and became the story, which wasn't good. And Mary does something that no one else does—she carries that big camera, she shoots, she edits and gets lost in the soul of the people."

Kopple's next documentary, due out in 2006, also deals with the war, but from a much different perspective; from that of popular country trio the Dixie Chicks. Kopple followed the Chicks around after head Chick Natalie Maines criticized President Bush over the Iraq War shortly after it started in March 2003. The comment led to a backlash; country radio stations across the country cut the trio from their playlists.

"Life really changed for them," Kopple said. "But the controversy brought the Chicks much closer together, and now people may really listen to what they have to say."

She's hopeful that *Bearing Witness* will have the same effect on its audiences. "I think that people will walk away after the movie feeling that it isn't enough to find the answer to the question of 'why war,'" she said. "If we continue to make our films and they are seen by large enough audiences, maybe we'll really be able to effect some change."

Indiewire Interview: Barbara Kopple, Co-Director of *Shut Up & Sing*

Brian Brooks / 2006

Originally published on *Indiewire*, October 24, 2006. Reprinted by permission.

Barbara Kopple is anything but a stranger to the world of documentary film, having accomplished notoriety in the genre, directing *Harlan County, U.S.A.*, which won the Academy Award for best documentary feature in 1977. Kopple again took the Oscar for best doc (shared with Arthur Cohn) in 1991 for *American Dream*. Both films delve into the plight of workers, in the case of *American Dream* at a meatpacking plant in Minnesota, while *Harlan* focuses on a bitter miners strike in Kentucky. Kopple has also turned the lens on celebrity, including *A Conversation with Gregory Peck* in 1999 as well as television doc *Fallen Champ: The Untold Story of Mike Tyson* in addition to many other titles throughout her career. In *Shut Up & Sing*, Kopple and co-director (and longtime collaborator) Cecilia Peck, turn the spotlight on the massively successful band the Dixie Chicks. At a London concert in 2003, lead singer Natalie Maines made what she believed was a fairly off-handed comment to the audience on the eve of the U.S. invasion of Iraq, "Just so you know, we're ashamed the President of the United States is from Texas"—their home state. The comment won cheers from the audience that night, but the fallout at home could not have been imagined.

Kopple and Peck explore the aftermath of CD burnings, censorship, insults, and death threats in addition to how the mayhem impacted the band's personal lives. The film also takes a look at how the trio catapulted themselves to their successful new album *Taking the Long Way* and having children. In this interview, Kopple talks about their approach in making the film and how they didn't want it to just be about "the incident," in addition to her early career working with Peter Davis and the

Maysles before striking Oscar gold. The Weinstein Company opens *Shut Up & Sing* in limited release beginning Friday, October 27.

Barbara Kopple recently participated in *indieWIRE*'s email interview series and her answers to our standard set of questions are published below.

Q: What initially attracted you to filmmaking, and how has that interest evolved during your career?

A: I've always been interested in how people think, how they react to challenges in their lives—what makes people tick. I've also always been passionate about social issues and causes, and I wanted to make films that addressed important issues in very human terms. I think that over the years my vision has evolved and has come to include things that I probably never would have guessed I'd be filming—like Woody Allen's Jazz Band, or Mike Tyson.

I think I still have that same drive and determination, the same curiosity and passion for filmmaking that I did when I first started. Every film brings with it unique challenges and experiences, and I approach every one with the same enthusiasm.

Q: Are there other aspects of filmmaking either on the creative side or industry side etc. that you would still like to explore?

A: Most of my films have been documentaries, but I'm also very interested in narrative filmmaking. I directed a few episodes of *Homicide* and *Oz*, and recently directed the feature film *Havoc*, as well as commercial spots. I hope to have more opportunities to direct features and I've got a few ideas in the works now. They include a film about the life of Dr. Jack Kevorkian, and another that tells a story about race and politics in America through the life story of Dennis Watlington, an amazing artist and writer. I'm excited to get started on these projects and others. Of course my main love is documentary films.

In another sense, though, every project brings with it surprises and unexpected turns. We never really know what's around the corner when we're filming—what turn a story will take, what a character will do or say to surprise us, how the events in the world will impact our story. That's what makes nonfiction filmmaking so interesting—just like life itself, every day brings something new.

Q: Please talk about how the initial idea for *Shut Up & Sing* came about, and how it evolved. . . .

A: Before the Chicks set out on their 2003 Top of the World Tour, this is pre-Bush comment, Cecilia Peck and I wanted to do a film of their tour with the idea of trying to follow them on the road. The Chicks already had a crew that was doing short web pieces for their homepage and didn't feel they could take us along. In late 2004 the Chicks came back to us saying they wanted to have a film created out of all the footage that was shot on that tour. I knew they were writing their new album and that it would be a response to their experiences from the backlash against them. I was of course extremely interested in their story but I didn't want it to be solely about the comment and its immediate aftermath, I wanted to see how this experience changed them as humans and musicians. So, we filmed them recording their new album and everything else that occurred so that the film will give a full picture from 2003 through 2006.

As the project evolved—in the field and in the edit room—I think we all came to see this experience of the Dixie Chicks as a lens through which to see the current political climate in America. We're living in a time when the freedoms we take for granted—the freedom of speech, the freedom to protest and dissent—are truly in danger. I think the story of the Dixie Chicks really encapsulates the risks we face—and at the same time shows that when you stand up for your rights, people will be there to support you, and follow your lead.

Q: Please elaborate a bit on your approach to making the film, including your influences (if any), as well as your overall goals for the project?
A: I like to approach my films with an open mind. I don't go into a film with any particular agenda—I rarely know how a film will end when I start filming. But [I] often do have a point of view on the subject—in other words, I know that I support free speech, and that I respect the Dixie Chicks for not backing down in the face of intimidation and threats. I felt that this film had a lot of potential to be fun and entertaining and also make some important points at the same time.

So I was excited to start shooting, and also to start sifting through the stock footage and the footage that had already been recorded. Some material dated back to before the famous "incident." We shot a lot of new footage—of the Chicks writing new songs, back in the recording studio putting together their very personal and artistic response to the last few years, and working with legendary producer Rick Rubin. We also filmed with their families in intimate moments that really get at the heart of who these incredible women are.

Like so many nonfiction films, the story really came together in the edit room. We had an amazing edit staff, and we were able to weave the two time periods (2003 and 2005) in a way that I think really highlights both the Dixie Chicks' personal experiences and the political significance of their story.

Q: What were some of the biggest challenges you faced in developing the project?
A: I think the biggest challenge was probably figuring out what not to include—there were so many interesting experiences and great moments captured on film that it was difficult to cut some out.

There was also so much great concert footage and music to include, and we did our best to satisfy people new to the Dixie Chicks and longtime fans as well.

Q: Who/what are some of the creative influences that have had the biggest impact on you?
A: One of the first films I had an opportunity to work on was *Hearts and Minds*, Peter Davis' chronicle of the Vietnam War. I recorded sound on a shoot with the parents of a soldier who had recently been killed in the war. These brave parents brought us into their home, and throughout the shoot I could feel the great sadness and loss they were experiencing. I also felt the excitement that comes with knowing you are telling an important story. The film was one of the first documentaries to get a wide theatrical distribution, and it influenced the entire national debate about the war. So that was a great experience to me and it really inspired me to keep working in documentary film.

I also had the great opportunity to work with Albert and David Maysles at Maysles Films. I'll never forget the creative, supportive, inspiring community that Al and David created. No matter what your position was—even if you were an intern or an assistant editor—your ideas were listened to. You felt important, like you were part of a team. It was a community that I'll never forget—one that I've tried to continue in my own filmmaking and encourage in others.

Q: What is your definition of "independent film," and has that changed at all since you first started working?
A: The rules are always changing, but what remains the same is that there are filmmakers who want to tell stories, and there are important stories to be told. I think we are seeing a real renaissance in nonfiction filmmaking, and it's a very exciting time. Films are getting more attention and

wider distribution, and there are more and more filmmakers bringing their unique viewpoints and experiences to the big screen . . . and the small screen . . . and the Internet and iPods and video blogs and on and on. The future is wide open.

Q: What are some of your all-time favorite films, and why? What are some of your recent favorite films?
A: My favorite film—and the film that really inspired me to be a filmmaker—is *The Battle of Algiers*. I'll never forget when the lights went down in that theater, and on came this exciting, exhilarating, in-your-face film, and everyone in the theater went through this unforgettable experience together. That's what a great film is all about.

Q: What are your interests outside of film?
A: I love to travel and to spend time with my family. I love to play tennis whenever I get the chance. And I'm also involved in social issues and volunteering, so I get involved whenever I can.

Q: What general advice would you impart to emerging filmmakers?
A: The best advice I can give to new filmmakers is this: Find a subject you are passionate about and just do it. Get out there and make your film. All over the country, there are classes, organizations, nonprofits, and rental houses who want to help new filmmakers. There are new digital cameras and editing systems like Final Cut. So get out there, find your story and start shooting—you never know where it will take you.

Q: Will you please share with us an achievement from your career so far that you are most proud of?
A: If I had to choose, I'd say I'm most proud of winning Academy Awards for two films that I had to work so hard to raise the money for, when it seemed like no one really believed in them.

But I knew that these stories had to be told, so I kept shooting. I was so inspired by the stories of people like the miners' wives in *Harlan County* who fought the coal company's gun thugs, got hauled off to jail, stood up to the local sheriff—all because they were sick and tired of seeing their husbands go down into the mines and never return, or come up only to develop Black Lung Disease. And the stories of the striking miners in the film *American Dream*, who did what they thought was right regardless of what their bosses or even their union said.

The stories of these incredible people—the way they put it all on the line for what they believed in—had a profound effect on me and continue to inspire me today. And in the end, the films found audiences and won Academy Awards. Those are the films and experiences that mean the most to me, and that had the greatest impact on me as a person.

Spirit in the Dark: Barbara Kopple on Filming the Group That Wouldn't *Shut Up & Sing*

Damon Smith / 2007

First appeared in *Bright Lights Film Journal*, issue 55, February 2007. Reprinted by permission.

New York native Barbara Kopple has been a vital and socially progressive voice in documentary filmmaking for the past three decades, bringing a compassionate and unblinking Mayslesian scrutiny to the lives of miners, meatpackers, professional musicians, journalists, and even disgraced boxing champ Mike Tyson. In her career-making hard-hat couplet *Harlan County, U.S.A.* (1976) and *American Dream* (1990), Kopple illuminated two of the more shameful episodes in recent U.S. labor history, demonstrating an abiding sympathy for the struggles of ordinary people and a gimlet eye for the ironies and ignominies of economic oppression.

One of the founding members of the collaborative group that produced the nightmarish anti-war testimonial *Winter Soldier* (1972), a soldier's-eye view of atrocities in Vietnam (and a doc with disturbing parallels to Bush Inc.'s recent misadventures in Iraq and at Guantánamo Bay), Kopple began making films while attending college. Starting in 1973, she spent a year living in a small Kentucky town filming the ugly, embittered, ultimately violent conflict between workers seeking a union contract from their overlords at Eastover Mining Company, and the gun-wielding scabs sent into their midst by greedy coal operators and their lapdogs in local law enforcement. Kopple, whose crew was targeted by one goon for hoisting a camera during an early-morning picket-line melee (a chilling incident plainly visible in the new Criterion DVD of the film), won an Academy Award for Best Documentary in 1976 when *Harlan County, U.S.A.* was released. Today, *Harlan* remains one of the most uncompromising depictions of class strife in American cinema, a gritty, fiery, visually dynamic testament to human dignity and the heroic spirit of resistance.

With her next film, *American Dream*, Kopple followed another labor standoff, this time between striking meatpackers at a Hormel plant in Minnesota and corporate negotiators who wanted to reduce their hourly wages and benefits drastically, despite a Reaganomically splendid year of profits. In contrast with the militant energy of *Harlan*, these workers' journey is arduous and dispiriting, especially considering the devastating toll exacted on blue-collar families who make big sacrifices out of a sense of what's right and fair, only to find themselves alienated, in financial limbo, and possibly worse off than before the contract dispute. Despite their own complicity in a factory system where bottom-line economics had become de rigueur by the mid-1980s (thanks to the advent of the almighty blockbuster), Academy voters responded favorably to Kopple's heartrending, quietly compelling *Dream* and honored her with another Oscar.

Since then, Kopple has been active as a director and producer, working with leftie media critic Danny Schechter on two projects, 1992's *Beyond JFK: The Question of Conspiracy* and the more recent political doc *WMD: Weapons of Mass Deception* (2004), which detailed how the mass media sold the war in Iraq to the public. Kopple directed a postmortem on the rebellious era of sixties music, *My Generation*, focusing on Pepsi-sponsored Woodstock '94. But her biggest commercial success came with *Wild Man Blues*, an intimate portrait of filmmaker/clarinetist Woody Allen as he leads his New Orleans-style hot-jazz band on their 1996 tour of Europe. In 2005, on the heels of *Bearing Witness*, a collaborative doc for A&E about female journalists reporting from war zones, Kopple released *Havoc*, her first fiction feature. Starring Bijou Phillips and Anne Hathaway, and penned by Stephen Gaghan (*Traffic*, *Syriana*), the film details the troubling escapades of two well-heeled, hip-hop-lovin' white girls from affluent Pacific Palisades who get out of their depth when they tangle with a group of Latino gangbangers from East L.A.

Her latest project, co-directed with Cecilia Peck, is *Shut Up & Sing*, a backstage portrait of the Dixie Chicks, the gutsy, wildly talented country-music sirens who told the Dark Prince of Pennsylvania Avenue and his neocon cohorts to take their war and shove it—sort of. In 2003, on the eve of the U.S. military's shock-and-awe campaign to oust Saddam Hussein, lead singer Natalie Maines mused to a London audience, almost worrying out loud, "We don't want this war, this violence." When the sold-out crowd at Shepherd's Bush Empire responded with cheers and applause, the Lone Star native added with a bit of southern gumption, "We're ashamed the President of the United States is from Texas," a puckish remark caught on tape by the Chicks' own video operators but never seen until the footage was given to Peck and Kopple. Within a week, Maines's comment—mentioned in a lone AP wire report—sloshed through the mephitic tributaries of right-wing-activist web portals like Free Republic, and eventually crested into a tsunami of indignation and outrage back home, a nasty turn of events that derailed the best-selling female artists just as they prepared to embark on the North American leg of their ironically named Top of the World tour. For better or worse, the Dixie Chicks had become, perhaps not martyrs for the cause of free speech, but cautionary emblems of the ominous watch-what-you-say attitude that was palpable in much of the nation in the lead-up to our then-popular unilateral war.

Shut Up & Sing toggles between the immediate aftermath of Maines's off-the-cuff Bush slap—protests, CD burnings, a country-music-radio ban, talking-head bitchfests, death threats, tour-date cancellations, and the loss of roughly half of their die-hard fan base—and their road to renewal in 2006 recording *Taking the Long Way* with producer Rick Rubin. Glimpsed backstage, at home, and in strategic meetings with manager Simon Renshaw, Maines and her partners Emily Robison and Martie McGuire come across like the badass, fiddle-and-banjo-shredding glamazons they are onstage, making tough business decisions and working to manage their now-controversial image while also, in more private moments, hanging out with their families. What's astonishing to see, aside from the strength of their sisterhood, is their tenacity in the face of crisis: Instead of cowing to the Nashville establishment that turned on them or issuing callow, insincere apologies to dismayed fans, the Chicks stick to their guns, declaiming their right to air a political opinion, however "inappropriate" it may be deemed to be.

Kopple and Peck wisely opt not to use voiceover and let these bold women speak for themselves, observing them work out the kinks in their career and, three years after the controversy, push ahead in a new creative direction. It's hard not to admire the trio's spunk and courage throughout the ordeal, especially the mercurial Maines. She'll crack a blowjob joke, flip the bird at Bush's image on TV, and put her foot down when it comes to "making nice" with radio programmers, CMT cable network, and others (like vapid C&W crooner turned Chick-bashing superpatriot Toby Keith) she now considers their enemies. But it's also obvious that the hailstorm of abuse and financial hardship she's brought down on their heads weighs heavily on her conscience. So when we see her finally bust out the lyrics to a new song, "Not Ready to Make Nice," and she sings the line "How in the world/Can the words that I said/Send someone so over the edge/That they'd write me a letter/Saying that I better shut up and sing/Or my life will be over," the grain of her voice—incredulous, defiant, resolute—and the cathartic release in her mad-as-hell refrain is literally hair-raising.

I spoke with Kopple, sixty, in October, a few weeks after the triumphant world premiere of *Shut Up & Sing* at the 2006 Toronto Film Festival, as distributor the Weinstein Company was gearing up for its nationwide theatrical release. Cordial, good humored, and very down to earth, Kopple talked about how she and Peck filmed the Chicks, why she was inspired by her subjects, and how the new film fits in with her body of work.

Damon Smith: Tell me the story of your involvement in this project.
Barbara Kopple: Cecilia Peck and I wanted to do a film about the Dixie Chicks even before "the comment." They had these web guys who were out there and they had just hired them to shoot little pieces for their website. So they thought, Why would anyone want to make a film about us? Then the comment happened, so of course we wanted to do it even more. "Oh, we could have been there, we could have done it!" Anyway, they still weren't ready for us. A bit later they decided yes, maybe what they have to say means something and that they would think about the idea of someone doing a documentary. So they spoke to us, and they spoke to other filmmakers as well, including Michael Moore and D. A. Pennebaker, and they picked us.

Q: Then you signed on to do the film and traveled to . . . London?
A: Los Angeles. We met at Simon Renshaw's office. He was out of town, so we didn't get the wonderful experience of his presence. [Smiling]

Q: At that point, what did you initially hope would come out of it?
A: You never think about that, doing a documentary. Because once somebody says to you, "OK, you can film us," you come to it with absolutely no agenda. You try to allow these characters to take you on a journey with them. And that's always the way that I approach filmmaking. When I got to do the Mike Tyson film [*Fallen Champ*], I just let every single thing I thought about Mike Tyson out of my head and started to

allow the story to emerge, to follow it along. The same with Woody Allen [on *Wild Man Blues*]. It's so key if you're going to do something real and sincere.

Q: We're accustomed to seeing these three women superstars onstage in all their glittery glory. But behind the scenes, they turn out to be savvy strategists, and hard-driving businesswomen juggling everything from tour-sponsor jitters to a radio boycott, death threats, and tour-date cancellations. Did that surprise you?
A: Yeah, especially their business savvy and how they are women in control. That nobody tells them what to do totally *fascinated* me, and I loved every minute of it. Plus, I learned a lot about how the business works. But I think if I had to pick one element about them that moved me as a person, it's their friendship and their bond. I look now at my life and think it is so important to connect with people. And that when things go wrong, not to run from it, but to pull together as a unit.

Q: It's amazing how rock solid they are. Martie says they are "a sisterhood" . . .
A: Two of them *are* sisters. [Laughs]

Q: Right, but they are truly "undivided," like Dan Wilson, the songwriter they're working with, says at one point. Their show of solidarity in the Diane Sawyer interview, for instance, and not breaking rank under so much pressure was impressive.
A: They're undivided in everything they do. Sure, they argue and discuss, but when it comes down to it, they are there for each other. And each one cares so much about the other. One of the most moving parts of the film is when Martie breaks down and cries and says "I would give up my career for Natalie"—if she wanted and needed it—to find some peace. What more of a friendship can you have than that, to give up everything you love for somebody else? The most intimate relationships between people aren't like that.

Q: Shortly after 9/11, press secretary Ari Fleischer said people should watch what they say.
A: Which *he* should have done! [Laughs]

Q: Well, it's interesting because I think in one sense his warning reflects the chill that came over the national media in the lead-up to the war.

And also, it immediately raises the issue of free speech. Martie says that dissent "had to come from an unlikely voice," from a place that is usually aligned with conservative feeling.

A: Right. The "all-American." That's so true. And that's probably why country music got so mad at them, because they didn't toe the line in a sense. Country music probably thought of them as very conservative [people], and when they came out like this I guess they felt betrayed by them. And then you also had groups like Free Republic and others doing massive organizing drives to boycott their music in many of the red states, and going online and saying some of the most horrific things about the Dixie Chicks imaginable. I spent many days reading the Free Republic website and was absolutely amazed. Last night, by the way, I was in Washington, and someone from Free Republic came and we put them on the panel! I couldn't for the life of me get them to really talk about their ideas and talk about politics. It's also an anonymous kind of group. But what he said was, he liked the film. He didn't like the politics, but he liked the family stuff and his favorite scene was the Halloween [sequence]. So it was pretty interesting. And he's going to write a review—a "good" review—of the film.

Q: That must have been interesting for you, coming into contact with one of the Chicks' nemeses.
A: Oh, I loved it. I mean, we were supposed to be talking to the audience, and there were quite a few people on this panel. And every time I got the mic, I would ask *him* a question. [Laughs]

Q: Do you think the backlash would have been as vitriolic if it had happened to a male artist of the same stature?
A: Well, it's hard to say, but I think probably not. I think they thought that they could set an example with the Dixie Chicks, that they would crumble. But I think they had no idea who they were dealing with.

Q: One of the things that comes across—one of the most powerful elements of the film—is the personal and artistic transformation that this incident set into motion for the Dixie Chicks.
A: Yeah. And also seeing them mature over three years and become totally comfortable within their own skin, writing this wonderful album [*Taking the Long Way*, 2006] that deals with everything from politics to infertility to love, all of the universal themes that are so much about who we are.

Q: I'm curious about something, because you followed that transformation, you captured it as it was happening. Did you ever think, when you first got involved after "the comment," that you might be observing a meltdown or a capitulation on their part instead of a show of defiance?
A: The magic of documentary is that you don't know and you just go with life and go with what happens. I mean, you would never come back from a shoot presupposing what you think would happen. The fascination and the excitement of documentary is that you don't know, so why guess? Just put your sneakers on and go. Go on the journey.

Q: Do you think that your presence emboldened them somehow?
A: No, they are emboldened all on their own. In fact, we tried to not be much of a presence. We tried to let them forget we were even there, because what they were doing in their lives and the things they were figuring out and the music they were writing or the relationships they were having with their families is what was important.

Q: Was there any sense in which you think you affected them by filming what was happening to them personally and professionally?
A: I don't think so. I think all of this would have gone on whether we were there or not there. I don't think we mattered. [Laughs] As much as I hate to say that.

Q: You have an amazing body of work that you have received commendations for over the years: two Oscars, and more recently, a Lifetime Achievement Award from the Human Rights Watch Film Festival.
A: Yeah, that was something. Alan J. Pakula gave it to me.

Q: A big moment.
A: For sure. And then a week later he died while driving up to the Hamptons. [Sad face]

Q: How do you see this film fitting into your vision, your overarching goals and themes, from *Winter Soldier* and *Harlan County* to *Wild Man Blues* and *Bearing Witness*?
A: Well, I think that maybe the majority of the films that I do—not so much *Wild Man Blues*—but with many of the other films, it's all about people who are fighting for social justice and people who are standing up for what they believe in, and people who won't be silenced. And I think if there was a theme, that would be it. It's also people whose stories

you might not know—or who you might think of in a totally different way. I'm sure many of the people who'll see this Dixie Chicks film would never have thought they would be so complex, so bright, such great businesswomen and so alive. They know that they're talented, but not all the different complexities that make them who they are. You see them in a different light. I'm hoping the people who don't agree with the Dixie Chicks, or with what they said, will see this film so they can understand where they're coming from. Because it seems like in this country, and I don't want to harp on about this, that we have a real sort of cowboy mentality. "You're either with us or against us," and that kind of thing. Dialogue has been lost, and communicating with another has been lost. So we need people like this more than ever to stand out there and say something.

Q: There is that strain of defiance in your work. You seem to gravitate naturally toward people who are insurgent in some way, who're resistant.
A: Or in crisis. [Laughs]

Q: And recently you seem to have taken an interest in female combat journalists, with *Bearing Witness* and your current project.
A: Well, I never know what my next project is going to be. I don't want to say too much about the new one.

Q: How did the temporal structure of *Shut Up & Sing* aid in telling the story you wanted to tell?
A: Actually, we started to edit as we were shooting. We accumulated a lot of stock footage, we found stuff that was really amazing, such as when they were playing in the club. We didn't leave a stone unturned. So it was very helpful to be filming still and editing at the same time. Not that it changed how the film was going to be, but the film was very hard to structure, because doing it in a linear way you really didn't get to know them. So it was very important to us as filmmakers to be able to allow you to get to know them, feel who they were, feel their talent enough so that you would care what happened to them in 2003. And we take you to 2003 three different times, so it was hard also to make that structural leap to get you there. It was tricky.

Q: Did it take you a long time to integrate into the Dixie Chicks operation?
A: No, we just showed up.

Q: As a socially conscious documentarian, do you think that the left-leaning, agit-prop documentaries that are popular now—like those by Robert Greenwald and Michael Moore—are a good thing for the form?
A: I think that having lots of different styles and ways of expressing yourself is always incredible, because what you are trying to do is tell a story. And whether you tell a story with very sharp, hit-you-over-the-head images to get people's attention, or you tell a story by allowing people's lives to unfold and look at people on a human level, and from the human level go to politics, it's all wonderful, whatever people take in. As documentarians, we are so supportive of each other and we care about each other and we look at each other's rough cuts and comment because we want each other to succeed, because it's been such a struggle to get our films out there. And finally, the public is catching up with our passion.

Q: *Shut Up & Sing* will certainly be seen by a lot of people. What for you is the most important thing you hope people will take away from watching it?
A: That it's really good to stand up for what you believe in and to never let anyone silence you or manipulate you. And no matter how bad you feel and how hard the times are, if you're true to yourself, that's what's going to be important.

Crossing Lines: Barbara Kopple

Michael Joshua Rowin / 2008

From *Stop Smiling*, March 2009. Reprinted by permission of Stop Smiling Media, LLC.

Since 1977, when her report on a Kentucky coal miners' strike—the tough, searing *Harlan County, U.S.A.*—won an Academy Award for best documentary, Barbara Kopple has been at the forefront of documentary filmmaking. With unflinching intensity, Kopple has taken on a broad range of subjects, from the working-class drama of *American Dream* (1990) to the dark side of machismo in *Fallen Champ: The Untold Story of Mike Tyson* (1993) to the musical odysseys of *Wild Man Blues* (1997), which trails Woody Allen on his jazz tour through Europe, and *Shut Up & Sing* (2006), a look into the travails of the Dixie Chicks after the fallout from their anti-Bush remarks.

Having ventured into fiction filmmaking with her work on the award-winning television series *Homicide: Life on the Street* and her fiction feature debut, *Havoc*, Kopple is now working on both fronts, planning a documentary on the possible fortieth anniversary Woodstock concert and directing a drama based on the events of Kent State. I sat down with Kopple in her Manhattan office on a hot July day last year to talk about her successful, varied, and sometimes dangerous career.

Stop Smiling: What attracted you to documentary filmmaking?
Barbara Kopple: When I got started there weren't a lot of women in filmmaking, and people cared less about documentaries. Men would go into feature films and a lot of women would go into documentaries. I couldn't have been happier doing that. Because how many times in your life do you get to really get into the soul of somebody, really see who they are and see what makes them tick?

I started working with the Maysles brothers. I was taking a course in cinéma vérité at the New School right out of college. There was a woman in my class who said, "Listen, I work with these people named the Maysles brothers. They're looking for an intern. Would you be interested?" And I said, "Are you kidding? Yes, absolutely."

So I went to the Maysles and did everything nobody else wanted to do. The Maysles were great because they treated us all like a family. We would all sit around and they would ask for our suggestions, so it empowered me and made me feel pretty incredible that somebody would actually listen to my opinion.

At night I would do the assistant editor's work. She would leave me stuff so I could start to learn. I was a voracious learner and wanted to do it all. So I learned assistant editing, I learned sound, I learned editing, and then I started my own company.

SS: What did you learn from the Maysles themselves?
BK: The Maysles brothers were very pure. They always believed that you should just go in there and allow the characters to be the main thing. And you shouldn't encumber them with lights, you should be almost invisible and just really allow people to be who they are and watch them.

SS: Was the use of vérité techniques in *Harlan County, U.S.A.*, for example, a political choice?
BK: No, more of what I was thinking about when I was there was staying alive. And also to just try to do the most honest piece of work possible. Something that's very important for me is to never bring my own agenda into anything, to let people be who and what they are and really watch how they change, never bringing in a political perspective. I mean, of course I really cared about the people—I wanted to film with them and I was a very political person at the time, but I think of myself more as a humanist than a political person, somebody who's instinctive and who cares about what people are going through, who has the patience and the perseverance to watch and be there.

SS: How did you adapt to the culture of Harlan County?
BK: Growing up in Scarsdale, New York, you're protected and taken care of. For me, I was able to go to Harlan County and totally adapt because I felt strong within myself that there was nothing I couldn't handle and couldn't do. It made it very easy, and I'm an easygoing person anyway and have a voracious curiosity about people and their lives. It was wonderful and incredible to meet all these different people seeing they could stand up for what they believed in, even if they knew they could die for it. They took care of us, they fed us, they protected us.

The first day I was in Harlan County I was asked what kind of gun I wanted—as you know, a girl from Scarsdale wouldn't have a gun for any reason. But I went along with it and picked some small little gun—later on I was carrying a .357 Magnum, of course never to use it but just to have it because people there lived and died by their guns.

The first day I was there two coal miners had a dispute. One coal miner was shot with a .38. Two days later he was driving around the coal fields with a sign on his car saying ".38s Ain't Shit." They also made me drink white lightning and chew tobacco. I did all those things to fit into the life.

SS: Did you feel close to the strong women of Harlan County?
BK: The women were amazing. Lois Scott, the heavyset woman who takes the gun out of her dress, was my role model, my hero of what women should be—women who weren't afraid to stand up, women who were courageous, women who really believed they could make a difference. At that vulnerable age when I was in Harlan County I looked up to her. Other women, too, each had their own identity. Susie Crusenberry, who looked very Native American, was a woman who had absolutely nothing. She had lost her home. She used to have to walk to school. She just stood up when people were saying "Oh, so-and-so is sleeping with so-and-so" and slammed her hand on the table and said, "I'm not after a man, I'm after a contract!" and then started weeping and telling the whole story of her life. Each one of these women had a great story—older women who had been around in the thirties, had seen how the gun thugs had killed their loved ones.

SS: *American Dream* came out almost fifteen years after *Harlan County*. It's about a similar struggle in Minnesota among meatpackers, and yet there are different conflicts in that film. One thing that struck me was that unlike in Harlan County, there are a good percentage of workers who are forced to break the picket line and go back to work to make money for their families. An incredible strain develops among these workers in coming to terms with that—we see grown men crying over this dilemma. What were the circumstances that caused something like that to happen?
BK: *American Dream* was a really tough film for me to make. The people were the same [as the ones in Harlan County]: your grandfather worked in the meatpacking plant, and your father worked in the meatpacking plant, and therefore you would. Hormel was almost like a parent figure,

so when they cut wages because it was the recession of the eighties, it was an act of betrayal to these people. They had given their hearts and souls. The main office of Hormel was right in Austin, the CEO lived right in Austin, and they felt as if everything they had been given hope for all these years was being totally dashed.

But then there was the problem with the international union. Lewie Anderson, who was head of the meatpacking division, had to contend with all the plants everywhere. Most of them were nonunion and he was trying to unionize them while they were having their wages dropped even lower than at Hormel. Anderson felt some people can't be way up here with high wages while others are down here, because it doesn't work with unionism. So he was against the Hormel workers going on strike to get their wages back up to what they were. That, of course, pitted the local union against the international union. Then on top of that you had the corporate entities that didn't want the strike to happen and that weren't going to be the only ones paying high wages.

It was also a period when people didn't care as much about unionism as they did during *Harlan County*. Coal miners have such a rich tradition of unionism, and even though they're geographically isolated they come out for each others' marches, they're always there for each other. I don't know if meatpackers have that kind of tradition. And there were so many new plants opening: IVP, which would bring over Asian workers and pay them the minimum wage, and many of the workers would take a piece of fat off the shoe of a foreman. They were competing with immigration and other people who would do anything to work at any price whatsoever. That doesn't happen so much with coal mines.

The people who crossed the picket line—for me that was one of the most incredible moments that I was able to film because I just felt at that particular time it was so important to be able to show what they were going through and how difficult it was for them to keep their heads above water. Minnesota men have a lot of pride, they're a little cut off from their emotions, and to watch these grown men cry because they couldn't feed their family or their family was all working and they were sitting at home—it just took everything about who they were and what their values were and just split them apart. It was a very profound moment for me as a filmmaker to be able to film that.

SS: What was your specific contribution to the Winter Film Collective and the film *Winter Soldier*, which documented the Winter Soldier hearings on American military atrocities in Vietnam?

BK: Sound. And also some editing. We were given this place in New Jersey, where we all lived together. Everybody contributed in the editing and two Vietnam veterans would come and watch. You'd shake them in the morning to wake them up and they'd be startled, still thinking they had their weapons in their hands. So it was pretty heavy, watching them watch material of people giving testimony and seeing if it was true and real, how we were putting it together.

SS: How were you prepared for your first shoot in such an intense environment where soldiers are sharing their experiences on the battlefield?
BK: Vietnam was part of my youth. I marched against the war, and it felt extraordinary to be doing something proactive and being there while all these guys and some of the nurses talked about what they were doing in Vietnam. What could be more remarkable than that? And then, at night, Jane Fonda and Donald Sutherland were there and were running the film, in a way. They were helping to raise money along with [producer] Barbara Jarvis's mother Lucy, who was a film executive. And at night they would question us about what we experienced and what we filmed and how that was changing us in a political way. It was one of the most extraordinary experiences—being able to verbalize and articulate what I was going through in hearing all of this, and doing something I knew would be out there forever so nobody would ever forget what these guys had gone through in a war we felt was wrong.

SS: Were you surprised that there was such controversy over these soldiers' accounts even four years ago when Kerry ran for president?
BK: No, I wasn't surprised, because when *Winter Soldier* was finished nobody would show it in this country. It only showed at the Cannes Film Festival, where it got an award for critics' choice, and on one local PBS station because some of their material had been canceled and they had to fill that slot with something. For some reason that film has always been controversial. For John Kerry, the political forces in this country were going to try to do anything to discredit him because they didn't want him to win.

SS: You've made very explicitly political documentaries but also many documentaries about celebrities and entertainers. At what point did you become interested in such different subject matter?
BK: Sometimes people call and ask if you want to do a film on Mike Tyson and Woody Allen, and how can you resist? It's really hard to continually

come up with the idea and struggle to raise money and do your own films, so it's wonderful when people call up and say, "We have a budget for this and would you be interested in it?" It takes you on an entirely different journey that you may not have thought to go on. Doing the film on Woody Allen was extraordinary. I mean, I loved it. A lot of my friends would say, "Why are you doing a film on Woody Allen?" And I'd say, "Are you kidding? I can't resist doing a film on Woody Allen!" And he let me film whatever I wanted.

It was also around the time of Soon-Yi, so there was a lot of controversy. They just seem to work together so well—they're still together, they've adopted children. I really got to see who Woody is, how Soon-Yi had to have him be polite to people and recognize people. He'll only talk to one person at a time. Even if the whole crew was standing around, he'd only talk to me; or if the band was standing around, he'd only talk to Eddy Davis. Just to see that the things about him that we think and feel are so real, that he's brilliant, except he's really introverted, into his own head a lot. He's actually very shy and really doesn't like to be filmed that much, but he allowed us to do anything we wanted to do. At times we wanted to say, "Come on, Woody, tell us we can't film because we want to go have a great Italian dinner." But being good filmmakers, of course we didn't.

SS: When did you start filming Tyson?
BK: He was in jail for the rape of Desiree Washington when I was asked to make the film by a woman named Diane Sokolow from Columbia TriStar. It was soon after *American Dream* was finished. The early footage—I had heard there was a German filmmaker who had come to Cus D'Amato's and he was filming this young boy who wanted to be a boxer but got so enthralled in all the different characters who would go to Cus D'Amato's that he filmed all of them, including Mike Tyson. I didn't know where to find him, so I hired a private detective to find him for me. He did, and I purchased all his stuff on Mike Tyson, which he had in a barn at that point.

I wasn't into boxing, really, and when Mike Tyson was put in jail for the rape of Desiree Washington I just thought, "Yeah, he probably deserved it." When Columbia TriStar and Diane Sokolow called and asked if I wanted to do a film on Mike Tyson, I let all of that out of my mind and tried not to go in with any preconceived notions. It also allowed me into that sacred world of men and of boxing, of tough critics and reporters. As a woman you're not expected to know anything about it, so you can ask whatever questions you want and they try to help you understand. I think if you're a guy you have to shorthand it, because you have to show that you know something so they don't think you're a wuss.

SS: You were hired by PolyGram to document the making of Woodstock '94 in *My Generation*, but the film deals very much with the corporatization of the ideals of the sixties. How did PolyGram react to that?
BK: The concert was going way over budget, and the only thing they could stop was the film. So they said they weren't going to give me any more money to keep going. And so of course I kept going anyway. I don't know if they were upset about it. I know we had a screening and people seemed to like it. It was on Starz Encore. And also, we just finished editing the footage from 1994 and then [concert organizer] Michael [Lang] decides to do '99. We weren't going to get any money [for the '99 show]. We went with two crews and filmed the whole concert, working 24/7. The feel of that show was so much different. It was so angry and hostile, toward women in particular. But at the end of it, everyone in a sense loves it no matter what age, whether it's '69, '94, '99, people all feel as if it's something sacred to them, that it's something sacred they experienced.

SS: Watching *My Generation*, I noticed that the movie doesn't really capture the full extent of the disaster of '99. Was that because of the circumstances of the shoot?
BK: I don't know, because we didn't hear people talk about being raped, and the film is all in real time, so I wasn't going to interview people after the fact. It was being there in a vérité way, and we tried to cover everything we could, from that woman being exploited, having her picture taken while topless, and the fires burning from within. It was a strange situation. Even Sheryl Crow was being asked to show her tits.

SS: Do you try to bring a documentarian's eye to fiction filmmaking and television work?
BK: I didn't know that I'd ever be making fiction films. Fiction films never really inspired me. I brought a lot of my work from documentary into fiction rather than just seeing something as a fiction narrative film. The most important thing for me was working with actors and getting that sense of truthfulness. That's where it came from, really, from working in documentaries for so long and being able to read when somebody's doing something real or not.

Barbara Kopple's Shortlist

Barbara Kopple / 2008

From Arts Engine: *MediaRights* "News," September 11, 2008. Reprinted with permission. This article is available for noncommercial use under an attribution, no-derivatives Creative Commons license. It was originally published on MediaRights .org, a project of Arts Engine, Inc.

The Shortlist article series is your opportunity to learn about the films that inspire intellectual, artistic, and activist leaders—leaders like Barbara Kopple. We asked Barbara to share her favorite films and her thoughts on the power of documentary to change the world. So what films make Barbara Kopple's Shortlist? Keep reading to find out.

Who Is Barbara Kopple?

Barbara is a two-time Academy Award–winning filmmaker for the documentaries *Harlan County, U.S.A.* and *American Dream*. Her other films include *Shut Up & Sing, Havoc, A Conversation with Gregory Peck, My Generation, Wild Man Blues*, and *Fallen Champ: The Untold Story of Mike Tyson*. Recently Ms. Kopple completed a pilot for TruTV called *The DC Sniper's Wife*. Also this year, she produced and directed a documentary for the Disney Channel entitled *High School Musical: The Music in You*.

Barbara is the recipient of the DGA Award for Outstanding Direction, the Human Rights Watch Film Festival Lifetime Achievement Award, Los Angeles Film Critics Award, National Society of Film Critics Award, the SilverDocs/Charles Guggenheim Award, New York Women in Film & Television Muse Award, the Maya Deren Independent Film and Video Award, and the Sundance Film Festival's Grand Jury Prize, Filmmakers Trophy, and Audience Award.

She currently serves as an advisory board member for the American Film Institute and as a board member of the American University Center for Social Media. She is a member of the Academy of Television Arts and Sciences, the Academy of Motion Picture Arts and Sciences, and the

Directors Guild, and she actively participates in organizations that address social issues and support independent filmmaking.

Barbara Kopple on the Power of Film

Great documentaries survive as lasting stories of people, their environments, the forces that shape their lives. They help us understand what we couldn't before and allow us to experience people and places that might at first seem alien to us.

When presented in a compelling and genuine way, a great doc can inspire others to act; whether that means running for political office, making a film, or anything else constructive.

One of the great joys of nonfiction filmmaking is discovery, finding some unexpected moment of truth in the seemingly mundane events of a person's life. In my films, I try to find what's at the heart of a story by going beneath the surface. With an increasingly homogenized popular media, it's especially vital for documentary films to present people with real, diverse perspectives and entertaining stories that are actually happening right now. The more I do, the more I realize how much there is to learn about people.

Barbara Kopple's Film Picks

Hoop Dreams: Certainly one of the greatest documentaries I've ever seen. It's hard to talk about this film because it's so rich and complex. It's a landmark in longitudinal documentary, spending the better part of four years tracing the arc of two young basketball prodigies—Arthur Agee and William Gates. The film is remarkable in its intimate involvement with the characters and their families, involving us in scenes of surprising euphoria, devastating frustration, unforeseen reconciliations. Peter Gilbert, Steve James, Frederick Marx are such great filmmakers, they know how to be in the moment and capture the dynamic at play. They must be commended too for using the film to speak to issues of race and class in America, showing us how the talents of young, poor people of color are exploited, how their families are threatened by their sometimes dire circumstances. I think the greatest compliment I can pay to the filmmakers is that when I think about *Hoop Dreams*, I don't think about the filmmakers at all: I think about the Agee and Gates families, how close I feel to them after having seen the movie and how much more I want to know. A testament to the tremendous power of film to truly connect audiences with the characters being filmed.

Salesman: A masterpiece of direct cinema. The film follows four door-to-door salesmen as they travel the country selling Bibles. The film takes us into the lives of ordinary people, the salesmen and their customers, as no earlier films ever had. Drawing on their own experiences as door-to-door salesmen, the Maysles Brothers gave us four real-life Willy Lomans, none more memorable than Paul "the Badger" Brennan. Through Paul's increasingly desperate attempts to make a sale, we see the dark side of sixties consumerism, more vividly than any fiction film could ever present it.

Al and David Maysles have the remarkable ability to disappear and to allow their characters to feel completely comfortable in front of the camera. Sometimes they open themselves to their most basic impulses—like when the salesmen go swimming in the middle of the night—and sometimes they are silent and still—a state Paul Brennan falls into as he grows increasingly frustrated with his struggles. The Maysles are such wonderful, sensitive filmmakers. They had the instinct to allow for both action and silence to play out in the film, showing us the breadth of people's experiences. Whether people are talking or not, we know what they're feeling because we have been allowed to live their story with them. An amazing document of changes in American culture and extremely influential in showing me how powerful a vérité film can be.

Roger and Me: I love *Roger and Me*. Michael Moore is perhaps without equal when it comes to blending politics with comedy. This is a witty and poignant documentary exploring the impact of the closing of a General Motors plant in Moore's hometown of Flint, Michigan. What unfolds is devastating as Moore captures the ramifications of corporate greed and its devastating effects on Flint and its people. Michael Moore is charismatic and entertaining, but he's also serious and convicted about what he's talking about. This was something of a revelation when it came out because nobody had so successfully used documentary film in such a peculiar, humorous but still profound way. A true classic.

Buena Vista Social Club: Appropriately understated, Wim Wenders allows the sensational music and its lively creators to take center-stage in this film. Jumping between Cuba, Amsterdam, and New York, we get to see the musicians in and out of their elements. The intimacy of following this aging group of musicians as they marvel at New York

City's skyline is so real, you realize that despite their talents, they're still humble and capable of being awed. You wonder if they really realize how huge it is that they're headlining Carnegie Hall! There's a real reverence on the part of Wenders and Ry Cooder for these musicians, they respect them enough to stay out of the way and let the relationships between the musicians play out so we can see that at the heart of their musical partnership lies a unique and unshakeable bond.

The Kid Stays in the Picture: Nanette Burstein and Brett Morgen captured a fascinating period in Hollywood, in America, presented it to audiences in a delightfully entertaining way that allows them to understand the glamour, the schmaltz, the kitsch, and the daring of Bob Evans and of that time. The artistic use of photos and animation is innovative and cool.

I think it's also something that is phenomenal for people who want to make films. This film inspires people to not be afraid, to go against the tide, to have perseverance to go with their instincts and the things they really feel. People are saying if this guy can do it, they can do it.

Hearts and Minds: Peter Davis made a profound and distressing portrait of the war in Vietnam and the heinous war-mongering attitudes of American political and military officials. This is really a film of powerful images—they are nothing less than arresting and absolutely necessary. Every war must have its visual documentation. It was images like these that horrified Americans and eventually brought an end to the war, now that the Bush administration has banned the images of American coffins returning home from television broadcasts, documentary films are more essential than ever. However "controversial" it was at the time, this stands as a brave and angry reaction to injustice. We should all strive to be so bold as artists and citizens.

Don't Look Back: Another touchstone in vérité filmmaking, D. A. Pennebaker takes us on a UK tour with Bob Dylan in 1965. We see how stunning a performer Dylan is—on and off the stage. Pennebaker is brilliant at capturing Dylan's contradictions—both irreverent and hostile toward reporters, loving and cruel with his girlfriend Joan Baez, wildly playful and deathly serious with his own music. Somehow, Pennebaker manages to keep up with Dylan's always unpredictable whims, whether he's suddenly sprinting from adoring fans or riffing with his inimitable wit. The film is important not only for its documentation of one of America's greatest artists during his creative height, but also for its ability to show us a story without trying to explain any of its mystery. A wonderful film.

Capturing the Friedmans: In *Capturing the Friedmans* Andrew Jarecki had the courage and insight to alter course from the initial subject matter of the film and go deeper, to create something quite different than he was probably initially intending. He started out making a film about New York City's premier clown, following his story, the final result is a brilliant portrait of a family self-destructing and an important challenge to the audience as to what the nature of justice and punishment and redemption is. Complex, disturbing, discomforting, this was a real breakthrough film that with difficult subject matter still brought new audiences to the theatre.

Woodstock: Michael Wadleigh's film documents the culmination of an ever-growing counterculture. He had the foresight to know the event would be something special, his talented filmmaking team wisely spent time filming all aspects of the concert, from the music to the fans to the police officers to the backed-up roadways and disgruntled locals. The performances are vital recordings of some of pop culture's great acts, the film is full of wonderful moments, like Country Joe rousing half a million people to their feet to sing his "Fixin' to Die Rag," or farm owner Max Yasgur who rented his field for the concert bridging the generational divide between hippie and adult. When I was working on my film *My Generation* about Woodstocks '69, '94, '99, I obviously went back to this film and was bowled over by how beautifully everything was shot and how much life there is in all the scenes. Absolutely essential viewing. A CLASSIC.

When We Were Kings: This is one of the best sports documentaries I've ever seen. It looks at the lead up to the "Rumble in the Jungle," the heavily promoted, 1974 George Foreman–Muhammad Ali boxing match in Zaire. The film expertly intertwines footage of Muhammad Ali at his most charismatic, a young Don King promoting the event, and the blistering music festival that inaugurated the fight. The interviews in this movie are priceless, with George Plimpton, Spike Lee, Norman Mailer, so many others offering their takes on the event and its significance, both athletic and political. The grandiosity of the fight itself, especially of Muhammad Ali, is amped up by Leon Gast's amazing eye for storytelling, blending commentary with beautiful footage. And, just like Muhammad Ali himself, the film is a great mix of sports and politics, and terrific vérité footage.

The Times of Harvey Milk: Rob Epstein chronicles the life and death of California's first openly gay public official, offering a vivid portrait of a hero. The film uses archival footage so brilliantly, evoking the feelings of an influential man and the political climate he was working to change. The vigil interviews with Harvey's friends and people inspired by him offer insight into the how much he meant to so many people. His tragic murder inspired a haunting, silent, 45,000-person vigil the night he was killed and later a riot when his murderer was given a light sentence. These images solidify the significance of who Harvey Milk was, and Rob Epstein wonderfully strings together this poignant story.

Woodstock Never Dies

Jacqueline Linge / 2009

August 14, 2009. This article first appeared in *Salon.com*, at http://www.Salon.com. An online version remains in the *Salon* archives. Reprinted with permission.

Forty years ago this weekend, over five hundred thousand people descended upon Max Yasgur's farm in Bethel, New York, for a three-day music festival. Miles of ink have been spilled in the years since then mythologizing the mud, the bad acid trips, and the music, and creating something fresh out of this cultural legend is not an easy task—even for an Academy Award–winning filmmaker like Barbara Kopple.

Nevertheless, this week VH1 is airing Kopple's new documentary, *Woodstock: Now & Then*, a historical portrait of the festival interwoven with a look at its impact on young musicians today.

For the "Now" portion of the movie, Kopple focuses on a group of young musicians from Paul Green's School of Rock. Their musical skills are impressive, and their nerdy knowledge of Janis Joplin and Keith Moon suggests that Woodstock's legacy stretches beyond aging hippies.

As for the "Then" segments, Kopple interviews many of the key figures of Woodstock, including festival producers Michael Lang and Artie Kornfeld, who conjure a compelling picture of the hectic days before, during, and after Woodstock, when it seemed like everything was hanging on a thread of pure happenstance. Kopple also uses memorable footage from Michael Wadleigh's Oscar-winning movie *Woodstock* in her film. The iconic scene of Jimi Hendrix playing his version of "The Star-Spangled Banner" to forty thousand people and fields of deserted trash never gets old, and Kopple uses it with resonant results. The guitar's wailing solos and frenzied feedback represent a decade of sadness and chaos, marked by assassinations, segregation, and the Vietnam War.

Salon spoke with Barbara Kopple over the phone about the ongoing interest in Woodstock, current-day festivals like Burning Man, and her documentary.

Q: Why did you make this movie?
A: What could be cooler than to do a film about Woodstock? It's got the greatest music, the best stories, and fascinating characters, and always an unexpected turn of events. Little miracles and moments that are funny or pure inspiration.

Q: Where were you during Woodstock?
A: I was studying and working. I was not at Woodstock, but I feel like I was.

Q: Why did you choose the "now and then" angle for this particular film?
A: Music, I think, is what bonds everybody together, and here were kids who just totally embraced the music of Woodstock—[the students of] School of Rock knew everything about it, loved it, and idolized Keith Moon. Loved Janis Joplin. It just seemed so natural that you would want something to happen with the next generation.

Q: Why do you think Woodstock is still relevant today? Why should kids who weren't born yet care about it?
A: I think Woodstock is still relevant today because people really care about what's happening in our world. People want to be part of something. People want to be part of a community. People want to have that same kind of ritual that everybody has, and to be able to see it with people who were really fighting for something. They were fighting against the war, they were fighting to have life be much better. They wanted to be free, they wanted to get away from their jobs, and to be able to stand in the mud and enjoy themselves and listen to great music. What can be more relevant than that? Because I think all of us want that in our lives. We still have some of the very same issues that we're dealing with. We're still dealing with war. We're still dealing with many of the same kinds of things that the generation of 1969 was dealing with.

Q: There's a section in the movie where you focus on the women's sexual liberation at Woodstock, and at one point, it's referred to as a "women's festival."
A: Yes, Greg Jackson, who was the reporter from ABC, called it a "women's festival." To me, it's like "yes!" That's what it made it so much different than Altamont and a lot of the other festivals that followed it. It was gentle, it was soft. Michael Lang and Artie Kornfeld and others picked

the Hog Farm [commune] as the people who were going to take care of the security. People would just come up to you and talk to you and hug you and stop any fights they could with laughter and with love. That's just a whole different way of thinking.

Q: What do you think the ripple effects of that were? How did it play into the political, social, and cultural realm after Woodstock?
A: I think every generation really searches for that common understanding. You know, to be able to shake off the rules, to be able to be together in a real community, and to take care of each other. I mean, in the way the film really talked about the drugs, and Wavy Gravy would help with one person, and that person, when he felt better, would help the next person. And it just kept going round and round, that whole sense of caring for your brothers and your sisters. And that's very rare, particularly when seeing four hundred thousand people together.

Q: I thought it was interesting that you included the election of Obama in the film. Are you saying that Woodstock set the stage for that?
A: Well, I think once again, we have that feeling of hope, that things are going to be OK. We had a really bad period. And now that Obama's been elected, and so many people from all different facets worked on it, young and old. People gave up their jobs to be able to be part of it. I think you're seeing something that's very different, that people realize that they have to go out and they have to do things, and they have to make change in their lives for it to happen.

Q: So why haven't we seen something like Woodstock duplicated?
A: Well, I think maybe it's happened in the Burning Man, and other festivals. But you know, it's so hard to duplicate something that happened in such a magical and spontaneous way. Each festival and each generation—I mean even think about [the Woodstock revival festivals of] '94 and '99 and how different they were. The amazing part of it was that each person said, "This is our Woodstock, this is our festival." And they took possession of it. People would pull up on a bus, as they were entering the grounds, and they would just yell, "This is our Woodstock! This is the one that we care about!" It's great to take possession.

Q: How did the original Woodstock movie, directed by Michael Wadleigh, fuel the continuing mythology of Woodstock?
A: Well, I think *Woodstock*, the movie, was one of the finest, grandest

movies imaginable. And if that movie had not been made, none of us would really know that this event happened. We wouldn't have felt the people, we wouldn't have seen the mud. We would've heard about the groups that played, but we wouldn't be up close and personal, right under them. I mean, Michael Wadleigh filming as well as the other DPs on the film—it was so intimate, it was so extraordinary. It just propelled you on a journey.

2010 IDA Career Achievement Award—The Magic of Being There: Barbara Kopple and the Subject-Filmmaker Relationship

Sara Vizcarrondo / 2010

This article originally appeared in the Winter 2011 edition of *Documentary* magazine, a publication of the International Documentary Association. © 2010 International Documentary Association. Reprinted by permission.

On the first day of her shoot at the Harlan County (Kentucky) coal miners' strike, Barbara Kopple and her crew were met with distrust. The miners were under threat from a company whose recklessness with their safety had gone unchecked for years. On top of that, the company had gotten crafty, hiring scabs and bullies to menace the strikers and placing spies on the picket line. When Kopple and her crew introduced themselves, the strikers gave them fake names. "They said they were Martha Washington or Florence Nightingale, but they left a door open," Kopple recalls. "'If you come tomorrow at four a.m. and be on the picket line. . . .' So we went up this mountain to find a place to stay, and we got up at three thirty."

The next morning, it was raining and the mountain road they travelled down lacked side rails; it's a dangerous situation if you know the mountain, but if you don't, anxieties are even higher. A car sped by the crew and Kopple's car toppled over into a ditch. "Everybody was fine," she says. "We got out of the car and dragged out the equipment. We knew we had to go to the picket line, so we walked. Harlan is small and news traveled and when everyone heard, they put their arms around us and embraced us and that was the start of something very special."

What was special, Kopple seems to suggest, was not the Academy

Award for Best Documentary that *Harlan County, U.S.A.* won in 1977, or the respect it earned in the industry, but the relationships she and the crew built with the miners. It was her integration into the community that this documentarian seems to value most.

Kopple got her start interning with Albert and David Maysles. Fresh off a course of study in clinical psychology, she came to New York and took a single class in cinéma vérité at the New School. One of the women in her class was the secretary at the Maysles Brothers' production house and told her that they needed an intern. "I was hired and I never went back to that class," Kopple says. What followed were stints as assistant editor working with Barbara Jarvis and then Larry Moyer, after which Kopple, like many socially minded documentarians of that era, made a film as part of a collective.

The collective, called Winter Film Collective, made one film together: *Winter Soldier*. "Vets coming out of Vietnam came to see us and we chose pieces of their interviews for the film," she reflects. "A woman donated a home in New Jersey and we all lived there, different people cooked. We were a collective but we weren't philosophically bound. Instead, our interest was showing you who these vets were." She adds, "Activism is a big word."

Kopple is known for her interest in social issues. While her attention to the Dixie Chicks' struggle with censorship in her and Cecilia Peck's 2006 film *Shut Up & Sing* "hints at a larger political issue," and her 1990 doc *American Dream* looks at a labor strike that pitted brother against brother, she emphasizes that her first priority is connecting with her subjects: "When you're with people for long periods of time, you're filming because there's a trust and a chemistry. Once they allow you in their world, it's wonderful—and that's what wonderful films are about."

This non-invasive tack leads to a clear but quiet politic. Kopple identifies that the goal is to "go with it. It's not as if I wouldn't plan [for a shoot], but you have to stick with the subjects. You just have to be there to take that on. If you do a film with an agenda, then it's just what's in your head and it's not really what's going on. You have to be loyal to the reality." And what loyalty to reality ultimately requires is a constant attention to the people you're filming.

Though Kopple's footage is commonly eye-catching, shooting itself is not always thrilling. "Lots of the time, not much is happening," she admits. "You're cooking or telling stories or playing music—that's what our lives are. Sometimes big things happen. Every project sort of brings with it surprises and unexpected turns." Clearly this kind of involvement in the everyday elements of her subjects' lives helps build the subject/filmmaker chemistry, and also lends to a feeling of greater proximity and access.

The sense of a cinematic backstage pass that informs *Wild Man Blues*, the 1998 doc on Woody Allen's sideline career as a Dixieland clarinet player, not only personalizes the cultural icon but softens his public persona in the wake of his messy divorce from actress Mia Farrow and his new marriage to Farrow's previously adopted daughter, Soon-Yi Previn. Were it not for her inclusive and necessarily neutral vantage, her subjects might not have trusted the filmmaker to shoot them. Muckraking would be a major obstacle to her goals, and frankly she doesn't need to seek out that brand of material; if you're ready, she suggests, it'll come to you. "I didn't know we were going to be machine gunned [in Kentucky]," she explains. "I didn't know when we were driving around with an organizer that we'd find out a miner had been killed. You just have to be there and be ready."

When Kopple found her way to the Dixie Chicks, it was partly because they seemed unlikely characters for debate and partly because their friendships and openness stood out so prominently. "The film touches on issues like free speech and the war in Iraq, but it's about these three beautiful women you'd never expect such controversy to happen to," Kopple maintains. "The situation became very politicized and the singers chose to not apologize and to stick to what they believe in. I connected with them through their friendship and caring for each other. If we have girlfriends in our lives that cared for us like that, it'd be fantastic."

Of late, Kopple's pupils are making a splash. "I taught one semester at NYU and my class was incredible: Lucy Walker, Brett Morgen, Nanette Burstein—they were all my students. *They* weren't lucky to train under me; it's me who was lucky, and they've done such wonderful things both for me and in their careers." Walker went on to make *Blindsight*, *Devil's Playground*, and the IDA Award–nominated *Waste Land* (winner of 2010 Best Documentary Feature and Pare Lorentz Awards). Morgen and Burstein's credits as a team include the Academy Award–nominated *On the Ropes*, as well as *The Kid Stays in the Picture*; Morgen later directed *Chicago 10*, and Burstein made *American Teen*.

When asked about Burstein's recent foray into fiction (the romantic comedy *Going the Distance*), Kopple says, "It's great: I did the same [her 2005 drama *Havoc*]. We all need ways to express ourselves. When you work with docs, you're always seeking what's real, and that's what comes out when you shoot fiction; you have an instinct and a pulse for that." Fiction, in this way, is a training ground for the doc aesthetic. "The film that inspired me most toward documentary was Gillo Pontecorvo's *The Battle of Algiers*. It wasn't a doc, but it was shot like one. You felt it was really happening and you were on the inside of it. It unfolded in small ways that made it feel so real."

Kopple says that, as new technologies have made filmmaking a more accessible form, the documentary community has been able to enjoy "a great diversity of storytelling—the past, family, personal stories. We need all of this to be able to continue in independent films. We can't become complacent; we need to let more and more people in to tell their stories. It's going to make us closer and help us understand each other."

Looking back, Kopple cites titles like Peter Davis' *Hearts and Minds*, Bill Jersey's *A Time for Burning* and Michael Moore's *Roger and Me* as inspirations. "I'm moved by docs that give a voice to the voiceless or tell a different side of a story than we thought we knew," she maintains. "By telling stories in a compassionate and compelling way, you can inspire others to act. When you do that, a hidden issue emerges and that comes to the forefront of our consciousness—and with that you can compel people and even inspire the mainstream media to open their eyes and respond." This is precisely what she's done, but not by casual means. To her obliquely activist statement, she adds that docs can affect audiences mightily—"If you make the film well, that is."

Exclusive: Barbara Kopple Talks HBO Gun Control Doc, *Gun Fight*: "Reason Is Lost"

Sophia Savage / 2011

Originally published on *Indiewire*. From *Thompson on Hollywood*, April 8, 2011. Reprinted with permission.

Academy Award–winning filmmaker Barbara Kopple (*Harlan County, U.S.A.*, *American Dream*, *Shut Up & Sing*) is premiering her latest, HBO Documentary's *Gun Fight*, on HBO April 13, three days before the fourth anniversary of the Virginia Tech shooting (thirty-three people killed including shooter's suicide) and a week before the twelve-year anniversary of the Columbine Massacre (thirteen people killed plus the two shooters' suicides).

In true Kopple form, *Gun Fight* is provocative and hard-hitting. Michael Moore's Oscar-winning 2002 documentary *Bowling for Columbine* looked at the state of guns and "gun control" in America. Now Kopple's film investigates where the issue stands in 2011. Below is our interview with Kopple, in which she states: "It's such a hot button issue that elicits passion from all sides, and often times reason is lost."

Question: What is the biggest misconception about gun control in the US?

Barbara Kopple: One big misconception about gun control is the very term itself. Some who oppose gun control view the term as a serious threat to their right to own any sort of gun. Others perceive gun control as enforcing things like background checks, cracking down on straw purchases, and closing the gun show loophole. Language is very powerful and I think we need to start out by making the term "gun control" less divisive. My hope is that all sides can somehow agree on a definition, eliminate misconceptions, and move forward together.

Q: Are there two clear opposing sides on the gun control issue?
BK: Some people and organizations like us to believe that gun control is an issue comprised of two extremes—banning guns completely or having unlimited access to firearms without any restrictions. In reality though, it's a far more complex issue that's impossible to break down into two sides. A person can be opposed to gun control, but also anti-NRA. Or pro-gun ownership, but in favor of thorough background checks. And the list goes on and on. I want this film to show that the issue is not so black and white and to make audiences aware of some of the different leanings and perspectives in the hopes of a greater understanding of this issue as a whole.

Q: What is your hope for *Gun Fight*?
BK: My hope for *Gun Fight* is that it inspires a common-sense conversation about gun ownership and gun control. It's such a hot button issue that elicits passion from all sides, and often times reason is lost. I sincerely hope there's middle ground somewhere that even the most ardent anti-gun individual and the staunchest pro-gun NRA member can agree on. For example, most everyone would agree that violent criminals shouldn't be able to purchase guns. I think together we should be able to figure out how this can happen, whether it's through background checks, waiting periods, or another method that would prove effective.

Barbara Kopple on Gun Rights, Freedom of Speech, and Virginia Tech

Eleanor Barkhorn / 2011

From *TheAtlantic.com*, April 13, 2011. Copyright 2011 The Atlantic Media Co., as published in The Atlantic Online. Distributed by Tribune Media Services. Reprinted by permission.

In her more than three decades as a filmmaker, Oscar winner Barbara Kopple has made documentaries about Kentucky coal miners (*Harlan County, U.S.A.*), the Yankees (*The House of Steinbrenner*), the Dixie Chicks (*Shut Up & Sing*), and more. Her latest project may be her most controversial yet: *Gun Fight*, a film about the gun rights debate in America that premieres tonight on HBO at 9:30.

She spoke with the *Atlantic* about the shootings at Virginia Tech and in Tucson, her personal views about guns, and the state of freedom of speech in America.

Q: When did the idea for *Gun Fight* first come about?
A: Four years ago. In fact, one of our first shoots was going to Virginia Tech a few days after it happened.

Q: And what drew you to the project?
A: Mark Weiss, one of the producers, called me up and said, "How would you like to make a film about guns and America?" I went, "Oh, I don't know about that. That's such a huge, huge issue, and I don't know that much about it."

We did a lot of talking, and then I started doing a lot of research, and I said, "Alright." And then we pitched it to HBO, and Shelia [Nevins] said, "Ok, go for it, go do it." And then the realization hit: "Ok, how do you get a handle on something like this, that is huge, and it's passionate. Because guns, you know, there's no coming back from it. People dying in a split second. It's such a major responsibility to do a film like this. So I guess that's kind of where it started.

Q: In an interview with *Indiewire* a few years ago, you said, "I don't go into a film with any particular agenda. . . . But [I] often do have a point of view on the subject." What was your point of view going into *Gun Fight*?
A: I think my point of view is I'm not a gun person. Although if you just looked at *Harlan County*, there were so many guns in *Harlan County*—everybody had guns. The first or second day I was in Harlan County, they taught me how to shoot. I would never carry a gun during the day, but during the nighttime we would all sleep on the floor with mattresses and stuff, because when the strike got really intense, they would shoot.

So it was sort of interesting for me to be able to be on the gun ranges and to really see people's love of guns. There was [former NRA lobbyist] Richard Feldman talking about, "This is Mr. Smith and this is Mr. Wesson, and I never go to the door without my two good friends."

It was very foreign to me—I was curious to see the other side, to see how people thought and felt and their whole passion about what freedom is. Even [executive director of Gun Owners of America] Larry Pratt, who's in the film, who talks about shooting the government, and then that horrible thing happens in Tucson. It's hard to wrap your head around it all. It's such a huge issue.

Q: Do you think people who support gun rights will feel that this film accurately represents their side of the issue?
A: I think it's both sides of the discussion. A lot of my films always surprise me: the people I think won't like them, like them. And I bet that they'll take quotes from this film to show their side, and their cause. And I think that's what's interesting about making a film is sort of the debate and the heat that the debate creates.

I think about [Virginia Tech shooting survivor] Colin Goddard in the Brady PSA that we use: "I want to see an America where people are safe no matter where they go." And I think that's a really great quote, and something that everyone can aspire to.

Q: You finished *Gun Fight* before the shooting in Tucson happened, and then went back and added some footage from that event to the beginning and end of the film. How does the Tucson shooting change the way you see the film?
A: What's so interesting abut Tucson: In some cases people die and then

everything closes—the shooter sometimes shoots his victims and then he shoots himself, as in Virginia Tech. And here, the shooter is alive, and also, thank God, Gabrielle Giffords is alive. And that in a way keeps the debate alive and keeps the issue alive.

Q: Another interesting thing you said in the *Indiewire* interview was, "We're living in a time when the freedoms we take for granted—the freedom of speech, the freedom to protest and dissent—are truly in danger." You've been making films for more than thirty years—do you think those freedoms are more in danger now than they were at the beginning of your career?
A: I think it's pretty consistent. It's so hard to tell because you go all the way back to *Harlan County*—I mean, I had no idea, here I was going to the coal fields. Who would know people would be machine-gunned with semi-automatic carbines, a miner would be killed by a company foreman—that kind of thing.

You just have no idea. With documentaries you have no idea what's going to happen, you don't know what's around each turn. But you're going to keep making films, and the films at some point start to lead you where you're going. And you just have to stick with it and have a lot of perseverance and compassion for what you're doing, no matter how hard it is, no matter how much people tell you not to do it.

You don't think, "Is this an issue about free speech?" You just know that it's a story about people, and hopefully it's a compelling story that people will want to see.

Full Frame Day 2: Barbara Kopple and Guns

David Fellerath / 2011

From *IndyWeek.com: Arts*, April 15, 2011. Reprinted by permission.

Last week I spoke to Barbara Kopple about her new film *Gun Fight*. It premiered earlier this week on HBO and will be rebroadcast and shown on demand through May 8. Although *Bowling for Columbine* remains the seminal doc on the topic of American gun policy (and it was a watershed in the commercial viability of documentaries, too), I find that I prefer Kopple's lucid, restrained, and non-sensationalist treatment of the issue.

But I also found it ironic: In 1977, the thirty-year-old Kopple shot to fame with *Harlan County, U.S.A.*, for which she won the Oscar for best documentary. This riveting film told the story of a Kentucky coal miners' strike and the women who assumed the backbone of the movement. The film achieved the force of a Western as the strikers faced off with the mine company's hired muscle in an armed standoff, and there perhaps was no scene as memorable as the meeting where one union firebrand, a middle-aged woman, punctuated a speech by pulling a pistol from her bra.

Harlan County launched Kopple on a career that has encompassed subjects such as Woody Allen, Mike Tyson, the Dixie Chicks, and George Steinbrenner, along with other labor films and the occasional foray into film and television dramas, including an Anne Hathaway indie vehicle.

When I mentioned *Harlan County* to Kopple, she laughed and said, "Yes, there are a lot of guns in that one. That film was made over thirty years ago and I wasn't looking at guns in the same way, but you're absolutely right. Everybody had guns, they open-carried them.

"And people used them. The first day, or second day, after I got to Harlan County, two miners got into a fight with each other. And then the next day, one of the miners—who'd gotten shot—was driving around in his car with a sign on the back of his car saying, '.38s ain't shit,'" she says with a laugh.

But three decades later, guns themselves come under scrutiny in *Gun Fight*. In an unintentional coincidence, it takes violence in the Appalachians—the Virginia Tech mass shooting—as its starting point. Her film follows several expert witnesses to this country's gun debate—such as it is. Colin Goddard, who survived the massacre of his French class on April 16, 2007, by a heavily armed and troubled fellow student and became a gun control advocate in its aftermath, is prominently featured in her film.

I tell Kopple that, as someone who keeps a modest farmer's arsenal, I can attest that there are plenty of gun owners who think American laws are scandalously lax. She laughs, "The NRA just hasn't gotten to you—yet."

While Goddard's credibility is unimpeachable, Kopple's film features powerful witnesses from the front lines of the carnage inflicted by the sea of three hundred million guns in this country—a crucial if unknown percentage of which are not in the hands of responsible, emotionally stable, law-abiding adults.

"One of the things I really care about in this film," Kopple says, "is to get a lot of different points across. I also really care about people whose lives change from guns in a split second, sort of a snap of your fingers. It happens everywhere, affects every community, people of every race and every class."

We meet Scott Charles, trauma outreach coordinator for Temple University Hospital in Philadelphia, who takes battle-hardened teenagers on tours of the hospital's trauma unit. Charles, who calls the vicinity the "deadliest neighborhood in one of the deadliest cities in one of the deadliest countries in the civilized world," later takes pains to point out that the country's suburban classes are largely insulated from the daily toll of gun violence.

"Occasionally you get the Columbines that happen, the Virginia Techs, but they're anomalies," he says, noting that ten thousand people have been shot in Philadelphia in five years, in a numbingly banal litany of domestic disputes and street corner altercations.

Indeed, viewers may come away from *Gun Fight* marveling at the disconnect in our culture, wondering if gun violence is another example of the gaping class divide in our culture. Kopple spends a lot of time with gun rights groups, who tend to be composed of middle-age people, mostly white and male, with a paranoid worldview. It's these people who are so uncompromising, and such effective fundraisers and organizers, that they wield influence so mighty that even Republican politicians are afraid of them, and law enforcement groups, which normally have politicians scurrying to their side, generally are frustrated in their efforts to encourage more stringent gun laws.

"They've made gun control like a poison, so that if you want to get elected or stay in office . . . no one wants to touch this issue," Kopple says.

Except for a pro forma montage of guns in American movies, Kopple's film avoids the showy pop culture invasion that marked *Bowling for Columbine* (Marilyn Manson! *South Park*!). Instead, her film is focused on the points of view of people with a stake in the debate. *Gun Fight* is bolstered by the courage of physician Garen Wintemute, who views gun violence as a public health problem, and the apostasy of Richard Feldman, a longtime P.R. man for the National Rifle Association, who has since denounced the organization as being primarily devoted to raising money for itself.

Kopple and her editing team were nearly finished with the film—in fact, they'd shown a final cut to HBO—when this country suffered another mass shooting, again perpetrated by a mentally ill person armed to the teeth, which nearly claimed the life of U.S. Representative Gabrielle Giffords.

"The editor and I got every piece of footage we could. We stayed up one night and put a little piece together," Kopple says.

I asked if the Congress, having seen one of its members shot in the face and nearly killed by a legally armed psycho, would summon the courage to face down the paranoid geeks of the NRA.

"I don't know," she said.

Shut Up & Sing: On Accidental Political Activists

Rahul Chadha / 2011

From Stranger than Fiction website (STFdocs.com), August 12, 2011. Reprinted with permission.

The Dixie Chicks were at the height of their popularity in 2003, when lead singer Natalie Maines told a London audience that she was ashamed that President George W. Bush was from Texas, sparking a controversy that would leave the trio taking heavy fire on the battlefield of the U.S.'s culture wars. Barbara Kopple and Cecilia Peck's expertly helmed film, *Shut Up & Sing*, shows us the fallout from that off-cuff remark—which fundamentally changed the lives of the performers—examining what happens when art produced for a mass audience runs full-bore into the overheated rhetoric of the political world. As the conservative country music industry turns to eat its young, Maines seems genuinely confused and angry, but not enough to stop her from apologizing for her comment and dismissing it as a blatant attempt to pander to an anti-war audience. On the other side, we see Dixie Chick decriers denouncing Maines's statement as—what else?—an assault on American ideals, oblivious to both the uselessness and irony of their protests. In a stunningly sharp insight, band member Martie Maguire crystallizes the controversy surrounding the Chicks, noting that it was perfect, allowing conservative demagogues a focal point at which jingoists could direct their vitriol, and providing the anti-war movement with a potent symbol of patriotic dissent from heartland America. *Shut Up & Sing* raises interesting questions about our expectations of our entertainers, and makes a solid case that—at least for musicians—unfettered economic success and freedom of speech are, at times, mutually exclusive. Following the screening Stranger than Fiction friend Hugo Perez spoke with co-director Barbara Kopple, editors Bob Eisenhardt and Jean Tsien, and producer David

Cassidy. [Note: Those questions marked Stranger than Fiction below were asked by Hugo Perez.]

Stranger than Fiction: How did you get involved with this project? Seeing the personality of Natalie, and how passionate she is, seems like a great fit for you. How did this all happen?

Barbara Kopple: Well, [co-director] Cecilia Peck and I decided we wanted to do a film on the Dixie Chicks. And this was even before they made the statement. And they went, no, no. They had a [Dixie Chicks] website crew with them that captured the statement, thank goodness. And we went back to them and said, now can we make a film with you? We had a whole discussion with them and they looked at our other films, and they said, you're on.

Audience: I noticed that you played around with time, between 2003 and 2005. Could you talk a little about that?

Kopple: We tried to do a linear structure, but it just fell flat.

Bob Eisenhardt: I think all the editors had a gut feeling that it couldn't be told chronologically. But we kind of had to prove it to ourselves, and for the longest time, it didn't work. It was very confusing, and it was hard to find the right jumping off point that sent you backwards. About three times during the process we strung it together chronologically to look at it. It made it for about thirty minutes and then everybody fell asleep. We finally got the time passages to work, then it was a question of getting the right moment to leap back and the right graphics and the right pacing.

Jean Tsien: As a way to help us edit this film, we had hundreds and hundreds of index cards made in the editing room. And there were days we were just staring at the wall in silence. . . .

Eisenhardt: Moving these cards around and looking at them and then arguing about whether it would work or not.

Kopple: And as always, there were certain things we wanted in, and that other people didn't. We were working with so many different editors and different sensibilities, but the discussions that we had were sensational, because you just couldn't say, no. You had to explain how it moved the story forward or what it gave the characters, so it was very egalitarian in the editing room.

Audience: It's such a well edited film, but it's also such a great verité film. So I'm guessing you spent a great deal of time with them. I'm curious about that, and how your relationship with the three women developed over time.

Kopple: I think, for me, the three women were so amazing. They were about transformation, they were about courage, they were about sisterhood. I really wanted to have friends exactly like the Dixie Chicks, because they were there for each other for all the big moments. The wonderful part of it was that most of the time we could just be there filming, and they just went about their lives. They were in so much crisis, or trying to write their songs, or having babies. And we were totally unimportant, and they just allowed us to film. So it was very good. But, Natalie does speak her mind all the time.

Audience: Did they ever get mad or frustrated with you?

Kopple: I think the heaviest thing was when they came to see the film for the first time, because we didn't let them see the anything until the film was in fine cut. I'll never forget it, it was my birthday, actually. We got wine and things for them to eat, but probably not enough wine. So they came in and they were looking at it. It was in Bob's editing room and we were watching them watch the film. And it wasn't as if after the film they went, oh, that was so great, or, we really loved it. It was as if they were watching their lives go by and remembering all those painful things and their body reactions were all doing different things. I remember that Natalie had never heard Martie say that she would give up her career for her. When she heard that, she touched her leg. I think it brought them together, but I think it really freaked them out to watch the film. It was as if somebody had climbed into their souls and exposed so much about them.

STF: Did you think about filming them watching the film?

Kopple: That would have been too hard. No, we didn't.

Audience: How did you decide when to stop filming and start editing? Because I was surprised that their big Grammy sweep, which to me was their "fuck you" to the whole industry, I was surprised that it wasn't in there. Was that a conscious decision?

Kopple: I think we said what we wanted to say. As filmmakers, we always want to put everything in. But the film had been finished by then, and we just cheered from the sidelines, and sort of enjoyed the moment of them being able to say, "screw you," to everybody.

Eisenhardt: We did film a whole other concert. We felt it would be important to show them coming back to the United States, not just seeing it in London. There was a fairly huge shoot in Detroit. And we took one look at it and said the other scene has all the emotion in it, and we didn't use it.

Audience: During the segment in Dallas, what was the mood with the crew?

Kopple: We didn't film that. The [Dixie Chicks'] website group filmed that. So I can only guess. But I know that Martie and Emily were petrified for the Dallas show. And they moved apart from Natalie, so she was sort of standing on the stage and they were at the far side of the stage. There was so much at stake for all of them with their families, but they did it.

STF: There are so many emotional moments in the film, and in that moment, Natalie is almost marching into battle as she walks onto the stage. She says nothing, but it's so powerful. Her shoulders are hunched forward.

Kopple: Also, the really beautiful part of that was her husband, Adrian [Pasdar], was there and just hugged her. He didn't really travel with her that much, but for this particular one he came because he just wanted to be there for her.

Audience: What was it about the Dixie Chicks that made you want to do a film about them before they made the statement?

Kopple: We knew Adrian really well. He had lived in New York. He would always tell us stories about the Dixie Chicks and how fascinating they were. Cecelia, who was also friends with Adrian, started hanging out with them, and she called me and said, come on, we've got to do this. We just thought they were fascinating creatures. They weren't political then, they were doing country music. It was looking into a space we had never seen before, we had never looked at before. Then it evolved into such a total transformation, and doing unbelievable creative work.

Audience: What was the film's reception in the country music world?

Kopple: We thought that this film was going to show in so many cities and really show theatrically in a lot of different places, and it did show in some. But in certain areas, it was never shown. The interesting thing is that the Weinstein Company, which distributed the film, did focus groups at the very beginning—in New York and I think Kansas. And it got the highest reviews that the Weinstein Company had ever gotten. Even in Kansas, they didn't like the politics so much, but they really loved the Dixie Chicks and their families and wanted to see more of it. I think if people went to see it, it touched them. I went to Washington, D.C., and one of the right-wing group members was in the audience. He started saying things before the film. After the film, I called him up and asked him to be on the panel with me so everybody in the audience could get a sense of why he felt the way he felt about the Dixie Chicks. At the end of the film he got up there and said, you know, I really love this film. He said, I shouldn't be saying this, but I really love it. For me, it's just getting out there and showing it and communicating with people. People fear what they don't know and what they don't understand.

Audience: Did the change in the political winds from 2004 to 2006 change how you edited the movie, or how the movie was promoted?

Kopple: I think we just wanted to make a good movie. We used all the scenes that we thought would do that. The distribution company, the Weinstein Company, wanted to make it more political. At the very end when it was decided they were going to distribute it, they asked us to put in a few political pundits, so we did that, but that was as far as it got. I think the Weinstein Company really thought this film would get the Republicans out of office. We just thought the film was about freedom of speech, it was about sisterhood, it was about feeling betrayed. It had so many larger, universal issues.

Tsien: When we first started the project, we were actually at the beginning of the making of the album. So there were five hundred hours from 2003 and we had no idea what was in the footage. So we really had to comb through every single frame. We didn't even know the statement was caught on film, we discovered that. We were just finding nuggets.

Eisenhardt: You could barely hear the statement, it was shocking that they captured it. It was a great gift to have the six hundred hours of footage, I don't know what we would have done without it. These guys were with the Chicks all the time, and we loved them because they pressed themselves up against the wall and were in the corners and didn't bother the Chicks at all. But they got all that stuff. The meeting in the hotel room after London. But for me, it wasn't really about the politics, it was about the friendship. Now, the political landscape has changed so much, it's strange seeing the involvement in that moment. What stayed with me was the sisterhood.

Audience: I was wondering what it was like to shoot Rick Rubin. Did you have any interesting experiences with him?

Kopple: He's very camera shy and laid down on the couch a lot.

STF: He had prayer beads that he used to help him in meetings.

Kopple: His iced lattes, he had his dog. Nothing outstanding other than he has the golden touch, and it seems like everybody he works with becomes megastars and their albums do so incredibly well. We weren't able to capture his magic, but I'm sure it's there.

Audience: Can you talk a little more about the dynamic between the three women. Was there tension between the band members?

Kopple: I think that if there was a conflict it was about the kind of music that they were going to play. I think Natalie wanted to go more into rock and for Emily and Martie country just meant everything to them. They were a little nervous, I think, when Rick Rubin came into the picture and were trying to figure out where they were in all of this and trying to preserve what they did best. Natalie was trying for a while to find herself and Martie and Emily just did a country album maybe about six or eight months ago where they were singing and playing, just the two of them together. Courtyard Hounds is the name of the group.

STF: This is a great film with a great story and great characters, but when did you know that you had something special? Or at what point in a project do you get this gut feeling?

Kopple: Sometimes we didn't know that, and sometimes we were wondering if audiences were ever going to really look at this. And then, I don't know, sometime it started to come together. It really leapt off the screen, and we felt that we had the right structure and the right dynamic. We loved it, and we knew if we loved it, maybe somebody else would.

Audience: Many times I've felt like within documentary, music films are considered a minor genre. Have you felt that way about the film?

Kopple: I've done a lot of films that could be considered music films, but I've never thought about them that way. We did *Woodstock Now & Then*, we did a film called *Wild Man Blues* about Woody Allen and his jazz band. But I don't look at this as a music film, I look at it as something about sisterhood, about friendship. It's about so many of the universal themes that we all care about that it goes far beyond being a music film. I don't think that we've ever really done a music film because there's always stories attached, and always human elements attached.

David Cassidy: We keep talking about the concept of friendship, and how fortunate can we be as filmmakers to have three extremely talented women who are trying to figure out what they just went through, and to find catharsis through their art. Thank goodness they are so talented because they did find peace. And how fortunate we are that we could find such a brilliant ending because that comment from Martie that Barbara spoke about before, every time I start to tear up a little bit because it's such a powerful statement. And I've seen it dozens and dozens of times. Every time I hear the music I think about what went into the writing process, and it's not just three women with pens and paper, but they're really trying to figure out what they just went through and who they're going to be at the end of it.

Filmmaker Barbara Kopple on *Running from Crazy* and the Burden of Legacy

Karen Kemmerle / 2013

From *Tribecafilm.com*, November 6, 2013. Reprinted by permission.

We spoke with Oscar-winning documentarian Barbara Kopple about filming her latest project, working with Mariel Hemingway, and her unique editing process.

Barbara Kopple's new documentary, *Running from Crazy*, celebrated its New York premiere at last year's Tribeca Film Festival. In this moving film, actress and icon Mariel Hemingway, the granddaughter of Ernest, fearlessly examines her family's personal demons and patterns of suicide as she tries to avoid the same fate for herself and her daughters. Aided by some remarkable footage shot by Margaux Hemingway before her death, Kopple explores the Hemingway family history, especially that of Mariel, Margaux, and Muffet, and focuses on their shared battle with mental illness.

We spoke with director Barbara Kopple about the famous family, the bonds of sisterhood, and the most dramatic change in documentary filmmaking that she has seen during her forty-year career.

Tribeca: Mental illness is a somewhat taboo topic in our society. Have you always been interested in making a documentary about the subject?
Barbara Kopple: No, I haven't, even though I actually studied clinical psychology in college and my son is studying psychiatry during his residency at St. Luke's Roosevelt. I got involved in the project because OWN actually called me and asked, "How would you like to do a film about Mariel Hemingway?"

Of course, I said yes, but what I didn't realize is that they were calling

Mariel at the same time asking if she'd like to do a film about her family. She responded: "Are you kidding me? They're crazy, why would you want to do a film about them?" OWN got us together for a breakfast meeting, and we just chatted away like girlfriends. I met her daughters, and we forged a bond. Mariel wanted to go as deep as I did into her personal history and that of her family. In my films, I really like to go under the surface, and because we both wanted the same thing, it was a good match.

Tribeca: The Hemingway family has been a subject of fascination for many people for nearly half a century. How familiar were you with the family already?
BK: Not at all. Like everybody else, I had read Hemingway books and I knew that Mariel was in *Manhattan* and *Personal Best*. I knew a little bit about Margaux, but my knowledge was pretty surface level. That's another thing that interested me about making the film. I really wanted to find out what this family was all about.

Tribeca: Mariel has two gorgeous daughters, Dree and Langley, who are just beginning to learn about their family history.
BK: Not only that, none of them knew much, including Mariel. They didn't read Ernest's books, and he was never talked about. They knew he was a great writer, but his life was ultimately kept secret. They understood that he was a WWI vet who hunted and fished, but his demons were never discussed by the family.

Tribeca: Is this documentary almost a cautionary tale for Dree and Langley? How do you think that they as sisters reacted to watching their own mother with her sisters?
BK: I hope they see it as a film about love and communication. I think the reason Mariel participated in the documentary was for her kids. She wanted to do it for others as well, but I guess you have to start at a certain spot. She was so insistent on telling all in this film. All of us know someone with mental illness, suicidal tendencies, or someone who actually has committed suicide. We're not going to change the problems these people face unless we talk about them. That's what this project was all about.

The Hemingway family in general was so complex—there was love, jealousy, illness, and unhappiness—so many different elements. For me, this is a film about family, relationships, and generations. More than a cautionary tale, it is the story of three sisters, and it's about hope, transformation, and being able to put yourself out there as who you are.

Tribeca: Though Mariel was not born before Ernest killed himself, the impact on her family, her life, and the lives of her daughters is staggering. Were you aware of the burden of his legacy?
BK: To have a family with seven suicides is just beyond belief. In the documentary, Mariel talks about how she believed they were somewhat of a WASP-y family. She thought every family was like theirs. Mariel thought everyone fought, threw glass, and slept in separate bedrooms. She thought that was the norm.

Tribeca: The footage from Margaux's unfinished documentary on the family was mesmerizing, and the audience gets to know her through her film. How did you find the footage? What was your initial reaction?
BK: That was the real treasure for me. Margaux had done an hour-long documentary; I think it was shown twice, called *Winner Take Nothing*, but there were forty-three hours of other material that we were able to look at. It was such amazing, powerful footage. You really get to take a step in to the Hemingway family and see what they're all about.

We really got to know Margaux as a person—how beautiful and warm she was. All she wanted was love. She was so charming, sultry, and talented, but so lonely. It just breaks your heart.

Tribeca: Throughout the footage, Margaux expresses resentment towards Mariel and other members of her family. Did this surprise you?
BK: Mariel expressed the same sentiment to me. They were all jealous of each other. They were all fighting for love, wanting to be adored, cared about, and embraced. Mariel confirmed this family dynamic without being aware that I had the material from Margaux's documentary.

So after I'd spent some time with Mariel, I'd go back and I'd find similar reactions and feelings in the Margaux footage. Once Mariel described a scene from her past with some very specific details about her mother sitting on the counter of their yellow and blue kitchen with her legs up on the counter.

When I showed Mariel the film in its almost final cut, she got very emotional when she saw all of this footage of Margaux and of her parents' kitchen. She just sat on the edge of her chair and was fascinated because she thought she had been imagining that image of her mother. She couldn't believe the memories were real. She also felt really good because her daughters had never seen their grandparents. It was quite amazing.

Tribeca: Though she's an actor, I was really surprised by Mariel's intimacy and honesty with the camera. As an interviewer, how do you go about making your subjects feel comfortable enough to share their experiences?
BK: I think that being honest with the camera is something they must want to do. Mariel already wanted to share her story, and, there was a great level of trust between us. When I make a documentary, I love my characters and the people I'm filming. I want to create an environment in which they feel safe and comfortable, so they can say whatever they need to say.

Tribeca: With the variety of different footage, what was the post-production process like?
BK: It was an exciting process. We had so many different levels of materials that we could go deep and find things out about all of the family members. The editors put little index cards along the wall with all of the different scenes on them. The first cut was five and a half hours so we knew we had to trim the film way down. We'd take things out and try things differently and argue. It's what you do in any situation where you take on a creative endeavor.

Tribeca: It must have been a challenge to whittle a story down from five hours to two.
BK: It's like taking a block of wood and crafting it into something. You can't have an agenda; you just have to let the film take you where it will. Sometimes you're in a terrible place with it, and then, suddenly, things become seamless.

Tribeca: It is no wonder that Mariel is so involved with suicide prevention and with raising awareness of mental illness. I assume the overall reaction to this documentary has been positive.
BK: Well, everyone has his or her own agenda. Some psychiatrists and therapists saw it and opined that we should have interviewed psychiatrists and therapists for the film, but that wasn't what the film was about at all. For me, the point of the project was being able to work with Mariel, who is one of the most positive people I know. She is so honest and brave and has an enormous capacity for self-reflection.

Tribeca: Established directors like Spike Lee and Paul Schrader have turned to Kickstarter to fund their latest projects. Would you ever use the crowdfunding site? How vital has this tool become for emerging/beginning filmmakers?

BK: Of course. It's a lot of work, but you need to keep your projects coming. I think Kickstarter and social media are positive because they get people talking and understanding what their projects are about. They are making all of our communications more fluid. I think this trend is wonderful.

Tribeca: You made your first documentary, *Harlan County, U.S.A.*, in 1976. Over your nearly forty-year career, what's the biggest change in documentary filmmaking you've witnessed?

BK: When I first started, I was shooting on 16mm. The equipment has always been the biggest change. But no matter how the medium or equipment changes, you still have to have the heart, soul, and ideas you bring to a piece. I don't think that will ever change. You have to always put storytelling first.

Tribeca: When making an independent documentary like this, how important is social media to start buzz?

BK: Very important because you want to build a community. You want this film to reach the people it needs to reach.

Tribeca: What is the best documentary you've seen this year?

BK: Filmmakers in a documentary community really support each other. So to say one work is better than another is really hard. [laughs] When one of us does well, we all do well. We'll look at each other's rough cuts and help each other because we all want each other be successful. So I really couldn't say.

Additional Resources

Anderson, Mae. "Barbara Kopple: On the Spot." *Adweek*, November 22, 2004, 30.

Bernstein, Paula. "Barbara Kopple on *Hot Type* and Why Being a Documentary Filmmaker is Easier than Ever." *Indiewire*, February 27, 2015.

Bloom, Daniel and David Ross. "MaDCap with Barbara Kopple, Director of *Running from Crazy*." MaDCapDC.org, November 28, 2013.

Brand, Madeleine. "Film Looks at Dixie Chicks on the Road, Under Fire." *NPR Day to Day*, November 3, 2006.

Brock, Pope. "Barbara Kopple: A Firebrand Documentary Filmmaker Moves to TV to Tackle Her Latest Subject: Iron Mike Tyson." *People*, February 15, 1993.

Bronk, Robin. "My 5 Minutes with the President—Filmmakers Would Talk with Obama about Issues Close to Them." *The Hill*, July 31, 2013.

Chadha, Rahul. "*Harlan County, U.S.A.*: Solidarity at Brookside." Stfdocs.com, March 19, 2011.

Chapman, Stacey. "*Shut Up & Sing*: An Interview with Director Barbara Kopple." Blackfilm.com, October 25, 2006.

Clark, John. "The Woman Who Reeled in Elusive Woodman." *Los Angeles Times*, April 19, 1998.

Colton, Michael. "Barbara Kopple Shifted Direction to Follow in Woody Allen's Footsteps." *Washington Post*, May 8, 1998, F1.

Crier, Catherine. *The Crier Report*: "Interview with Barbara Kopple." *Fox News Network*, April 15, 1998.

Dunning, Jennifer. "A Woman Film Maker in the Coal Fields." *New York Times*, October 15, 1976, 59.

Eagan, Daniel. *America's Film Legacy (The Authoritative Guide to the Landmark Films in the National Film Registry)*. Bloomsbury Academic, 2010.

Edwards, Bob. "Interview: Barbara Kopple on Her Mini-Series *The Hamptons*." *NPR Morning Edition*, May 31, 2002.

Elder, Robert K. "Steve James: Harlan County U.S.A." *The Film That Changed My Life: 30 Directors on Their Epiphanies in the Dark*. Chicago Review Press, 2011, 110–22.

Goldberg, Danny. "Chapter 8: *No Nukes* and 'Nick of Time.'" *Bumping Into Geniuses: My Life Inside the Rock and Roll Business*. Penguin, 2008.

Goldberg, Danny. *How the Left Lost Teen Spirit.* Akashic Books, 2005, 99–109.

Goldsmith, David. *The Documentary Makers: Interviews with 15 of the Best in the Business.* Rotovision, 2003, 74–85.

Goodale, Gloria. "A Woodstock for Everyone in *My Generation.*" *Christian Science Monitor*, August 17, 2001.

Goodman, Amy. "*Shut Up & Sing*: Dixie Chicks' Big Grammy Win Caps Comeback from Backlash over Anti-War Stance." DemocracyNow.org, February 15, 2007.

Gregory, Mollie. *Women Who Run the Show.* New York: St. Martin's Press, 2002, 132–34.

Green, James. *Taking History to Heart: The Power of the Past in Building Social Movements.* University of Massachusetts Press, 2000, 172–74.

Hall, John. "Interview with Barbara Kopple." *Latent Image: A Student Journal of Film Criticism*, Spring 1992.

Hansen, Liane. "*Gun Fight* Relives Va. Tech Shooting, Revives Debate." *NPR Weekend Edition*, April 10, 2011.

Herbert, Steven. "Sweeps Punch: NBC Looks for a Knockout with Documentary on Mike Tyson." *Los Angeles Times*, February 7, 1993.

Holmlund, Christine, and Justin Wyatt. "Ordinary People, European Style." *Contemporary American Independent Film: From the Margins to the Mainstream.* Taylor & Francis, 2004.

Hurd, Mary. *Women Directors and Their Films.* Westport, CT: Praeger, 2007, 83–92.

Jolliffe, Genevieve, and Andrew Zinnes. *The Documentary Film Makers Handbook: The Ultimate Guide to Documentary Filmmaking.* Bloomsbury Academic, 2006/2012 editions.

Kelleher, Ed. "Kopple's Award-Winning Dream Explores Harsh Labor Dispute." *Film Journal*, April 1992.

Kennedy, Dana. "Where the Livin' Is Easy [Sometimes]." *TV Guide*, June 1, 2002, 24+.

Knowles, Harry. "Capone with Barbara Kopple and Cecelia Peck, Directors of (the Dixie Chicks') *Shut Up & Sing.*" *Ain't It Cool News* (www.aintitcool.com), November 15, 2006.

Kotek, Elliot. "Mariel Hemingway and Barbara Kopple from *Running from Crazy.*" DailyMotion.com, January 25, 2013.

Kopple, Barbara. "Be There: Barbara Kopple on Making Documentaries and *Running from Crazy.*" *Movie Maker Magazine* (moviemaker.com), November 6, 2013.

Kopple, Barbara. "Commencement 2010: Barbara Kopple." American University School of Communication. American University, 2015.

http://www.american.edu/soc/resources/commencement-2010-kopple-speech.cfm.

Kopple, Barbara. "Guest Column: Filmmaker Barbara Kopple Goes Inside *High School Musical.*" *TV Guide*, January 14–20, 2008, 34.

Kopple, Barbara, and Roger Ebert. "Panel Discussion from the 2005 Sundance Film Festival." Included on *Harlan County, U.S.A.* Criterion Collection DVD, 2006.

Leiberman, Paul. "Power of the Pen: HBO's Gritty Prison Drama *Oz* Finds Its Cast and Writer-Creator Taking a Hard Look at the Hard Time Known as Life." *Los Angeles Times*, August 8, 1999.

Le Peyron, Serge, and Louis Skorecki. "Interview with Barbara Kopple (*Harlan County U.S.A.*)." *Cahiers du Cinema*, November 1977, 62–64.

Legiardi-Laura, Roland. "Barbara Kopple." *Bomb* 38 (Winter 1992).

Linfield, Susie. "Cameos—Director Barbara Kopple." *Premiere*, April 1992, 60–61.

Martin, Marcel. "*Harlan County U.S.A.*: Interview with Barbara Kopple." *Ecran*, October 15, 1977.

Martin, Reed. *The Reel Truth: Everything You Didn't Know You Needed to Know about Making an Independent Film.* New York: Faber and Faber, 2009.

McEnteer, James. "Chapter 4—Barbara Kopple: Intrepid Pioneer on the Front Lines." *Shooting the Truth: The Rise of American Political Documentaries.* Westport, CT: Praeger Publishers, 2006, 3–78.

Meyers, Kate. "Barbara Kopple's KO Punch." *Entertainment Weekly*, February 12, 1993.

Mitchell, Elvis. *The Treatment*: "Barbara Kopple." KCRW(.com), April 24, 1998.

Moore, Frazier. "AIDS Documentary Is for All Ages." *Associated Press*, November 30, 1998.

Neary, Lynn. "American Dream: True Film about Labor Dispute." *NPR All Things Considered*, April 5, 1992.

Nelson, Rob. "Anything to Get the Story: Doc-maker Barbara Kopple Goes to War for *Bearing Witness.*" *(Minneapolis) CityPages.com*, May 25, 2005.

Orvell, Miles. "Documentary Film and the Power of Interrogation: *American Dream* & *Roger and Me.*" *Film Quarterly* 48, no. 2 (Winter 1994–1995): 10–18.

Oumano, Ellen. *Film Forum: Thirty-Five Top Filmmakers Discuss Their Craft.* New York: St. Martin's Press, 1985.

Powers, Jessica. *Tell Me Something: Advice from Documentary Filmmakers.* New York: Film First Co., 2013.

Rausch, Andrew J. *Fifty Filmmakers: Conversations with Directors from Roger Avary to Steven Zaillian.* Jefferson, NC: McFarland, 2008.

Rocca, Mo. "Barbara Kopple on the Documentary *Running from Crazy.*" *CBS News Sunday Morning*, October 28, 2013.

Rose, Charlie. "A Conversation with Barbara Kopple." *Charlie Rose*, April 22, 1998.
Rosenthal, Alan. *The Documentary Conscience: A Casebook in Film Making*. University of California Press, 1980, chapter 18, "*Harlan County, USA*: Barbara Kopple and Hart Perry," 303–16.
Rowat, Alison. "Kopple Plans to Go On Revealing the Facts of Life." *(Glasgow) Herald*, October 10, 2013.
Rule, Sheila. "In Film, a Career of Trying to Balance the Inequities of Life." *New York Times*, March 24, 1992.
Salovaara, Sarah. "Following the Legacy's Lead: Barbara Kopple on *Running from Crazy*." *Filmmaker*, October 31, 2013.
Sandomir, Richard. "A Poet of the Proletariat Finds an Unlikely Subject." *New York Times*, February 7, 1993.
"Setting the Record Straight." *People Magazine*, March 8, 1993.
Simon, Scott. "Interview: Barbara Kopple Discusses Her Life's Work as a Documentary Filmmaker." *NPR Weekend Edition Saturday*, June 19, 2004.
Stone, Judy. *Eye on the World: Conversations with International Filmmakers*. Silman-James Press, 1997.
Stubbs, Liz. *Documentary Filmmakers Speak*. Allworth Press, 2012, 63–78.
Tallmer, Jerry. "Barbara Kopple: Documentaries That Sing, Shout, and Speak for Themselves." *Thrive NYC*, Community Media, LLC, 1, no. 23 (April 2007).
Warren, Charles. *Beyond Document: Essays on Nonfiction Film*. University Press of New England, 1996, 113–23.
Watlington, Dennis. *Chasing America: A Memoir*. Macmillan, 2006.
Zacharek, Stephanie. "'Everybody Needs an Honest Shake.'" *Salon.com*, October 27, 2006.

Index

A&E, 101, 110
Abramson, Michael, 22
Academy of Motion Picture Arts and Sciences, 125
Academy of Television Arts and Sciences, 125
Agee, Arthur, 126
Ali, Muhammad, 129–30
Allen, Woody: documentary filming, 67–69, 73, 77, 99, 137; music, 72–73, 104, 153; personal life, 69–71, 75, 123; tour, 74
Alliance for Justice, 64
American Dream: awards, 41, 49, 78, 95; concept, 50–51, 62, 110, 120; filming, 54, 58; financing, 55; goal, 63, 107; history, 45; music, 46–47; release, 48, 56–57; violence, 52–53
American Film Institute, 22, 125
American Playhouse, 41, 50
American Teen, 137
American University Center for Social Media, 125
Anderson, Lewie, 42, 43, 47, 51, 52
Armour, 50
Aronson, Letty, 68, 73, 75
Arquette, Patricia, 79

Baez, Joan, 128
Baker, Nancy, 23
Battle of Algiers, The, 65, 107, 138
Bearing Witness: collaboration, 97; concept, 96, 101–2; release, 93; subjects, 98, 100; theme, 115; title, 96
Beautiful Girls, 79
Beyond JFK: The Question of Conspiracy, 50, 110
Bill Moyers Journal, 13
Bingham, Molly, 96, 97, 101, 102
"Black Lung," 17
Black Sunday, 38
Blaine, David, 73
Blindsight, 137
"Bloody Harlan," 12, 23, 27
Bowling for Columbine, 139, 144, 146
Boyens, Phyllis, 17
Boyle, Tony, 7, 11, 12, 36
Brando, Marlon, 79
Brennan, Paul "the Badger," 127
Brookside Mine, 11, 14, 22
Brookside Women's Club, 16, 23, 28
Broomfield, Nick, 97
Buena Vista Social Club, 91, 127
Bunny Bunny, 67
Burning Man, 131, 133
Burns, Ken, 95
Burstein, Nanette, 128, 137

Cannes Film Festival, 62, 122
Caplan, Cathy, 45
Capturing the Friedmans, 129
Cassidy, David, 148, 153
Charles, Scott, 145
Chicago 10, 137

Chicks. *See* Dixie Chicks
China Strikes Back, 20
Civil Rights: The Struggle Continues, 41, 50
CMT, 111
"Cold Blooded Murder," 17
Collando, Jesus, 64
Collins, Basil, 8, 25, 27, 35
Columbia Tristar, 123
Columbine, 139
Colvin, Marie, 96, 97, 100, 102
"Come All You Coal Miners," 33
Conversation with Gregory Peck, A, 103, 125
Cooder, Ry, 128
Corporate Campaign, Inc., 43, 52
Courtyard Hounds, 153
Crumb, 78
Crusenberry, Susie, 120

D'Abo, Maryam, 101
D'Amato, Cus, 123
"Dark as a Dungeon," 17
Davis, Bill, 41
Davis, Eddy, 72, 74, 122
Davis, Peter, 90, 103, 106, 128, 138
DC Sniper's Wife, The, 125
Deconstructing Harry, 71
Defending Our Daughters, 64, 78
Dershowitz, Alan, 59, 60
Devil's Playground, 137
Dickens, Hazel, 17, 19
DiGiovanni, Janine, 98, 100, 101, 102
Directors Guild, 126
Dixie Chicks: comments, 102, 103, 111, 147; documentary, 105, 110, 112, 137, 148; group dynamic, 149; persona, 116; publicity, 114
Donovan, Dick, 22
Don't Look Back, 128

Doumanian, Jean, 73, 78
Dreiser, Theodore, 33
Dykstra, Len, 73
Dylan, Bob, 128

Eastover Mining Company, 35, 109
Eisenhardt, Bob: collaboration, 96, 100; commentary, 101, 102; editing, 148, 150, 152
Epstein, Rob, 130
Evans, Bob, 128

Fahrenheit 9/11, 97
Fallen Champ: The Untold Story of Mike Tyson, 58, 59, 73, 112
Farmington Mine, 12
Farrakhan, Louis, 60
Farrow, Mia, 75, 78, 137
Feldman, Richard, 142, 146
Film Fund, 19
Film Preservation Act of 1988, 41
FilmColumbia, 101
Filmfest DC, 72
"Fixin' to Die Rag," 129
Fleischer, Ari, 113
Fonda, Jane, 61, 122
Foreman, George, 129
Free Republic, 111, 114

Gaghan, Stephen, 110
Gast, Leon, 129
Gates, William, 126
General Motors, 127
"Generations," 75
Geo. A. Hormel & Company, 44, 45, 49, 51, 121
Giffords, Gabrielle, 142, 146
Gilbert, Peter, 94, 126
Gimme Shelter, 49, 77, 95
Goddard, Colin, 142, 145

Going the Distance, 137
Gonzalez, Juan, 64
Good Morning America, 34–35
Grapes of Wrath, The, 46
Green, Paul, 131
Greenwald, Robert, 117
Grubman, Lizzie, 87
Gun Fight, 139, 140, 141, 145, 146
Gunning, Sara Ogan, 33
Guyette, Jim, 47, 51

Hamptons, 85–86, 88, 95
Hamptons, The, 87–88, 89
Haneke, Tom, 45
Haney, Evan, 61
Harlan County, U.S.A.: awards, 41, 55, 109, 136; concept, 11, 67, 78, 144; editing, 45; film technique, 119; filming, 53–54, 58, 69; historical element, 45; music, 46–47; portrayal of women, 57, 107; release, 48; screening, 18–19, 42; starting film, 13, 62; theme, 42, 50, 51–52, 109, 115; unionism, 121; violence, 102, 142, 144
Harlan Labor News, 23
"Harlan Miners Speak—Report on Terrorism in the Kentucky Coal Fields," 33
Hathaway, Anne, 93, 110, 144
Havoc, 91, 93, 118, 137
HBO, 90, 91, 141, 144, 146
Hearts and Minds: inspiration, 138; Kopple participation, 38, 106; plot, 128; release, 90; theme, 39
Hemingway, Ernest, 154, 156
Hemingway, Margaux, 154, 155, 156
Hemingway, Marial, 154, 155, 156, 157
Hemingway, Muffet, 154
Hendrix, Jimi, 131

High School Musical: The Music in You, 125
Hog Farm, 133
Hollywood on Trial, 20
Homicide, 79, 104
Homicide: Life on the Streets, 75, 93, 118
Hoop Dreams, 91, 94, 126
Hormel. *See* Geo. A. Hormel & Company
Hot Docs, 96
House, Laura, 92
House of Steinbrenner, The, 141
Human Rights Watch Film Festival, 115
Hurwitz, Tom, 72

I Married . . . , 93
"In Harm's Way," 96
In the Boom Boom Room, 75, 79
indieWIRE, 104, 142, 143

Jackson, Greg, 132
James, Steve, 126
Jarecki, Jared, 129
Jarvis, Barbara, 122, 136
Jarvis, Lucy, 61
Jersey, Bill, 138
JFK, 50
Joe Glory, 75, 79
John Birch Society, 35
Johnson, Richard, 88
Jones, Lawrence, 18, 27
Joplin, Janis, 131, 132

Keeping On, 41, 50
Keith, Toby, 111
Kennedy, John F., 50
Kent State, 118
Kevorkian, Jack, 98, 104
Kickstarter, 158

Kid Stays in the Picture, The, 128, 137
King, Don, 59, 129
King Kong, 30, 38
Knowlton, Richard, 43
Konigsberg, Alan Stewart, 73
Ku Klux Klan, 34, 35

Lang, Michael, 83, 84, 124, 131, 132
Lee, Spike, 129, 158
Lewis, Anne, 23, 25–26, 27, 35
Lewis, Anthony, 64
Lewis, John L., 11, 12
Little Republic Steel Strike, 20
Living Daylights, The, 101
Local P-9, 50, 52, 56

"Macaroni Minutes," 92
Mailer, Norman, 129
Maines, Natalie: London comments, 102, 103, 110, 147; political position, 147; portrayal in documentary, 111
Mandela, Nelson, 78
Manhattan, 155
Marathon Man, 30, 38
Marx, Frederick, 126
"Matmington," 17
Maysles, Albert and David: films, 127; influence, 77, 106; work with Kopple, 3, 41, 49, 95, 118–19, 136
McGuire, Martie: group dynamic, 113, 114, 149, 153; London comments, 147; performance, 150; portrayal in documentary, 111; separate work, 152
Milk, Harvey, 130
Miller, Arnold: leadership, 28–29, 36; miner movement, 3, 13, 39; portrayal in documentary, 5–6, 13, 21
Miller, Peter, 68, 72

Miners for Democracy: development, 12, 21, 36, 39; hiring Kopple, 11; leadership, 28–29; portrayal in documentary, 3, 24
Miramax-Prestige Films, 41
Moon, Keith, 131, 132
Moore, Michael, 97, 127, 138, 139
Morgen, Brett, 128, 137
Morris, Errol, 79
Morrison, John, 56
Movie of the Week, 49, 73
Moyer, Larry, 136
My Generation, 80, 82, 83, 110, 124, 129

National Film Registry, 41
National Miners' Union, 33
National Rifle Association, 140, 145, 146
Native Land, 20
NBC, 58
Nevins, Sheila, 141
"New Kid," 92
New School, 77, 118, 136
New York Entertainment Town, 80
New York Film Festival, 19, 38, 41
No Nukes, 41, 50
Northeastern University, 75
"Not Ready to Make Nice," 112
NRA. *See* National Rifle Association
Nyberg, Chuck, 43

On the Line, 20
On the Ropes, 137
Ornitz, Samuel, 33
Out of Darkness: The Mine Workers' Story, 41, 49
Oz, 93

Pakula, A. J., 115
Paris Is Burning, 48

Pasdar, Adrian, 150, 151
Passos, John Dos, 33
Patrick, Harry, 12, 21
Peck, Cecilia: collaboration, 103, 110, 136; concept, 105, 148; filming, 111–12
Pennebaker, D. A., 112, 128
Perez, Hugo, 147, 148
Perry, Hart: commentary, 22–23, 25, 27; filming, 8, 15, 25, 35
Personal Best, 155
Phillips, Bijou, 93, 110
Plimpton, George, 129
PolyGram, 83, 124
Pontecorvo, Gillo, 138
Portman, Natalie, 79
Power, Duke, 22
Pratt, Larry, 142
Previn, Soon-Yi: controversy, 75, 123, 137; participation in documentary, 78, 99; personal life, 68–69, 70
Propoganda Films, 83

Rabe, David, 75
Radner, Gilda, 67
"Red Ball," 92
Reece, Florence, 17, 33, 34
Renshaw, Simon, 111, 112
Robben Island, 78
Robison, Emily, 111, 150, 152
Rocky, 38
Roger and Me, 48, 127, 138
Rogers, Mary, 98, 101
Rogers, Ray, 42, 47, 51
Rubin, Rick, 111, 152
"Rumble in the Jungle," 129
Running from Crazy, 154

Salesman, 3, 41, 49, 77, 127
Salt of the Earth, 28, 29

School of Rock, 131, 132
Schrader, Paul, 158
Scott, Lois, 120
Scottsborough Boys, 20
Shut Up & Sing: collaboration, 147; concept, 103, 104–5, 110–11; goal, 117, 147; release, 104, 112; structure, 116
Sighvatsson, Joni, 83
Silk, Larry, 45
"Soccer," 92
Sokolow, Diane, 123
"Solidarity Forever," 44
Springsteen, Bruce, 78
Sprint, 92
"Start Something," 93
Steinbrenner, George, 144
Stern, Jim, 67, 73
Stevens, J. P., 10, 20, 42
Stone, Oliver, 50
Sundance, 80
Sutherland, Donald, 61, 122
Sweetland, 73

Taking the Long Way, 103, 111, 114
Target, 93
Temple University, 145
Terminator II, 48
"They'll Never Keep Us Down," 17
Thin Blue Line, The, 79
Tiger Woods Foundation, 93
Time for Burning, A, 138
Times of Harvey Milk, The, 130
Toronto Film Festival, 112
Travis, Merle, 17
Trbovich, Mike, 12, 21, 29
Tribeca Film Festival, 154
TruTV, 125
Tsien, Jean, 147
Tyson, Mike: documentary, 49, 73, 78,

109; filming, 123; Kopple's preconceptions, 112–13; persona, 59–60

UFCW. *See* United Food and Commercial Workers
UMWA. *See* United Mine Workers of America
Union Maids, 20
Unionism, 5, 15, 33, 45
United Food and Commercial Workers, 50, 51, 52
United Mine Workers of America: filming, 3; movement for democracy, 21, 36; participants, 12, 22; portrayal in documentary, 11, 23, 33

Variety, 30, 48
Versace, Gianni, 71
Virginia Tech, 139, 141, 142, 145

Wadleigh, Michael, 129, 131, 133, 134
Walker, Lucy, 137
Washington, Desiree, 123
Waste Land, 137
Watlington, Dennis, 104
Weinstein Company, 104, 112, 151
Weiss, Mark, 22, 141
Welsh, May Ying, 100, 101–2
Wenders, Wim, 127–28
When We Were Kings, 129
"Which Side Are You On?," 17, 33
Why, 61
Wild Man Blues: commercial release, 78, 110; concept, 72, 95, 137; filming, 71; theme, 115, 153; title, 72
Wilson, Dan, 113
Winner Take Nothing, 156
Wintemute, Garen, 146
Winter Film Collective, 121, 136
Winter Soldier: concept, 55–56; financing, 61; Kopple participation, 13, 50, 109, 121; production, 136; release, 122; theme, 115
Witness. See *Bearing Witness*
WMD: Weapons of Mass Deception, 110
Woodstock, 118, 131, 132, 133
Woodstock, 133
Woodstock: Now & Then, 131, 153
Woodstock '69, 83, 124, 129
Woodstock '94, 83, 110, 124, 129
Woodstock '99, 84, 124, 129
"Woodstock Two," 79
Woodstock Ventures, 83
Workman, Nimrod, 17
Wotton, Marijana, 96, 100, 101

Yablonski, Joseph "Jock," 12, 21, 36
Yasgur, Max, 129, 131
Year of Living Dangerously, The, 96

Zarintash, Shane, 22
Zwigoff, Terry, 78

www.ingramcontent.com/pod-product-compliance
Lightning Source LLC
Chambersburg PA
CBHW021841220426
43663CB00005B/348